Die
Broke

Die
Broke

Die Broke

A Radical, Four-Part Financial Plan

Stephen M. Pollan and Mark Levine

HarperBusiness
A Division of HarperCollinsPublishers

A hardcover edition of this book was published in 1997 by HarperBusiness, a division of HarperCollins Publishers.

HarperCollins books may be purchased for educational, business, or sales promotional use. For information please write: Special Markets Department, HarperCollins Publishers, Inc., 10 East 53rd Street, New York, NY 10022.

First paperback edition published 1998.

Designed by Elina D. Nudelman

The Library of Congress has caatalogued the hardcover edition as follows:

Pollan, Stephen M.
    Die broke : a radical, four-part financial plan / Stephen M. Pollan and Mark Levine.
  — 1st ed.
    p. cm.
    Includes index.
    ISBN 0-88730-867-8
    1. Finance, Personal. I. Levine, Mark, 1958– . II. Title.
HG179.P555433 1998
332.024—dc21   97-38118

ISBN 0-88730-942-9 (pbk.)

98 99 00 01 02 ❖/RRD 10 9 8 7 6 5 4 3

The authors would like to dedicate this book to their heirs

Contents

Acknowledgments

The authors would like to thank all the friends, clients, peers, authors, and experts who freely lent us their wisdom and their ears.

Special thanks to Laurence Hooper, John Koten, and all the editors at *Worth* for their willingness to let us explore contrarian ideas and their insistence that we back up our theories with solid factual arguments.

Thanks to Gary Ambrose, director of Personal Capital Management, Charles B. Goldman, executive director of the UJA Federation of New York's department of planned giving and endowments, and Neal P. Myerberg, vice president of Sanford C. Bernstein & Co. for their patience in providing us with an education.

Thanks to Jane K. Morrow, Michele Landes, Kim W. Mendola, Anthony Scamurra, and Leslie Burleigh for their continuing support and help keeping so many balls in the air at the same time.

Thanks to our agent, Stuart Krichevsky, and to our editor, Adrian Zackheim, for ensuring we didn't die broke while writing this book.

Thanks to Michael, Lori, Tracy, and Dana for proving the greatest legacies are your children.

Finally, we'd like to thank Corky Pollan and Deirdre Martin Levine for helping us live rich.

—*Stephen M. Pollan and Mark Levine*

Introduction to the Paperback Edition

I've always said that I learn the most by speaking with my clients. Since the hardcover publication of *Die Broke* I've had to expand that statement to include my readers.

I've been overwhelmed by the positive response to *Die Broke*. I knew my contrarian advice worked for my clients here in New York City, since I see the positive results every day in my office. But in all honesty, I wasn't sure how my ideas would play in other parts of the country. The results have been, to say the least, gratifying. Clearly there is a need for a fresh look at personal finance issues, a reexamination of our entire approach to assets.

One of the most fulfilling things about being a personal consultant is having clients say you've changed their lives for the better. Since the original publication of *Die Broke*, readers have given me joy by telling me about the impact the book has had on them. I cannot tell you how rewarding it is to have people you've never met offer you thanks for something you've written.

I've learned a great deal from those who've offered suggestions and amplifications to the *Die Broke* philosophy. As you'll learn as soon as you start reading chapter 1, I'm always open to new ideas. Some of the applications offered by readers have actually found their way into my practice, so the process has now come full circle. I look forward to more input from readers of this paperback edition. You can either write to me, care of HarperCollins, or, if you're online, send email directly to me at mark4smp@aol.com.

The realization that my iconoclastic personal finance advice works for Americans outside the metropolitan New York area led me to sit down with Mark Levine and write another book about the other half of my practice: career and business consulting. It's called *Live Rich* and brings the same kind of contrarian approach to earning money that *Die Broke* brings to spending money.

What I've learned from writing both of these books and from speaking with readers is that there's a secret to being happy. It's freedom. That sounds very simple, but it's true. Having the freedom to earn and spend your money when and how you choose is more than just empowering, it's physically, psychologically, and even spiritually liberating.

Die broke.

Live rich.

Be happy.

Stephen Pollan
Little River Farm
Sharon, Connecticut

Part I

The Die Broke Philosophy

An Immigrant's Guide to the New Age

Die broke. Turn the phrase over in your mind. At first it sounds insane. Instinctively it's something to avoid at all costs, not something to pursue with a vengeance. It immediately conjures up images of Dickensian poverty; of Depression-era families having their mortgages foreclosed on by Lionel Barrymore. But fight off those instinctive responses and reflex images and think about it for a minute, really think about it.

What's wrong with dying broke? What good will money do you when you're dead? Isn't there something ironic about hoarding money for a time when you can't spend it? But what about your family, you worry; how will they get by? Well, why can't you take care of them when you're alive? Isn't it daft for them to have to wait for your death to be taken care of? Okay, you say, but what about those images of poverty the concept instantly brought to mind. You just can't shake them. Don't. In fact, look at them really closely. There's something very important about them you need to focus on. They're from the past.

STOP LIVING IN THE PAST

Are you living in Victorian England? Does your hometown look like Bedford Falls? Of course not. You're about to enter the twenty-first century. Your home, regardless of where it's located, is probably closer to that of the Jetsons than that of the Cratchits. Yet the images of financial ruin that instantly spring to your mind are from the turn of the *prior* century. That's because your entire approach to money and career, and much of your approach to life, is based on principles and beliefs that sprung from the experiences of the past. Your fear of dying broke is an early-twentieth-century fear carried forward to a twenty-first-century life.

Rather than running your twenty-first-century life by up-to-date rules, you're using outdated nineteenth- and twentieth-century ones. You're taking practices designed to deal with the shift from an agrarian to an industrialized society and trying to make them fit the shift to an information world. You're following financial patterns sketched out in the Great Depression at a time when the Dow Jones is over 7,000. You're managing your career based on advice formulated when every man still wore garters to hold up his socks and the only women in the corporate world were in the secretarial pool. And you're still running your life as if your family looked and lived like the Cleavers. That's why you're experiencing an overwhelming sense of uncertainty, insecurity, and fear.

YOU'RE NOT ALONE

I can make these generalizations about your feelings because I speak with people like you every day. I'm a financial and legal consultant on New York City's Upper East Side. Most of my clients are baby boomers from what used to be called the upper middle class. While only a few of them would have felt at home in Tom Wolfe's *Bonfire of the Vanities,* almost all of them aspired to be masters of the universe in the 1980s. Today they have combined incomes of well over $150,000, live in apartment buildings with doormen or rural homes on more than an acre of land, take European vacations, go out to Thai restaurants, shop at Barney's, and buy wine by the case. They belong to health clubs and send their kids to after-school programs. They grind their own coffee beans.

While there are some uniquely New York elements to my clients' personas, they're just like lots of other successful baby boomers . . . including you. They've succeeded in acquiring more possessions and experiences than their parents had at their age. They hold down decision-making and policy-setting positions in corporations, are running their own successful small companies, or have made a name for themselves in a competitive creative field. At work they have staffs and personal assistants. They read *The Wall Street Journal*. They have accountants to prepare their taxes, therapists to help them with their psyches, nutritionists to help them with their diets, and personal trainers to help them build up their pecs.

And they have me to help them with their fears. In fact, on the conference table I use for an office desk there's a name plaque—a gift from a grateful client—that reads "Stephen Pollan: Professional Fear Remover."

I really am an expert on fear. Not the life-threatening kind, but the gnawing doubt kind; the kind these people are feeling; the kind you're currently feeling.

For more than two decades I've been very successful at helping people solve their problems and achieve their goals. Much of my practice deals with traditional legal matters, like real estate transactions, wills, divorces, business negotiations, and workplace issues. But what makes my practice different is that I see these problems as elements of a much larger project: the Business of Living. I try to put my clients' financial, legal, and career problems in the context of their entire lives, and help them draft "life plans" tying all these elements together into a cohesive whole. I spend much of the time empowering clients by providing the kind of advice and backup they need to overcome their fears. Basically, I teach them the rules for succeeding in the Business of Living.

And my clients are very good at following rules. You probably are too. For all their rebelliousness, boomers are excellent at following rules. After all, they've been achievers all their lives, and to achieve you've got to follow the rules. My clients learned the education rules and won one or more degrees. Most learned the career rules and landed good jobs and climbed the corporate ladder, sometimes making larger salaries than their fathers ever could have dreamed of. Some learned the entrepreneurial rules and started successful businesses. They learned the rules of real estate and bought apartments and homes far more expensive than their parents could have managed at the same age. They learned the rules of juggling and were able to keep two careers and their family lives in the air simultaneously. They certainly learned the rules of credit—often teaching me, a former banker and venture capitalist, a thing or two in the process—since that's often what enabled them to do and have so many things so young. They were all doing quite well following these rules . . . and then one day something happened.

Actually, it wasn't one thing, and it didn't happen in one day, yet that's how it seems today. I don't think anyone is ever going to be able to put a finger on exactly when our economic world shifted axis. It's like we were all on autopilot and missed it. You know the feeling. You're on a long drive. The weather is clear. The sun is out. There's almost no traffic. You're familiar with the route so your mind begins to wander. Suddenly you snap out of it. You don't consciously remember the past couple of minutes of the trip. For a few seconds you worry about the missing time . . . but then you shrug it off. After all, everything's okay.

Well, sometime during the past few years we all fell into that same kind of trance about our own economic lives. Except now we've snapped out of it and everything's not okay. In fact, everything now seems precarious and frightening. Rather than cruising on a newly paved, three-lane interstate you're suddenly on a narrow dirt road on the side of a cliff . . . and there's no guardrail.

All of a sudden your job is temporary no matter how long you've held it, how hard you work, or how good you are at it. In the blink of an eye owning real estate in some cases has become a curse rather than a blessing. What was once going to be the key to your long-term financial success now seems an albatross around your neck. Credit, once your lifeblood, is now hanging over your head like the sword of Damocles. Retirement, which you once thought you'd reach in middle age, now seems impossible. And estate planning? Hey, it looks like the kids will be lucky if you can help them pay the tuition at the local community college, let alone pass on wealth.

Because I'm in the business of solving the problems of people like you, all these issues end up in my office. In fact, one thing I do remember is the first time I was confronted with this situation. It was September 1989.

PLAYING BY THE RULES . . . AND LOSING GROUND

Mitch and Janet Peters[1] were long-term clients of mine. Mitch was, at the time, forty-two years old and working as a sales and marketing

---

[1]The names and personal details of these and other clients mentioned in the text have been changed somewhat in order to protect their privacy. However, the essential details of their situations have been retained.

executive for a consumer electronics company. Janet was thirty-seven back then and working as an account executive in an advertising agency. They'd met ten years earlier when her agency worked on a campaign for Mitch's company. They had a combined income of about $150,000. They shared a two-bedroom apartment on New York's Upper West Side with their four-year-old daughter, Sara. I'd helped them buy their apartment, set up their finances, and negotiate raises over the six years they'd been coming in to see me.

At first, the visit seemed typical. They came in together. (I always request that both members of a couple come in to see me.) They were both dressed well, since they'd just come from their offices. Anthony, one of my assistants, greeted them at the door, took their coats, and offered them coffee. While he went to make their coffee, my law associate, Jane Morrow, came out of her office to say hello. (I was, as usual, on the telephone.) She asked about how Sara was doing in preschool. When I came out to say hello they were all smiles, regaling Jane with tales of Sara's "galloping" proficiency.

But as soon as I ushered them into my office, sat them across the table from me, and shut the door, the mood changed dramatically. A host of fears and anxieties came pouring out.

There had been another round of layoffs at Mitch's company. And while he wasn't touched, the ax had fallen pretty close. He no longer felt secure. Janet's job seemed a bit less uncertain—the managing partner was reassuring her weekly—but she hadn't gotten a raise in two years and was told none were in the offing.

They wanted to move out of the city since their apartment was getting pretty tight and Sara was about to enter school. But the real estate market was down—they knew they'd be lucky to get their money back, let alone make enough of a profit to buy something bigger or better.

With their rising bills and stagnant salaries they hadn't been able to put any money away in their 401(k)s during the past tax year. Mitch laughed bitterly and said retirement was out of the question. His open anger was the key that unlocked Janet's frustrations. "We wanted to have another baby, but how can we now?" she sobbed. "Why are things getting worse rather than better?" The emotional floodgates had opened. "What are we doing wrong?" she asked. "How can we get our lives back on track?"

Mitch appeared to be ashamed, not of Janet's behavior but his own inability to answer her questions, his perceived financial impotence. "We've followed all the rules," he said in frustration. "We've done everything we were supposed to." Unsaid but clearly heard by me was that they'd done everything *I* had told them to do. "We took charge. Our lives were supposed to keep on improving," Mitch said. "What happened?"

These are the kind of situations a personal consultant dreads. Don't get me wrong: I'm not uncomfortable with emotions—my office probably goes through as many tissues as a psychotherapist's office. It was the hopelessness and the desperation in their voices and the implicit message that I'd somehow failed them that struck home.

What could I tell them? Well, when someone is drowning you don't ask them how they fell overboard, you throw them a life preserver. That's what I did. I comforted them. I instinctively told them they weren't to blame. (Only later did I realize my instincts were right.) But I quickly said that worrying about how or why they'd gotten into this situation wasn't productive. The key was to concentrate on the practical problems they were facing. "Forget about the 'why' and focus on the 'how,'" I said. "Let's just play the cards we've been dealt." With that I began talking to them about shoring up their jobs.

As we got into the details of their employment situation, much of the drama and emotion receded from the situation. It hadn't been eliminated, but by moving from introspection to action a great deal of angst can be set aside. It's just like the planning of a funeral. People can lose themselves in the details so they don't need to face the emotional issues.

However, I hadn't forgotten about the fears and frustration they'd expressed. My other clients wouldn't let me. From that time on not a week went by when I didn't have a similar client meeting. After the fifth or sixth incident I knew I was going to have to come up with answers to their questions.

GETTING BEYOND CRISIS MANAGEMENT

Crisis management (that's actually what I was urging them to do by focusing on the problems at hand) is not satisfying in the long term. On the practical level, we can only bail so fast. Unless we figure out what's punching the holes in our lifeboats we'll eventually sink and

drown. On the emotional level, we all need answers to such fundamental questions. We need to feel we're standing on a firm foundation, a set of rules. We need to feel there's some order to the universe.
We need to feel we are in charge of our lives, or at least that we can be
if we choose to seize the reins.

That's why almost all the personal finance and career advice offered
today is like a bad Chinese meal: Not only are you still hungry an
hour after consuming it . . . but it also leaves a bad aftertaste.
Honestly, I don't mean to denigrate my fellow financial advisers and
authors. But it's just that they're all still practicing crisis management; they're trying to fix a system that's beyond repair. I'm saying,
throw out the system and get a new one.

It has taken me six long years to come up with the answers to those
questions first asked of me by Mitch and Janet Peters, and subsequently asked by hundreds of other clients, friends, and family members; to come up with a new system for the new world. I now know
why things aren't getting better for those who are playing by the
rules. I now know what's causing all those fears and frustration. And
more important, I finally know what they, and you, can do about it.

I've gotten beyond offering tips on crisis management and have, for
the past two years, been preaching an entirely new, proactive approach
to personal finance. An approach that promises greater physical, emotional, and psychological satisfaction than the outmoded rules of the
past. It has worked for my clients. They're back to feeling they can be
masters, this time of their own universes. It can work for you too. It's
an approach I call Die Broke.

THINK OF YOURSELF AS AN IMMIGRANT

It's an approach that requires an open and hungry mind, a mind like
those of your wide-eyed ancestors who first came to this country.
You're just like them, except you're an immigrant in a new economic
world. The rules and ideas you brought with you from the old country,
while they worked for your family for generations, no longer work
here. The goals you were told to pursue might have made sense in the
old country, but here they're beyond reach. You're frightened because
the passage from one world to another, from one age to another, is
always scary. But despite the fear, you can't keep playing by the rules
of the old world, following the maps you were handed years ago. They

were representations of a world that is long gone. Using them would be like trying to navigate modern Manhattan Island with a map drawn by Peter Stuyvesant.

In the old world, real estate soared in value, credit cards were tools that let you painlessly live out your dreams, jobs were secure as long as you did your work, retirement was an idyllic reward for years of toil, and money was made to be saved and passed on to the next generation.

In the new world, real estate values are stagnant, credit buying can lead to financial ruin, we are all free agents in a job market where security can come only from within, retirement at any age may be foolish, and trying to build up and maintain an estate can be downright dangerous.

In the old world, you lived by some simple rules: climb the ladder in your company; use credit to maximize your comfort; retire into a leisurely lifestyle as early as you can; and die rich, leaving an estate for your children.

In the new world, you need to learn four new but equally simple maxims:

- Quit today
- Pay cash
- Don't retire
- Die broke

Together these four simple axioms form a mantra for living in the new world.

QUIT TODAY

When you were growing up you were always told that if you got a good education you'd get a good job; if you did what was asked of you in that job you'd be secure; and if you did your job well you'd get raises and promotions. Under such circumstances it became easy for your job to represent yourself; somehow what you did for a living reflected on your value as a human being and the values you held. "Job" became an old-fashioned, blue-collar kind of word, a term used by your grandmother, which you replaced with more abstract terms like "career" and "work."

This made a lot of sense at a time when government was subsidizing higher education through low-interest loans and when corporations were expanding the ranks of middle management. As a nation, our attitudes toward work had shifted from it being for God's glory or our own individual comfort to it being a way to judge our status in society or to achieve personal growth. With such a work ethic in place, organizational loyalty and identification with our jobs made perfect sense.

But in the new world, a world in which there's no such thing as corporate loyalty, a world where young people graduating from good colleges can land positions only as temps, a world where raises are rare and barely keep pace with the cost of living, viewing yourself and your job as one is dangerous psychologically and financially.

The answer is to quit today: mentally separate yourself from your employer and realize that you're on your own. Abandon any remaining tinges of loyalty to your employer (who long ago abandoned any sense of obligation to you) and instead think of your job and yourself the same way free-agent athletes do: They retain their integrity by doing their best and being part of the team, but they're also focused on getting the best financial deal they can. You should do the same. Once you've quit in your head, being fired is no longer a real threat: You're already a free agent on the lookout for your next opportunity.

I also think most of us are making far too many demands on our jobs. It's rare today for a job to be secure and rewarding both emotionally and financially. I suggest you instead adopt a mercantile approach: focus on what you're doing as a job—that word your grandmother used—not necessarily a career, and view your job as primarily an income-generating device; any other benefits are purely secondary. Having a mercantile approach doesn't mean obsessing over money. It simply means using your job to generate the money you need to pursue your personal goals, rather than looking to the job itself to fulfill those goals. A career is simply a series of such jobs viewed from above and placed in some kind of context. And a life's work need not be what is done on the job.

PAY CASH

Since the end of World War II we've become a nation of debtors. Americans in the eighteenth century had Ben Franklin's Poor Richard as their role model. We're ending the twentieth century trying to emulate conspicuous borrowers and spenders and refinanciers like Donald Trump. Powerful advertising promotes the joys of consumption, increasingly available consumer credit, and a mass psychology of self-indulgence and immediate gratification, turning us into a country that, collectively and individually, lives beyond its means.

Years ago it all seemed to make a lot of sense. Real estate was soaring in value. By borrowing as much as possible and buying a home as soon as possible you could jump on the bandwagon. Buy a starter home or condo and hold it three years. Then sell it for a profit and buy another, more expensive home. Hold that until the kids were out of the house, then sell it and buy a luxury apartment in the Sunbelt overlooking the green at the seventeenth hole.

Inflation was high, so credit card buying looked like a brilliant idea. After all, incomes were rising. I used to tell my clients, "Why wait until you can afford to pay cash for that trip to Paris? By that time you could be too old to climb the Eiffel Tower. Charge it instead." We all bought into this consumerism. If you're brought up using a dishwasher rather than a Brillo pad, and the only time you're inside a coin-operated laundry is to use the pay phone, it seems only right to buy appliances right away—even if you have to charge them. And when new, more sophisticated or stylish appliances (or cars, or furniture, or clothes, or anything) come along, you can buy them, on credit, even if you haven't finished paying for the one you just replaced.

But you're now in a new world: a world where real estate values are generally stagnant; a world where most incomes are shrinking or disappearing altogether; a world where excessive borrowing is the seed of financial ruin. The maxim for such a world is to pay cash whenever you can. To not reach beyond your grasp. To save and wait and then buy something—whether a home or a car or a dishwasher—that will last long enough to justify either the cost of borrowing or the time spent saving.

Look at real estate as primarily an emotional, quality-of-life purchase (with some tax ramifications) and therefore make fewer compromises. Wait longer and buy your second home first—in effect the second home you would have bought in the past. And apply this approach to all your big-ticket purchases. Wait, study and research, and then use cash to buy something that will last you for a long time, rather than jumping to buy today's hot item—whether a sport utility vehicle or a CD-ROM drive—using credit.

Frugality really does have longer-lasting psychic rewards than immediate gratification. But more important, it offers dramatic real-life financial benefits—it's a life preserver that can keep you from drowning in a sea of red ink on your voyage to the new world.

DON'T RETIRE

It's remarkable how pervasive the relatively recent notion of retirement has become. Retirement as we now know it didn't exist prior to the 1930s. Social Security was developed and promoted by FDR and his New Dealers as a way to convince older workers to retire in order to open up jobs for young people during the Great Depression. Since then Social Security benefits have been expanded dramatically. From the 1930s to the 1980s private pension plans also boomed. The financial services industry saw money to be made and began relentlessly promoting retirement. In less than half a century it had evolved from a social experiment to a presumed entitlement.

Retirement made a lot of sense at a time when you weren't going to live much longer than age sixty-five, when your job was backbreaking, when you got less productive as you got older, and when society had to make room in the job market for lots of young people. And an idyllic retirement was actually possible for your parents' generation, who could take those expanding benefits and pensions and add to them a windfall profit from the sale of their real estate.

But in this new age, retirement is not only not worth striving for, it's impossible for most—and something you should do your best to avoid. The notions it's based on are simply no longer true.

When age sixty-five was chosen as the retirement age, most people died at sixty-three. Today, not only are you likely to live into your eighties or nineties, but your older years are going to be active and productive ones. Retiring at age sixty-five would mean your spending two decades doing needlework and gardening.

When retirement was first developed, everyone thought leisure was automatically more fulfilling than work. You know better. You take pride in a job well done, enjoy being part of a team, and know that work—of one form or another—is as integral a part of your life as play.

When retirement took hold in the American mind, most work was physical in nature. It was obvious then that older workers were less productive than younger workers—they simply couldn't lift as many bales of cotton or carry as many bricks. Today the most physically demanding part of your job probably is pushing the buttons on your telephone or tapping on your keyboard. There's absolutely nothing that indicates older workers are less productive. In fact, most evidence indicates they're *more* productive.

When retirement was first being promoted, America had a large generation of young people that it had to absorb into the workforce. It made some sense, therefore, to open up spots. Today, however, the twenty-somethings waiting in the wings are a small generation. They don't need to have lots of spots opened for them. In fact, there aren't enough of them to fill all the jobs your generation is doing.

Finally, the financial trends that made it possible for your folks to retire have been reversed: Social Security is shrinking, private pensions are vanishing, and real estate values are barely keeping pace with inflation.

Forget about retirement. Believe me, giving up this living death is actually an empowering act that opens up undreamed-of opportunities for your personal, professional, and financial growth. Emulate the ancient Greek hero Ulysses rather than model yourself after a lemming. Look at your working life as a lifelong journey up and down hills rather than as a single climb up a steep cliff that ends with a fatal step off the edge (and into the abyss) at the arbitrary age of sixty-five.

FINALLY, DIE BROKE

Ever since economists and the media began focusing on what they heralded as potentially the single largest generational transfer of wealth in history—bequests to baby boomers from their parents—my clients caught patrimony fever. Even if you could inherit a small fortune (and I don't think you will), I don't think it's something you should plan on or dream of. And it's certainly not a process you should try to replicate with your own children.

Inheritance made sense when it consisted of fixed assets—like a family farm, a business, or a set of tools—and was part of an implicit contract between generations—oldest son Jeb gets the farm when Dad dies in exchange for supporting Mom. But when it consists primarily of mutual funds and treasury bills and carries with it no obligations, it's nonsensical.

Creating and maintaining an estate does nothing but damage the person doing the hoarding. It will force you to put the quality of your death before the quality of your life. You'll be forced to choose not to spend on something for yourself so your kids can use the money.

Inheritance also hurts society. Funds maintained in an estate are generally kept in frozen investments that contribute very little to the productivity of the economy.

Estates and potential inheritance can also hurt families. By inserting economic self-interest into emotional decisions, they can damage family dynamics and relationships. Suddenly, your son views your purchase of a new sailboat not as your lifelong dream being fulfilled but as money coming out of his own pocket. You begin to suspect the motivations behind your daughter's trip to visit you for the holidays: "Does she really want to see me, or is she just worried about maintaining her share?"

There's even evidence that inheritance hurts the recipient. Studies show that the expectation of an inheritance erodes the drive and motivation to work. And what do you think it would do to your soul to have a reason to look forward to the death of a loved one?

Finally, inheritance is an incredibly inefficient means of passing along wealth, since it's subject to significantly more of a tax bite than any other type of income.

Rather than looking to acquire assets in some futile quest for immortality, in the new world you should focus instead on getting the maximum use out of your assets and income. There are financial tools available that can ensure you won't outlive your money while guaranteeing you'll leave nothing behind. Free from the burden of building an estate, you can use your money to help your family and improve your own life.

You can help your children when they're young and need it most. Rather than leaving them money when you die, you can send them to Europe for the summer, help them buy a car, supply the down payment for their first home, or provide start-up capital for their own business. Given wisely, such lifelong gifts can have a far greater long-term impact on their lives. When your child is twenty-five, $10,000 from you could spell the difference between renting an apartment and buying a home. When your child is fifty, that $10,000 could end up funding a two-week European vacation. Besides, if you give the money while you're alive, you'll be around to see their joy and receive their thanks.

By giving up the goal of maintaining an estate, you can also lead a far richer life of your own. You can take that month-long trip to England, study Renaissance art in Italy, buy a summer home in the Berkshires, renovate your kitchen, or simply just go out to dinner and the theater more often. I tell my clients that the last check they write should be to the undertaker . . . and that it should bounce. Ironically, by striving to die broke you guarantee you live well.

A CHANCE TO FINALLY PICK OUT YOUR OWN CLOTHES

Following these four maxims, and adopting the Die Broke program, will do more than just ease your fears and frustrations. Those four principles are actually keys that can unlock an incredibly rich future for you, one far better than was possible under the old rules.

It's not that I'm some kind of financial guru coming down from the mountaintop with the secret to life. It's just that there's a fundamental philosophical difference between the new axioms and the old rules that makes all the difference in the world.

The old rules were based on a whole litany of values, some of them good, some of them not so good. Underlying the advocacy of the climb up the corporate ladder is the concept that what others think of you is more important than what you think of yourself, and that the only rung that's worthwhile is the top one. Implicit in the promotion of buying on credit is the belief that something earned is no more valuable than something simply acquired. Urging full and early retirement is tantamount to saying work is a curse to be avoided if at all possible. And pushing for estate creation and the transfer of wealth through inheritance is based on the belief that money is the most important thing you could leave your children.

The new precepts are based on just one underlying principle: set your own goals and do the best you can do to achieve them. In this philosophy, every job "is just a job." You choose what to buy when you "pay cash." You can do anything you want if you "don't retire," just so long as you *do* something. And you can spend your wealth throughout your life however you see fit, just as long as you use it all up and "die broke."

What the Die Broke program offers most of all is freedom. Just as those earlier immigrant generations came to America and found their freedom, you can find freedom in the new economic world. Free from living the kind of life you've been told to lead, you can start to lead your own. It's as if your parents had been picking out your clothes and dressing you for years, and now, finally, you can pick out your own clothes. All those tapes that have been playing in your head, telling you what you had to do to measure up, what you couldn't possibly do, can now be thrown out and replaced with digital disks you write yourself.

Okay, real estate is no longer an investment. But did buying a starter home and then moving soon after *ever* really make sense? Weren't you taking what should have been an emotionally enriching part of your life and turning it into a commodity? Now you have an opportunity to buy a home rather than just a house, a place you and your family can love and afford, a wonderful space that can last your family for generations.

Sure, job security is gone. But weren't you killing yourself, physically and spiritually, by pursuing the company's goals rather than your own? Now you have a chance to stake a claim to your own dreams.

Yes, retirement may be out of reach. But was it ever really worth the stretch? Wouldn't it just ruin your physical and mental health and make you old before your time? Now you can view work as a lifelong journey that fits your own unique life.

Passing on wealth to the next generation might be possible for some, but why do it? It wouldn't be good for you, your child, or society. Now you can use your money while you're alive, doing good for yourself and others.

By choosing to Die Broke you turn the future from something to fear to something to embrace and rejoice over. Dying Broke offers a way out of your current misery and into a place of joy and happiness.

By giving up the outmoded rules of the past, by abandoning the quest to do what's impossible, and by establishing your own goals and paths, you can stake a claim to your own hopes and dreams. You can have a chance to follow your own bliss and uncover paths that truly bring you joy, satisfaction, and even prosperity.

Having finally learned to see the economic world as it is, you'll be able to look at the rest of your life with this same empowering candor. You'll be able to see clearly and objectively the new world facing you and find your place within it. This program will change your life for the better. I know, because I see it happen every day in my office.

You do have a choice, of course. You can choose to adapt to this new world, or you can remain locked in the ways of the past. You can look ahead and greet the new century joyously, or you can fear it and cling to archaic rules. You can become a living relic, sitting around and talking about how good it used to be, griping about the new world, and staying hidden in a ghetto of your own creation, or you can get out from between your ears, roll up your sleeves, and get to work carving out a niche for yourself in this new land.

The journey I'm asking you to take won't be easy. While you won't risk drowning on the trip, you will have to take a hard look at yourself and your place in the world. It might not be as bad as a week in steerage, but it could get uncomfortable. But I promise you, by the end of this book you'll have all the information and advice you need to make it. And believe me, the twenty-first century really is the promised land. To get there all you have to do is turn the page.

Quit Today

2

Need proof you're living in a new economic world? Just look around your office. I bet it's a lot less crowded these days.

Those folks who used to type the sales reports, deliver the mail, lay out the brochures, and do most of the grunt work around the place are long gone. Not only that, but the people who supervised the grunts have bit the dust too. Some of your peers whose departments weren't cash cows or who weren't averse to speaking their minds or who were entering the home stretch toward retirement have vanished as well. And I'll bet those of you who are left are a lot less chipper. No more long lunches with talk about the kids and golf, am I right? Instead, there's a lot more eating sandwiches at the desk, alone. When you do go out with someone, the talk seems more like networking than conversation. Instead of asking how the Yankees did yesterday you want to know how the company's stock did yesterday.

Want even more conclusive evidence? Just examine your feelings about your career.

Ten years ago you (and your spouse) were probably eagerly working from sunrise to sunset . . . and then some. You brought work home at night and on Friday. When you socialized, the number one topic of conversation was work . . . because you went out with people you worked with. Basically, your career was your life. You and everyone else were sprinting up, not just climbing, the ladder. It was go, go, go and you were going to be successful, successful, successful, and rich, rich, rich.

Today you (and your spouse) are probably still working from sunrise to sunset . . . but a lot less eagerly. You're still bringing work home too, but now it's because you're doing the work of three. The number one topic of conversation when you go out is still work, but now it's how much you hate it. You're still sprinting, but now it's on a treadmill. You're having to go faster and faster to just stay in place. Forget about success and wealth—now you're worried about holding on to your paycheck. Rather than the focus of your life, your career is now the bane of your existence.

Believe me, you're not alone.

THE STORY OF ANDREA DREESON

When I first met Andrea Dreeson in 1985, she could have been the cover girl for *Yuppie Magazine*. She and her husband, a prominent plastic surgeon, came to me for help in buying an apartment on Sutton Place—one of New York City's most exclusive areas. A graduate of the Wharton School of Business and Finance, Andrea was a rising corporate star. Sacked in one of the most notorious boardroom battles of the 1980s, she was snapped up by a leading international financial services firm, given a $200,000 salary, and named executive vice president. It was understood that she was being groomed for the presidency. It was easy to see why.

Andrea was striking. Tall and thin, with high cheekbones and an aquiline nose, she reminded me of a magnificent bird of prey. There was that kind of intensity about her. While she wasn't rude, you could tell she wasn't interested in any more small talk or pleasantries than courtesy dictated. Andrea didn't mince words, nor did she show any self-doubt. She was looking to hunt down and seize all that she wanted from life.

It wasn't easy working with Andrea and her husband. They both worked twelve-hour days. They hardly saw and spoke with each other, so it was rare they had the time to sit and chat with me about apartment hunting. Actually, that worked out for the best, since before we even got around to contacting brokers they were contacting divorce lawyers. Andrea remained my client, and while the divorce was being finalized, I helped her find an apartment of her own on the Upper

East Side, not far from where she worked. After finalizing her apartment purchase, I'd see Andrea every January for a financial and career checkup. She never spoke of anything personal. Her career was her life.

That made it especially difficult when in 1993 her company had two bad quarters in a row. The primary shareholders—an English investment banker and an Asian financier—had both invested in the firm because of its ability to generate cash. After it had been in the red for six months they pressured management to downsize and simultaneously boost revenues. Andrea's position wasn't in danger, but she was given the job of hatchet woman. Even though she already seemed to be living in the office, it was subtly made clear she'd have to redouble her efforts if she wanted to remain "next in line" to the throne.

Right around that time she came to me for her annual "checkup." She didn't look well. She'd crossed over that line that separates "striking" from "sickly." Her intensity no longer seemed to come from a place of self-confidence; it smacked of desperation. We went about our consultation in the same businesslike manner we'd always taken. She explained what was happening at the office in her usual detached and analytical style. Then something happened that was totally out of character. "That's Vivaldi, isn't it?" she asked.

(Let me back up and explain that I always have classical music playing in the office. It can be crowded and chaotic in the converted apartment I use for my practice. Phones are always ringing, and people are always working on at least three things at once. I've found that classical music—particularly from the Baroque and Romantic periods— helps to subliminally soothe nerves. That's why when I get into the office one of the first things I do is load the CD player with enough disks to take us through lunch.)

Andrea was right: It was Vivaldi. I was surprised because it was actually a fairly obscure concerto, not *The Four Seasons* or some other well-known work. "You know music," I said in response. She chuckled and told me she'd studied the cello for most of her life, giving it up only after college. She then went on to tell me how much she'd loved playing Vivaldi. Her whole face lit up, not with the intensity I'd grown used to seeing but with a warmth I'd never seen her display before. But just as suddenly as the change in her appeared, it vanished. With her usual no-nonsense attitude she finished telling me about her on-the-job problems and pressures. "What are your suggestions?" she asked.

"Quit," I said.

JOB SECURITY IS DEAD

It's obvious the relationship between employers and employees has changed. The first signs were easy for us to ignore. When America's top five hundred manufacturing firms laid off almost five million blue-collar workers during the 1980s, those of us wearing suits wrote it off as just one more in a long line of "course corrections." Then, when layoffs began to reach into middle management in the early 1990s, we blamed them on the recession and incompetent corporate management. But the recession ended and the layoffs continued. More and more middle- and upper-level managers are being "downsized" each day, and there's no end in sight.

What makes this particularly troubling is that there's really nothing you can do to make your job secure. In the old days of corporate paternalism, performance and seniority were enough to ensure your security and advancement. In the 1980s and early 1990s it looked like security would be based on continued corporate profitability. While you had less control over that, you could still impact it somewhat, or at least show you personally were a "profit center," theoretically ensuring your position. But now that's not even enough. Companies are simultaneously declaring record profits and slashing payrolls. That's the final straw: There is now absolutely nothing you can do to make your own position secure.

White-collar, middle-class, college-educated folks are seeing their standards of living and prospects for employment drop for the first time since the Great Depression. Sure, there are new jobs out there, as the economic boosters will rush to tell you. But they're not as good as the jobs that are being eliminated. They're part-time rather than full-time. They're fry cook jobs at a local Taco Bell rather than executive spots at PepsiCo's corporate headquarters. The biggest employer in America is no longer General Motors, it's Manpower, a temporary employment agency. That just about says it all. The days of climbing ladders, of jobs that were rewarding, both financially and emotionally, are gone forever.

So what's the solution?

THE MERCANTILE ETHIC

The same solution it has always been: change your attitude toward work. That's what I meant when I told Andrea to quit. Let me explain.

Historically, Americans' attitudes toward work have always evolved to fit changing socioeconomic patterns. Social scientists point to five distinct, often overlapping, trends in Americans' attitudes toward work.

First there was the Protestant Ethic—we work happily for the glory of God—which grew out of the predestination of Calvinism and the individualism and asceticism of the Quakers.

That was secularized by Benjamin Franklin, among others, into what's called the Craft Ethic: We work diligently for ourselves. It made a great deal of sense in a nation where 80 percent of the population were self-employed farmers and craftsmen. As Franklin said, "God helps those who help themselves."

In response to the risk taking of the frontier and the dawn of the Industrial Revolution, attitudes toward work began to change again. Replacing Franklin's taciturn craftsmen were the smart-talking risk takers popularized by Horatio Alger. This Entrepreneurial Ethic, that a person with the right attitude could make it on his own, helped rationalize the growing inequality in society.

Technological advancement and the further development of corporate bureaucracies made it harder and harder for the Ragged Dicks of the world to go it alone and succeed. As a result, a new attitude toward work developed. Rather than hoping to establish their own businesses, people began to seek jobs in large organizations and move up the bureaucratic ladder to positions of greater responsibility and higher status. This Career Ethic led to an entire generation of Organization Men.

But as your generation began to enter the workforce in the 1960s and 1970s, you brought with you a further change. Raised in a large group, you sought desperately to carve out some individuality, both at home and at work. Concerned with personal growth, you looked for work that was "challenging" and that allowed for "self-expression." This Self-Fulfillment Ethic makes a great deal of sense, if it's built upon a foundation of job security. But today, with insecurity the rule, the continued pursuit of self-fulfillment leads to incredible frustration . . . as I'm sure you know.

These changes in Americans' attitudes toward work have been coming quicker and quicker, mirroring the speed with which American society is changing. The Craft Ethic lasted more than a century. The Career Ethic lasted fifty years. And now, after only two decades, it's time to abandon the Self-Fulfillment Ethic and adopt what I call the Mercantile Ethic.

In conditions of economic expansion and security it's easy, and probably healthy, for work to represent the self and for people to tie themselves closely to their employer. Such attitudes made sense at a time when government was subsidizing higher education through low-interest loans and when corporations were expanding the ranks of middle management. For the past two decades, what we did for a living and who we worked for reflected on our value as human beings and the values we held. "Job" became an old-fashioned, blue-collar kind of word, replaced by more abstract terms such as "career" and "work."

But in a time when there's no such thing as corporate loyalty, when anyone can be laid off for any reason, with no regard to their performance, when kids graduating from Ivy League colleges are taking positions as temps, when raises are as rare as Chicago Cub pennants, viewing yourself and your job as one is a tremendous financial and emotional risk.

I'm telling my clients to quit today: to instantly separate themselves from their employer mentally; in effect, to begin acting as if they were unemployed. I'm telling them to pay as much, if not more, attention to their own bottom lines as the company's. I'm suggesting they focus on what they're doing as a job, not necessarily a career, and view it as being primarily an income-generating device. Any other benefits are purely secondary. I'm not saying they, and you, should obsess over money. I'm simply urging you to abandon the single-minded pursuit of self-fulfillment through employment. I think you should use your job—and I use that word intentionally—to generate the money you need to pursue your personal goals rather than looking to employment itself to fulfill those goals. Start practicing bifocal vision: look at both your own needs and the company's.

LOOKING FOR ROLE MODELS

You want a role model for this new work ethic?

Look to professional athletes. They do their best and are part of the team, but they're primarily focused on getting the best financial deal they can. They know that their tenure with any one team is temporary—in their case for as long as their contract runs. And even with that contract, they accept they could be traded tomorrow to another team, or they could be cut from the squad or placed on waivers.

They see their work as a tool to generate income, whether in salary or endorsements. Free agents insist that their pay must relate to their performance. They compare their statistics to others playing the same position and insist the team pay them the market value for their labors. It's only after they've "taken care of their families for life" that they will even consider taking a pay cut in order to play for a potential champion. Do their employers think less of them? Not at all. That's because an owner can trade or cut a player for any reason, and doesn't think twice about offering a contract for less money if the player's performance drops.

I know. You're thinking it sounds good in the abstract but can't really be put into practice if you're not a six-foot nine-inch 315-pounder who runs a 4.2-second 40-yard dash. But it is being done, right now, by people you know very well: your younger brothers and sisters, that much-maligned group called Generation X.

Unlike you, they never experienced corporate loyalty, so they have no "good old days" to look back to. Far from coming of age in booming economic times, they've had to face depressing job prospects from day one. They're the ones that grew up with McJobs. They saw you and your folks work yourselves to death, have little or no "life," and then get repaid with layoffs. They hate corporate politics, distrust institutions, and are motivated primarily by money. As one young fellow told me recently: "It's easy to avoid obsessing over money when you've got it. When you're twenty-seven and still living at home, money is everything."

People love criticizing Gen Xers, but they're exactly the kind of workers we need in the current economy. They're self-directed, techno-literate, empowered, and flexible . . . that's every management guru's wish list. I'm urging all my clients to quit today, adopt the Mercantile Ethic, learn the workplace rules of Gen Xers, and put them into practice. What's the alternative? Extinction.

MAKING IT IN THE TWENTY-FIRST-CENTURY WORKPLACE

Follow these principles and you won't end up like the dinosaurs. (More specific advice on these and other topics can be found in Part Two of this book.)

It's Just a Job

Forget about the pursuit of a holistic work life. You cannot successfully integrate your work and the rest of your life. Your work is not your life. Your work is what you do so you can *have* a life.

Mary Stallone was one of my most driven clients. A well-known advertising executive, she was earning nearly $200,000 at the age of thirty-seven. But when her youngest daughter, age five, was more upset when the nanny took a vacation than when Mary had to go to Europe on business, she knew something was wrong. After it was made clear to her that she couldn't possibly keep her current position and salary without putting in endless hours, she found another job with a company that didn't demand twenty-four hours a day, seven days a week. She's making the same money, but now she's home for dinner with the kids every night.

Jump Ship

Quit in your head. The only way to definitely increase your job satisfaction and/or your income is to get another job. The more you move from job to job, the more likely you are to continually increase your income. Job hopping is the future. The secret is for you to find a new job before they can fire you. That's why you should always be looking for a new job.

Danny Kennedy had been the art director of one of America's most popular travel magazines for more than nine years. He was making decent money but hadn't gotten a raise in four years. With a baby on the way, he and his wife needed to buy a larger apartment. It was clear the only way Danny and his wife could afford a larger apartment in the kind of neighborhood they wanted was to make more money. It took some doing, but Danny eventually accepted that the best way to do that was to leave his comfortable niche and jump ship. He found another art director's job that paid 5 percent more in salary. And now, rather than getting too comfortable, he's already looking for his next job after being there only ten months.

Short Term Is the Only Term

Long-term benefits, like pension plans, are worthless. Most of you will be fired long before you're fully vested. It's short-term benefits that count: things that improve your present quality of life, like health insurance, company day care, parental leave, telecommuting and flex-time options, even company health club memberships.

Lateral Is Better Than Vertical

It's better to make a lateral move that offers a chance to expand your skills than it is to take a position with great responsibility. There's probably no increase in pay to go with the greater responsibility, just a new title and a greater chance to become a scapegoat. Added skills will make it easier to jump ship.

Gary Leopold had been working his way up the ladder at a major retail chain. He'd always loved marketing and promotion and had made those his specialties. So when he learned there was an opening in the national marketing department, he automatically applied. However, when he spoke with the human resources executive in charge of recruiting, he learned there was also an opening in the regional finance department. After learning the new rules, he knew that a chance to broaden his skills was more valuable than climbing another rung up a crumbling ladder. He took the finance job instead. Eighteen months later he was able to jump ship and take a job as regional general manager of another retail chain.

Will This Be on the Test?

Learn exactly what's expected of you and do it the best you can. Forget about filling company vacuums and creating new power bases. Such behavior will take time away from your personal life and will do nothing to increase your security. Do your job well, however long it takes, and then go home.

Just Do It

Don't pay attention to company politics. Who gets credit doesn't matter. The rising star and the brownnoser are going to be on the unemployment line alongside the quiet performer and the loner. Any time spent talking and not doing is time you could have spent on your personal life, or finding another job.

There Are No Dues

There's no point in paying dues. By the time you're a full member of the club it could have vanished. Getting your foot in the door and learning a business or industry from the bottom used to make sense. Today the whole industry could be dead before you get out of the mailroom. You've no time to pay dues. Jobs must now make economic sense from day one.

Show Me the Money

The work reward that matters is what you're paid. Remember: Everything other than money can come from the rest of your life. Your job is the only part of your life that can give you money, so you need to maximize that.

When it comes to raises, remember your value as a free agent is based on the value the market places on your skills, not the company's bottom line or your seniority. If other top assistant wallpaper hangers are earning $15,000, that's what you should be earning. If other top executive vice presidents in your industry are earning $250,000, that's what you should be earning. You are your skills. Make it clear to your current employer that if they don't pay the market rate for your services, they won't be able to replace you when you leave. That will make them "show you the money."

Richie Gudderson came to me when he was laid off from a major media company. It was a long struggle, but after nearly a year of unemployment he received two job offers in the same week. One was from an entertainment company with a reputation for innovation and being a fun place to work. The other was from a publishing house, known to be a steady but conservative, almost stodgy organization. A dynamic person, Richie's first instinct was to opt for the innovative firm. But then he focused on the bottom line. The stodgy publisher was offering $10,000 more a year. He took it and focuses on getting his thrills at home.

AN ADDED BONUS

If you quit today and then follow the Mercantile Ethic, you'll discover it has an added bonus: It increases your chances of being happy with your life. There's nothing magical about this. It was probably always a mistake to look to work to answer any of our needs other than just money. When you view work as primarily a means to make money, it's easier to put your other needs in perspective and pursue them through the areas that offer the greatest chance of success.

If you want spiritual rewards, look to your spiritual life. You'll be far more likely to find God in a church, mosque, temple, or through meditation than in an office.

If you want love and a sense of belonging, look to your family and friends. You'll be more apt to find it among them than with coworkers brought together temporarily by circumstance and coincidence.

And if you want self-actualization, look for it in all that you do outside of your work. Be the best spouse, parent, child, neighbor, friend, and citizen you can be, and you'll be far closer to reaching your true human potential than if you concentrated on being the best accountant you can be.

ANDREA DREESON: PLAYING OUT HER OPTION

After suggesting Andrea quit, I explained to her my ideas about the Mercantile Ethic and jobs being just tools to generate streams of income, not emotional and psychological satisfaction. She laughed it off at first, but I could see the wheels in her head start spinning.

When next we met again, six months later, Andrea seemed happier and far warmer and more personable than I'd ever seen her. She laughed and said it was all my doing. She had quit in her head and had actually started playing the cello again. She and some other skilled amateurs had organized a little string quartet. Andrea was still putting long hours in at the office, but she'd given up her all-consuming pursuit of the company's presidency. She'd stopped defining herself by her job and her employer. She was occasionally taking time off work for rehearsals and performances. I begged for, and received, an invitation to her next concert.

By the next time we met—four months later at one of her concerts—an even greater change had come over Andrea. She had gotten up the nerve to contact an old boyfriend from college who she learned had recently divorced and was teaching high school in Connecticut. It was love at second sight. They were already talking marriage and sketching out plans to sell their apartments, buy a home in Greenwich, and start a family.

Today, Andrea and her husband, Jack, are the parents of twin girls. Jack's still teaching high school, and Andrea's still working at the financial services firm. She's no longer viewed as the next likely president. But what's more important is that she's feeling totally in charge

of her own life. She's still working at a job she's good at, but she
knows it's not her whole life. If she lost her job tomorrow she'd certainly be disappointed, and she and Jack would have to make adjustments, but it wouldn't affect her sense of self. After all, she'd quit over
a year ago.

Pay Cash

3

There are only three things that could keep you permanently trapped in the twentieth century. The first is an unwillingness to change your attitude and approach. Since you've already bought a book called *Die Broke* and have read this far into it, it's safe to assume you're not that stubborn . . . or foolish. The other two are a bit more difficult to dismiss.

That's because you carry them with you almost everywhere. They're the vital organs of life in the 1990s. In fact, you can't even imagine life without them would be possible, let alone preferable. Yet these perceived necessities are actually vestigial, even cancerous. If you don't cut them out of your life right now, they're going to spread deadly disease to the rest of your financial life. Of course, I'm talking about your ATM and credit cards.

Think I'm exaggerating? Well, let's take a look at how convenient your financial life has become; how instantly your wants are being satisfied.

How do you pay for your groceries? If you're like many of us you probably whip out your ATM card and slide it through the scanner at the checkout line. The only time you focus on exactly how much you spent is if you remember to enter the transaction in your checkbook or on your PC. It wasn't so long ago that you wrote checks at the supermarket . . . and your mom paid for her groceries with cash. Convenience. Instant gratification. No pain.

Speaking of your checkbook, when was the last time it even left the house? It was such a pain writing checks, wasn't it? Sure, when you got your first checking account freshman year of college it was pretty neat. But by the time you were out in the real world, it was passé. Filling in all those lines, updating the register, pulling out your driver's license, and having the clerk write down that absurdly long number in addition to the Social Security number of every member of your extended family. Now you get a bit annoyed when you're stuck in line behind someone paying by check. They're so retro, you think. Why don't they just put it on their credit card or go to the cash machine first? Convenience. Instant gratification. No pain.

ATMs really are amazing, aren't they? Do you even remember back to when you had to make sure to get to the bank before it closed to get money for the weekend? Seems like decades. In fact, can you even remember how to get cash from a teller? Oh, yeah, you need to write a check out to cash. But of course your checkbook is back at home, and who remembers what hours the bank is open? You've got your little ATM card instead. That magic wand you can wave and get cash anywhere at any time. You used to have to take money out before a trip, since banks wouldn't cash your out-of-town checks. Now you can get money instantly, even overseas. Hey, need a few bob to buy a pint at a pub near Covent Garden, just remember your PIN number and you've got constant access to a seemingly endless stream of cash . . . in multiples of $20, or £10 only, of course. Convenience. Instant gratification. No pain.

On the way back from the ATM you can just pull into a gas station and fill up the Subaru. Pull right up and pay at the pump with either your ATM, credit, or gasoline card. No waiting. By the way, do you know which station in your town charges the least for gas? Convenience. Instant gratification. No pain.

When was the last time you actually saved up to buy something? When you were a kid you put quarters in a jar. When you were a teen you probably stashed some of your allowance in a savings account. Today? Banks don't even want to look at savings accounts—unless they've got balances of over $500—on which they'll charge fees that add up to more than the interest they pay. And what can *your* kid buy for a quarter? Now we let Visa or MasterCard do our savings for us. The VCR chews up your tape of *Spin City*. Rather than setting aside a certain amount from every one of your paychecks until you've got enough to pick up a new VCR, you simply go to Circuit City and slap down the plastic. Convenience. Instant gratification. No pain.

Lately you've been thinking about doing even more of your banking on-line. Your bank sent out a mailing last week saying that if you use Quicken or Microsoft Money, and subscribe to the bank's on-line service, you can pay your bills directly from your PC. No more need to buy those expensive stamps and return address labels. No more worries about whether or not the check arrived on time. Hey, in a couple of years you may not even need checks at all. In fact, for the ultimate in utility your friendly creditors and bankers will set up a system where they just take the money out of your account automatically. No more of those nasty bills clogging your mailbox. Convenience. Instant gratification. No pain.

All this convenience, instant gratification, and lack of pain come with some strings attached—strings that at first are as hard to see as fishing line, but once spotted become as apparent as chains.

On the most obvious level you're charged fees for convenience. Individually they may not seem like much, but added together over a year they can be quite substantial. For instance, my bank charges $.35 every time an ATM card is used to make a purchase. It charges $1.00 every time money is drawn from another bank's machine. (Sometimes the other bank charges its own $1.00 fee as well.) It charges $5.00 a month for its on-line banking services.

Let's go through a typical year and see how much convenience could cost. If you go shopping once a week, that means $.35 times fifty-two weeks for a total of $18.20. Let's say you go to the ATM once a week. But one of those times each month you use a different bank's machine; that's $12.00. And maybe half of those times the other bank slaps on a charge too. That's another $6.00. Finally, let's assume you subscribe to the on-line banking service. That will run you $60.00 a year. Your grand total for banking convenience is $96.20. Okay, it's not a fortune, but it isn't chump change either. That would pay for an awfully nice dinner out for you and your spouse.

You're also charged fees for instant gratification, namely interest on your credit cards. On a rational level I'm sure you're aware of how absurdly high these can be. We're talking about anywhere from 12 percent on up to nearly 19 percent on purchases; it's even more if you take out cash advances. Since the interest compounds monthly on unpaid balances, it's easy to end up paying a couple of grand a year if you just pay the minimum. Add to that the interest you're losing by not taking that two grand and investing it and we're talking a nice chunk now. But still, that's not the most damaging thing about convenience and instant gratification.

What really makes the pursuit of convenience and instant gratification dangerous is that they anesthetize you to the pain of spending. And like any effective painkiller they're both habit forming and constantly require greater doses for you to get the same effect. The further removed you become from the actual spending of cash, the easier it is to spend. I'll bet you don't even know what most of the items you buy at the supermarket cost. And I'll wager you couldn't tell me how much you're paying per gallon for gasoline. That's because you just hand over a piece of plastic. The whole transaction has become abstract. That has made impulse buying a snap. See something you like in the store? Just hand over the plastic and it's yours. See something you like in one of the ten thousand catalogs that arrive in your mailbox each day? Spot something interesting (for $19.95) on television when you're up late one night with insomnia? Call the twenty-four-hour telephone line and read them your card number. Can't be bothered even talking to an operator? Just fax or E-mail your order.

Can't pay the whole balance when the bill comes at the end of the month? Don't worry, you can just pay 5 percent of your new charges. Your pals at Visa or MasterCard will let you slide for the rest . . . while charging you interest. Want to buy something that will more than max out the limit on you card? No problem. Call customer service, twenty-four hours a day, and they'll be able to instantly increase your credit line. Before you can max out the new limit you'll have gotten two new automatically preapproved cards in the mail. It's like they're just sending you money.

To a certain extent they are—but in the same way drug dealers give kids free crack, or cigarette makers hand out samples of new brands on city streets. They're just trying to get you hooked. And once you've got that plastic monkey on your back, it's tough to shake him off. He'll drain the cash flow right out of you. He'll keep you trapped in a twentieth-century credit-shooting gallery while those of us who are clean move into the twenty-first century. Just ask Ken Schoenfeld.

THE STORY OF KEN AND MARY SCHOENFELD

Ken Schoenfeld looks a lot like the actor Kevin Kline . . . and he knows it. Relying on his creativity as well as his charm and good looks, the forty-two-year old native New Yorker has had a meteoric rise in the advertising industry. Starting out as an account executive when he graduated from college, over the course of twenty years he has hopped from agency to agency, getting a pay jump each time. When I first met him two years ago, he'd finally put down some roots as creative director in a medium-sized agency that was paying him a little over $300,000 a year.

In a good year, his wife, Mary, thirty-eight, could make almost as much. A successful photographer, she had met Ken on an assignment ten years ago. They made for an interesting couple. Mary wasn't nearly as outgoing as Ken, but she radiated a substance and solidity that you sort of felt he lacked. Similarly, Ken seemed to provide the drive and energy that made them both successful.

Mary made her early reputation doing fashion shoots, but after marrying Ken and having a baby—Juliet—two years later, she shifted her focus to product photography, since it didn't require travel. Of course, it did require a fairly large studio space. But Ken and Mary were lucky in that right after Juliet's birth they were able to find a large and affordable (for New York City) loft space downtown. The space was large enough that when they got pregnant again two years after Juliet's birth, they were able to steal space from Mary's studio and the living room to make another room. By the time Penelope arrived, she and Juliet both had their own rooms.

But taking care of two little girls was a lot more work than Mary anticipated. Even though she worked from home, it was soon clear she'd need help if she was going to continue working full-time. After two years and a few failed attempts at getting day care help on their own, they decided to contact an agency and look for a live-in nanny. It took them only a week to find a wonderful girl named Siobhan. They moved Juliet and Penelope into one room and gave Siobhan the other, but they knew that was only a temporary fix. Clearly, they needed more space. That's when they came to me.

The first thing I do when clients come to me for help in buying a new home is develop a list of prioritized goals. With Ken and Mary that was the easy part. They needed sufficient space for two children (they didn't plan on having any more), a live-in nanny, themselves, and Mary's business. They wanted to be near enough to Manhattan so Ken wouldn't spend more time commuting than with the kids, yet they wanted a safe area with good schools. I knew that was a tall order, but not impossible, considering they had a combined income of anywhere from $400,000 to $600,000 a year, depending on how well Mary's business did. The shock came when we went over their expenses.

Ken and Mary had accumulated more than $75,000 in credit card debt. Just making the minimum payments each month was costing them $2,000. I'm used to seeing large credit card balances, but this was extraordinarily large. I probed to find out what was behind it. I didn't have to dig too deep to discover that Ken was a compulsive clothes shopper. He came home with a new designer suit at least once a month . . . and along with the suit there was a custom-tailored shirt, a silk tie, new shoes, and perhaps a sweater or vest. He had no trouble rationalizing his wardrobe as a cost of doing business. "In order to *be* successful in advertising you need to be perceived as already *being* successful," he said. "It's just the cost of packaging," he explained with a charming grin. Mary had to have similar "packaging" in order to "look right" on Ken's arm when they went out with his clients, she explained, with a lot less conviction than Ken. And of course, the girls were just as well wrapped.

It wasn't just clothes, however. Ken and Mary had dined out nearly every night before they'd had children. Having a family didn't turn them into cooks; they just become takeout fanatics. And we're not talking Pizza Hut and Boston Chicken. They brought meals in from gourmet shops and fine restaurants—the same places they'd eaten in before they'd started their family. They went on luxury vacations, paid for by credit card. They furnished and refurnished the loft, with their credit cards. The more I learned, the more it became clear they were simply buying everything they wanted. As their income and family grew, so did their lifestyle. Despite an income that averaged about half a million dollars a year, they literally had nothing in the bank . . . they were living in a house of cards.

Ken had become so used to this lifestyle that he couldn't see anything wrong with it, even after I pointed out the tremendous strain and burden it was putting on their stream of income and the handicap it was to their buying a new home. "My income has jumped up every year, why wouldn't it jump next year?" he asked, not really wanting an answer. "We're paying our bills and at the same time, we're living a great life." Clearly he was so heavily invested in his credit card lifestyle that he couldn't see the trees for the forest. But Mary's blinders didn't fit quite as well. It was obvious from her body language and expressions that the borrowing was causing her emotional stress. She just needed an outsider to confirm her feelings and confront Ken.

Mary's own income was erratic, and knowing the nature of the advertising industry, she thought Ken's income could dry up as quickly as it soared. "You're so wrapped up living in the present," she blurted out, "you never give a thought to our future. That was okay when it was just the two of us, but what about the girls? We don't have a dime in the bank."

Before our financial planning degenerated into a marital counseling session, I jumped into the fray. "Ken's no victim," I said, "but it's not entirely his fault."

BLAME IT ON THE CREDIT PUSHERS

We have become a nation of spenders and debtors rather than a nation of savers. One recent study found that 20 percent of Americans had no net worth beyond consumer goods. If you ignored real estate, the number jumped to 55 percent. Basically, most Americans have nothing other than the home they live in and the stuff they put in it.

Sure, all of us, including Ken Schoenfeld, have free will. We're not being forced to spend and consume rather than scrimp and save. However, for more than fifty years we have been encouraged to consume rather than save, not just by those who are selling us things but by our national leaders.

Prior to the 1930s the dominant capitalist economic theory was that espoused by Adam Smith. In a nutshell (the only way anyone can understand economic theory), Smith preached that it was savings that led a country into prosperity. In fact, he believed the instinct to save was rooted in human nature. But Smith's "thrift philosophy" was called into question by the Great Depression.

FDR and his New Dealers, desperate to get the country going again, adopted a different theory, one associated with John Maynard Keynes. He believed that it was consumption (spending), not thrift (savings), that led a country to prosperity. This fit in well with the

New Dealers' understandable desire to do something, anything, to get the country back on its feet. Government began spending rather than saving.

While the American response to the Great Depression was to shift economic theories within a democratic framework, the German, Italian, and Japanese response was to turn toward fascism. Among its many other monumental impacts on history, World War II gave the U.S. government something to spend its money on.

The American economy boomed both during and after World War II. Even though savings were down, the economy was growing as never before. John Maynard Keynes had displaced Adam Smith.

Savings was no longer considered human nature. Instead a new "life cycle theory" of savings, developed by Franco Modigliani, was adopted. It said that people saved when they had surplus money *and* a specific reason to save. In other words, when they'd already bought the house, the car, and the dishwasher; had put the kids through college; and had gone to Europe; then in middle age they'd start saving for their own retirement. Until then they should just spend and borrow and spend some more.

As you can imagine, it didn't take much arm-twisting to get people behind these new theories. Consumerism was not only fun but patriotic. Advertising became an industry. Phrases like *conspicuous consumption* and *planned obsolescence* entered the vocabulary. We fell into an apparently endless cycle of borrowing and buying, linking our national and individual self-images to our level of luxury.

At first it was the families with televisions that had status. Then it was a new car. Then there were all those new kitchen appliances. Then color televisions, followed by stereo systems, VCRs, answering machines, personal computers, cellular phones . . . and whatever comes next. This all-consuming frenzy reached its apex during the 1980s, when spending more than you earned was enshrined as both a national policy (Reaganomics) and a lifestyle (yuppies).

Incredibly powerful advertising—of both products and policy— promoted the joys of consumption. Consumer and commercial credit was readily available for everyone either through credit cards that just appeared in your mailbox or junk bonds. The national psyche was obsessed with self-indulgence and immediate gratification. It all actually seemed to make sense. It was part and parcel of the American way.

Real estate was soaring in value. By borrowing as much as possible and buying a home as soon as possible, you could jump on the bandwagon. Buy a starter home or condo and hold it three years. Then sell it for a profit and buy another, more expansive home. Hold that until the kids were out of the house, then sell it and buy a luxury apartment in Aspen overlooking the ski slopes.

Inflation was high, so credit card buying looked like a brilliant idea. After all, incomes were rising, weren't they? Why wait until you could afford to pay cash for that trip to Ireland? By that time you could be too old to hike up Croagh Patrick. Charge it instead. If you were brought up using a food processor rather than a grater, and if the only time you ever saw a service van was when it arrived with a new stove, it seemed only right to buy appliances right away—even if you had to charge them. And when new, more sophisticated or stylish appliances (or cars, or furniture, or clothes, or anything) came along, you bought them on credit, even if you weren't even finished paying for the one you just replaced.

The problem is you were living beyond your means. We all were, both individually and as a nation. But that only became clear when we had, without recognizing it, crossed over into the new economic world.

Suddenly we are in a world where real estate values are flat, not rising like a rocket; a world where inflation is low, not high; a world where incomes are shrinking or disappearing altogether, not climbing. In this world the "life cycle theory" of savings no longer works. Today you're putting your kids through college at an age when your parents were saving for retirement. Your income is at its most precarious at an age when your parents' income was its highest and most secure. And you can't rely on your home to bail you out, as they could. When it was time for them to sell, there were only a few houses out there, but millions of baby boomers in the market to buy. When it comes time for you to sell there will be millions of boomer-owned houses on the market and only that handful of Gen Xers looking to buy.

What's the solution? Simple. Pay cash.

MAKE SPENDING DIFFICULT AND UNCOMFORTABLE

You've got to banish credit and convenience from your spending life. In fact, you've got to make spending as difficult and uncomfortable as possible. You must resolve to no longer reach beyond your grasp. If you don't have the cash on hand or in your checking account to buy something . . . don't buy it.

You need to save and wait and then buy something—whether a home, car, or a suit—that you need rather than just want. Having to physically hand dollar bills over can do a great deal to help you determine the difference. When you've got to physically go and pull $20 out of the bank, or write a check, going to that first-run movie no longer seems as pressing. Maybe you can wait for the video. When you've got to pull $200 out for a new food processor, cleaning up and repairing the old one don't seem so bad. And when you've got to write a check for $6,000 for that trip to France rather than just slapping down the Visa card, a weekend in Gettysburg starts looking a lot better.

And when you do buy something, you've got to make sure it's going to last long enough to justify either the cost of borrowing or the time you spent saving the cash to buy it. Phrases like "the newest," "the latest," and "the hottest" need to be banished from your mouth and, perhaps even more important, the mouths of your kids. Replace them with terms like "classic," "timeless," and "traditional." You simply can no longer afford to replace items just because they're out of fashion.

Worried about what everyone else will think of you when you're no longer cutting edge? Don't. First, you shouldn't care what people think of you. Second, pay cash and you *will* be cutting edge. In the twenty-first century frugality will be hip. Conspicuous consumption will be out. You can already see the trend starting if you look close enough. There are lots more used-book stores and vintage-clothing shops appearing around cities. Gardening is becoming America's number one hobby, and composting is suddenly cool. Third, everyone else will be paying cash too. Why? Because they'll have either realized the wisdom of the approach or they'll have gone broke. Need further reassurance? Ask your grandparents.

LOOK BACKWARD FOR ROLE MODELS

Assuming you're a baby boomer, your parents came of age during the post–World War II boom. Your folks entered the workplace when the economy was expanding, when jobs were more secure than ever before, and when incomes moved in only one direction: up. They could start a family early in life and support that family in middle-class comfort on just one income. They could look to an expanding welfare state that provided assistance when they went to buy a home and send their kids to college. They were the first generation covered by generous public and private pensions. They were able to buy real estate when it was abundant and inexpensive and sell when it was in demand and expensive.

Your economic life is, and will be, nothing like your parents'. Look at your grandparents' economic lives, on the other hand, and you'll feel like you're staring into a mirror.

They came of age and reached maturity in a time of economic uncertainty. They were in the workplace at a time when the economy was shrinking, when jobs were insecure, and when incomes fell more often than they rose. They waited until later in life to start their families and often needed two incomes to keep a roof over their heads. They received little or no government assistance when it came to buying a home or sending their kids to college. They had a meager government pension (Social Security without cost-of-living adjustments) and no private pension to rely on. And they didn't make money on the sale of their real estate. What did they do to get by? They repaired rather than replaced. They mended and made do. They saved for everything they bought and avoided borrowing. They did what you should be doing: They paid cash.

SAVINGS AND SPENDING IN THE TWENTY-FIRST CENTURY

That's why they'd be familiar with many of these guides for saving and spending in the twenty-first century. (More specific advice on these and other topics can be found in Part Two of this book.)

Melt Your Plastic

Remove every credit card from your wallet, including gasoline cards. There's absolutely no reason you need to carry them around. The only things they do is make it easier for you to ignore prices and buy things you don't need and can't afford.

Get a pay-as-you-go charge card, like American Express, if you don't already have one. Keep that with you in case of emergencies. Since you have to pay the entire bill when it arrives at the end of the month, you'll soon be cured of any mistaken belief it's just like a credit card. Start paying cash for your gasoline and you'll soon discover which station has the lowest prices.

Meanwhile, transfer any and all credit card balances onto one card with a low interest rate. Put that card in your closet. Cut up all your other cards. Pay the balance off as soon as possible and when you do, cut up that card. Now, apply for a new closet credit card with no annual fee. You don't care about rates anymore because it's just for emergencies and you won't be maintaining a balance.

Bank with People

Remove the ATM card from your wallet and put it in the closet with your emergency credit card. Once a week go to a real live bank teller and withdraw sufficient cash for all your normal spending needs by writing a check out to cash. You'll end up spending less when you're forced to recalculate your balance.

What if you need emergency spending money? Why do you need emergency spending money? You've got your American Express card for emergencies.

Don't have enough cash to buy a spontaneous lunch out, or to pick up that new CD you heard on the radio? Then save for it.

Worried you won't have enough cash to go out to the movies Sunday night? Plan ahead. Then, when the money is in your wallet, make sure you remember it's there for an already defined purpose, not for a sudden whim. If you do succumb to that spontaneous buy, you'll have to skip the movie.

Practice Cognitive Spending

Take out your last checking account statement. Add up all ATM withdrawals. Now, tell me where the money went. If you've got a really good memory you can probably recall $.75 of every dollar. Most of my clients have a hard time remembering more than half their cash expenditures. Since the best—in fact, the only—way to cut back on unnecessary spending is to figure out exactly where your money is going, you've got to improve that percentage.

Keep a blank index card in your wallet. Every time you spend money, write it down. At the end of the week categorize your spending. Then at the end of the month do the same. After two months I guarantee you'll be able to track every dollar, if not every penny. That will give you a chance to come up with lots of little ways to save money—like having a cup of coffee at home rather than buying one with your morning paper. Do that for a year and you'll have saved more than $300. Even more important, you'll have gotten into the habit of thinking about how you're spending your money.

Buy Your Second Home First

Owning real estate will still be a good idea in the twenty-first century. However, it will be for different reasons than in the past. In the foreseeable future real estate will *not* increase in value as it did during the 1970s and 1980s. The real estate boom was an anomaly directly traceable to the uniquely huge baby boom generation driving up the demand for a limited number of houses. However, ownership of real estate will remain an excellent tax shelter—one of the only ones available anymore—as long as mortgage interest and taxes are tax deductible. Real estate will also, in all likelihood, increase in value at, or slightly better than, the rate of inflation. That means it will remain an excellent form of forced savings, one which, as I'll explain in future chapters, you'll be able to use to generate an income. Most important, home ownership will continue to offer emotional and psychological security in an age when that will be a very rare commodity.

Since real estate is no longer an investment, you can't count on practicing what I call serial home ownership: buying a starter home, selling it for a profit and buying another for your growing family, selling that for another profit and using the proceeds to buy a retirement home. In this new economic age you should wait longer to buy and then buy your second home first—in effect the second home you would have bought in the past. And you should buy a home you can live in for the rest of your life. That means it's either large, or expandable enough for you to accommodate more children, your aging parents, or a home business. And it should be located in an area where you'll feel comfortable as both a young parent and an empty-nester.

Obviously that makes the purchase of a home much more dramatic. But that's as it should be. You're not buying a pair of sneakers or even a car. This is the single largest transaction you'll ever make. It's not just a house, it's a "home."

Avoid "Everest" Buying

When someone asked the famous English mountaineer George Leigh Mallory why he was going to try to climb Everest, he responded: "Because it is there." Well, if you're like most of my clients, you could probably respond the same when asked why you buy something. Do you really need it? Or are you buying it because "it's there"? If you're going to survive and thrive in the new economic age, you're going to have to stop this "Everest" buying. From now on, simply wanting something isn't sufficient reason to buy it; you must need it as well.

Believe me: I'm not an ascetic urging repentance and self-denial. I'm just suggesting a more thoughtful approach to spending. I'm willing to define "need" rather broadly, certainly encompassing more than just subsistence. Let me give you an example.

No one "needs" a magazine to survive. However, they can be informative and entertaining. I think it's fine to buy a magazine . . . but only when you've finished reading all your other magazines. In other words, when you "need" a new magazine. Just because *The New Yorker* publishes an issue a week doesn't mean you have to subscribe. And just because you spot a new issue on the newsstands doesn't mean you have to buy it. Buy an issue only when you're done with all the magazines piled on the floor in the bathroom and "need" a new one to read.

This same approach must be applied to all your purchases. Buy a new winter coat, or stereo, or briefcase, or whatever, only when your old one no longer fits, can no longer be cleaned, or is beyond repair. If you follow this strategy, the natural result will be savvy shopping and utilitarian buying.

Ignore the New

Those who feel they've got to own the latest device or product are going to have a hard time making it in the twenty-first century. New products now appear almost daily and are often obsolete within a month—just look at the computer industry. Remember the previous rule and don't buy something new unless it answers a real need. People didn't need electronic personal organizers until they suddenly came on the market. Until then, inexpensive little notebooks were fine. No one cursed about how terrible those diaries were. No one was praying for an electronic replacement to come on the market . . . except the person selling them.

And even if you do "need" something new, I'd urge you to wait at least until the third generation of the product is on the market. By that time all the bugs should be cleared up and the price will have dropped from "fad" to "staple" level. Of course, at that point it will have been replaced by something else as the hot new product. This absurd consumption is a sucker's game you can't afford to play in the twenty-first century.

Repair Before You Replace

I have an old Macintosh Plus computer at home that I use to do my personal bookkeeping and correspondence. It has been upgraded as far as possible, which admittedly isn't much, but it continues to serve its purpose well. A few month ago the "7/&" key stopped working. I brought the machine into the local computer shop for repairs. They looked at me like I was nuts. "We use those as door stops," the sales clerk joked. "It's going to cost you about $200 to repair and clean that up," he said. "Don't you think it's time to buy a new one?" "Sure," I said, "if you've got one for $200."

Of course they didn't, but that was my point. If I could have bought a brand-new replacement for the same price as repairing my old Mac Plus it would have made sense. But since it cost less to repair it than replace it, and it was still serving its purpose fine, why buy a new one? Retailers, distributors, and manufacturers all make far greater profits selling new things than repairing old things (that's why so many of them don't even offer repair or parts services anymore). You, on the other hand, will generally profit more by repairing rather than replacing. Remember and focus on that fact and you'll do better in the new economic world.

Pay Yourself First

Most of my clients put themselves last when it comes to paying out money. Each month they write out checks to pay their credit card bills, mortgage, telephone, utilities, cable television, and everything else. They tell themselves that if there's anything left over after paying their bills, they'll try to save it. Of course, there's never anything left over.

In the new economic age you've got to turn the process on its head. The first thing you need to do every time you get paid is to pay yourself, not everyone else. That means putting the most you can in a tax-free savings plan like an IRA, a 401(k), or an SEP. Sit down with your accountant, calculate your maximum allowable contribution, and have it automatically deducted from your paycheck and invested accordingly.

AN ADDED BONUS

Paying cash means making some lifestyle sacrifices. However it has a concrete financial benefit: It will keep you from drowning in a sea of red ink on your voyage to the new economic world. But it also has an added emotional benefit: It adds meaning and value to the things you do buy.

How often have you told your kids that they'll appreciate something more if they earn it rather than just get it without effort? How often have you heard that guy hoisting the Stanley Cup say the triumph was so sweet because of all the effort it took to achieve it? You know what? It's true. When you have to work hard to get something, you're making an investment, not just buying something. All the time and sweat and sacrifices made on the way add to the value of the object being pursued. When you finally get it, it's worth far more to you than if it was just handed over without any effort. It's really yours because you earned it. No one can take it from you. You'll find yourself caring for your possessions, perhaps even cherishing them, rather than ignoring and maybe even abusing them.

Now, I don't expect you to accept this right away. Just as your children have to learn the rewards of hard work, you have to relearn them. But trust me: Frugality really does offer greater psychic rewards than conspicuous consumption. Start treating the little things in life with more respect and it will carry over to the bigger things. When you start having an increased awareness of the value of your possessions, you can't help but have an expanded cognizance of the value of other human beings.

KEN AND MARY SCHOENFELD: MELTING THE PLASTIC

I explained all this to Ken . . . without pulling any punches. I said that he was not only jeopardizing his family's financial security and his daughters' futures, he was putting his marriage at risk, all for a Hermès tie and some takeout Thai noodles. While it seemed to sink in, I still urged both him and Mary to make spending as inconvenient and painful as possible.

I knew they wouldn't suddenly start bringing their lunch to work in brown paper bags, but in the eight months they've been paying cash there has been a remarkable transformation. While they haven't suddenly become models of frugality, they have stopped their extravagant buying. For the first time in their married lives they're finally living within their means. They've stopped adding to their debt load, and are planning to use the proceeds from the sale of their apartment to pay off their credit card balances. That will free up their credit for use where it can do some real good—in the purchase of a home, one in which they'll be happy spending the rest of their lives.

Just as important, if not more so, their attitude toward their lives has changed. They're no longer living solely in the moment. They're beginning to feel they have a future, not just a present. Mary's starting to feel a bit more secure, and Ken is realizing that he doesn't need a new Armani suit every three months to show the world he's a success.

Don't Retire

4

I'm continually amazed at how obsessed people are with retirement. One of the first things nearly every new client who comes to see me wants to talk about is retirement planning. Either they're upset they aren't putting anything away, they're afraid of not putting enough away, or they're worried they're not putting their money in the right places. This fixation is doubly ironic. First, because with all the obsessing, most of them are simply not going to be able to retire in the same manner as their parents. Second, because they're insane to even want to.

Despite its widespread acceptance (people now think it's a fundamental part of the American Dream), retirement is a fairly new concept. It's an idea that worked for one generation only, and that was because of a demographic fluke. Far from being a natural part of the life cycle, it's a form of social engineering—and an outdated one at that. Rather than helping society, it's damaging our nation. And far from being a blessing to individuals, it leads to unhappiness and ill health. Abandoning the idea of retirement isn't a sacrifice—it's an empowering act that opens up incredible opportunities for personal, professional, and financial growth. How has everyone gotten things backward? Well, in order to answer that we've got to go back to the beginning.

WEAVING THE SAFETY NET

Prior to the Civil War and the industrialization of America, there was no such thing as retirement. Older people remained a vital part of agrarian society, offering insight and advice born of their experience. Wisdom more than compensated for any lessening of physical prowess. But that wisdom didn't count for much on the industrial assembly line. You didn't need insight to be a cog in a wheel—all you needed was a strong back.

That attitude naturally led to ageism. America *was* an aging country at the turn of the century (as it is now). These folks were considered a drain on the nation's growth and a cause of the newly discovered malady, unemployment. (The word wasn't coined until 1887.) In 1905, William Osler, one of the nation's most respected physicians, gave a much-heralded speech urging that everyone over sixty stop working so that younger people could take their jobs. He even cited a "charming" novel by Anthony Trollope (*The Fixed Period*) in which men of that age retired to a college for a year's contemplation . . . after which they were chloroformed. But since chloroforming an entire generation wasn't practical, something had to be done to support these folks after they'd been put out to pasture. Enter the concept of pensions.

Private pension plans caught on when the Taft administration began pushing them as a way to get rid of the old folks and therefore increase industrial efficiency. From 1910 to 1920 more than twenty plans were created each year. Then in 1920 changes were made in the tax law to make setting up pensions more advantageous for employers. From 1920 to 1930 about forty-five new plans were created each year. Still, only about 15 percent of American workers were covered by private pensions at the end of the decade, a time when the issue came to a head.

In 1933 around thirteen million Americans—one quarter of the labor force—were unemployed. Crowds of unemployed young men have made politicians nervous ever since the French Revolution. With this perceived threat in mind, FDR and the New Dealers came up with the idea of a universal public pension. They called it Social Security. They had two big issues to deal with, however: Who should pay for it, and when should people become eligible?

Remember, the idea was to get those masses of young men off the street and into jobs. That meant the system had to work from day one. Since you can't tax people to pay for their own pensions once they're out of work, the solution was to tax those who got the jobs. In other words, kids would be taxed to pay for their parents' pensions. As long as there were lots more people working than collecting pensions, workers wouldn't have to pay too much.

That led back to the eligibility issue. Retirement had to be set at an age where there would be enough people around to actually open up jobs, but not so many that it would bankrupt the system before it got started. The solution: sixty-five, a number Chancellor Otto von Bismarck of Germany first picked earlier in the century as the age when civil servants could collect a government pension. What was good enough for German bureaucrats and Bismarck was apparently good enough for Americans and FDR. At the time, the average American died at sixty-three. That meant most people wouldn't live long enough to collect, and those who did wouldn't collect for too long.

Even though the Social Security Act of 1935 was the cornerstone of the nation's retirement obsession, it was still a pretty rickety structure. Benefits provided, at best, a subsistence lifestyle. The stereotypical image of a retiree from this first Social Security generation was a widow eating cat food. It would take another two decades for that image to change.

FROM SAFETY NET TO LIFESTYLE

During World War II most wages were frozen. In exchange for workplace peace, organized labor won wider pension coverage. It wasn't too tough a fight, since pensions were tax deductible and, as future obligations, they didn't show up on a company's books. Meanwhile, government was catching flak for letting Social Security recipients fall below the poverty line. Politicians boosted benefits, got kudos, and were reelected. Improving Social Security benefits became politically expedient. Coverage was extended to the husbands of women in the private sector, members of the armed forces, the self-employed, farmworkers, and even some government employees. Benefits were expanded to include disability and health insurance and welfare for the blind and disabled. And all these benefits were subjected to cost-of-living adjustments so they'd keep pace with inflation.

The boom in private pensions and the increasing Social Security benefits were backed up by perhaps the greatest public relations campaign in history. Business, labor, government, and the financial services industry marketed the heck out of retirement. The recipe was laid out by H. G. Kenagy of Mutual Life Insurance at a 1952 meeting of the National Industrial Conference Board: fill company newsletters with stories of happily retired people, people who stuck with the company and hired the financial services industry. Just like in so many other religions, the church of retirement preached that stoicism was the road to paradise. Labor loyally at a job you may not be too fond of and you'll be rewarded in your golden years. Kenagy's formula transformed that image of the cat-food-eating widow into a tanned, healthy couple living in the Sunbelt, playing lots of golf. Retirement had become a lifestyle.

THE ENABLING MIRACLE

Why were older Americans willing to be led like lambs to the Sunbelt? First, they didn't know they had a choice. No one told them that continuing to work was an option: not the unions, not the AARP, not the media, and certainly not the companies who were kicking them and their high salaries out the door. Second, they'd received an extraordinary financial windfall, one so large that continuing to work seemed . . . silly. What was this miracle? Two words: real estate.

After World War II and Korea a grateful nation—with cash to burn—decided to reward its returning veterans by making it very easy for them to buy homes. Visionaries like builder William Levitt and planner Robert Moses created the suburbs just for them. They settled in and started having kids . . . lots of kids—including you.

Fast-forward thirty years to the 1980s. You and your peers have now graduated from college, gotten jobs, and started families. It's time for you to buy homes. You and the rest of the horde start looking to buy homes in the kind of places where you grew up. This unprecedented demand drives prices through the Andersen skylights in the den ceiling. The second generation of retirees—your parents—who bought their homes in 1950, with government help, for $15,000 sells them to you and your friends, thirty years later, for $150,000.

With their living expenses already covered by their pension and Social Security, and their medical bills covered by Medicare and their

AARP Medigap plan, your parents can take their $135,000 profit and spend it all on early-bird specials. Thanks to you and your fellow baby boomers they can actually live the lives they were being sold. You, however, can't count on your kids to return the favor.

THE IMPOSSIBLE DREAM

If someone is rich enough, they'll be able to retire at age sixty-five—or any age for the that matter—and lead the same lifestyle they led when they were working. That has always been true and will always be true. But for you, for most of my clients, and for subsequent generations of average Americans, the traditional notion of retirement is impossible.

That's right. Impossible. Not just improbable and not just incredibly difficult. Forget all those formulas you read about in the personal finance magazines. Don't bother with those personal finance books that say they'll show you how to make it work. It's hopeless. For you, retirement is a pyramid scheme you've got no chance of winning. How can I be so sure? I've looked at the numbers.

Remember that only one generation in American history has been able to make this dream—luxurious retirement—come true. They're doing it by drawing on five income streams. The average retiree gets 42 percent of their income from government assistance, 20 percent from their personal wealth, 20 percent from their pensions, 15 percent from current wages, and 3 percent from other sources. Let's look at your chances of drawing income from those same five streams.

Government Assistance

You simply will not be able to receive the same kind of help from Uncle Sam that your parents are getting. When it was launched, each Social Security recipient had forty workers supporting him. Up until 1949, the maximum each of those workers was being asked to contribute was $30 a year. Things have changed. Longevity has increased so there are more people than ever collecting benefits—benefits that have expanded dramatically. In 1993 each Social Security recipient had just three workers supporting him, and those workers were kicking in up to $3,757 a year. Around one-third of American workers now pay more to Social Security than to the IRS. And baby boomers haven't even started to retire yet. The way it's currently constructed, Social Security simply won't be able to provide you with the same benefits at the same time as your folks. There are lots of potential fixes being suggested. But the bottom line of every single one of the schemes is that baby boomers will have to get less money, start getting it later, and not get it for as long.

Personal Wealth

Your folks saw their incomes increase 524 percent, in real terms, between the ages of twenty and thirty. Yours increased 34 percent. Your parents were able to take advantage of government help in buying a home and sending children to college. Those programs haven't been there for you. Your parents had their kids early so they hit their peak earnings years after the kids were grown, allowing for savings and investment. You had your kids much later and will be paying child-related expenses into and beyond your peak earnings years. Your parents got a windfall when they sold their homes. For you there's no such real estate bonanza on the horizon. Add it all up and your personal wealth will not equal that of your folks.

Pension Income

Most current retirees are receiving pensions from plans in which their former employer or their union guarantees them a specific income. These plans are now as rare as New Orleans Saints victories. Your pension, if you have one, is a 401(k) plan that relies on your contributions and management. Less than half of those eligible for 401(k)s actually participate, and most of those who do don't invest as much, as aggressively, as they need to in order to come close to their parent's pension income.

Other Sources

Here's where a few optimistic folks think boomers may rescue their retirement dreams. It has been projected that boomers may be the recipients of the largest generational transfer of wealth in world history. According to this hopeful scenario, all those benefits their parents received will come to boomers in the form of inheritance. Sorry, but I don't think so. Yes, current retirees are the richest generation in American history. But they're not rich enough to bail you out. The average net worth of a couple from your parents' generation is $290,000. The average family size is three children. That's a nice chunk per kid, but certainly no magic bullet. Besides, I think it's doubtful that money will be there after the estate has been ravished by health care costs during your parents' final years. Whatever they've managed to save will probably end up going to doctors, nursing homes, and hospitals, not you.

Wages

Let's recap. You're not going to get as much government assistance as your folks. Your personal wealth is not going to be as high as theirs. It's almost impossible for you to get the same kind of pension income. You may get some inheritance, but it's clearly not going to be enough to make up for all the other drops in income streams. That leaves you with only one income stream that you can draw from: wages. That means working longer or living on less. And that's not the vision of retirement you've been brought up with, is it?

That's okay, however. You won't be able to retire in the same manner as your parents. But after looking at things objectively, I don't think you'd even want to.

A FICTION BUILT ON FOUR LIES

Forget all the hype and marketing. Retirement isn't a golden age. It's not about doing what you want where you want. It's not a dream—it's a nightmare.

More than 40 percent of retirees say the transition into retirement was difficult. If that doesn't sound too bad to you, consider that only 12 percent of newlyweds say marriage was a difficult transition and only 23 percent of new parents say having a child was a tough transition. Obviously, retiring is the single most difficult lifestyle change you can make. Why? I think it's because it's built on four lies—four assumptions that whatever their past validity aren't true today, and that certainly won't be true in the twenty-first century: age sixty-five is old; leisure is more fulfilling than work; older people should make room for the next generation; and people over sixty-five are worse workers than young people. Once you realize none of these are true, you'll be able to say good riddance to retirement.

1. Age sixty-five isn't old.

As I mentioned earlier, when FDR picked sixty-five as the retirement age, the average American lived to sixty-three. Today the average

American lives to seventy-five. And by 2040 the average American will be living to eighty-one. When it was first developed, retirement age wasn't even reached by most people. Today, retirees live about a decade after retiring. If you retire at sixty-five, you're apt to live two decades more. And thanks to advances in nutrition and medicine, those added years will be far more active than prior generations' later years. Far from being a time of decrepitude, they could be years of just as much activity as the rest of life . . . unless of course you choose to spend two decades sitting in a rocking chair muttering about past glories. Age sixty-five will not be the onset of old age for baby boomers. For you, it will be the beginning of middle age.

2. Leisure isn't more fulfilling than work.

Having read chapter 1, you know I don't believe you are your job. However, that doesn't mean you are a set of golf clubs. Work, of some form or other, is an integral part of human life, a reason to get up in the morning. Many who shift suddenly from work to leisure become ill, both physically and psychologically: Post-retirement heart attacks and bouts with depression are extremely common. That's why almost 25 percent of today's retirees say they're unhappy not working. Nearly a third of today's male retirees return to work, mostly within less than a year of retirement, and more than two-thirds to full-time employment. Even if you didn't like your job, retirement isn't necessarily better. It's clearly not the only option—there are other jobs and careers out there.

3. Older people don't need to make room for the next generation.

And there's no need to feel guilty about taking those jobs: You won't be leaving a young person out in the cold. Universal retirement actually hurts the economy. Not only are there fewer workers out there in the next generation than there are jobs, but if all you boomers retire, the country could go down the tubes economically. Not only will the costs of whatever public assistance is available go up, but the nation will have lost the output of all those productive workers. If we become a nation with lots of nonworkers being supported by a fewer number of workers, our national standard of living will certainly drop. And if you all retire, that's exactly what will happen.

4. People over sixty-five are worse workers than young people.

When jobs consisted of toting barges and lifting bales, strong backs were what counted. But when was the last time your boss asked you to lift any bales? Crunching numbers doesn't take a strong back, just a strong mind. We are in the information age, not the industrial age. According to most studies, age doesn't affect mental powers until the mid-seventies. And even then it's just a decrease in short-term memory. Carry a notebook and appointment calendar and you'll be a more productive worker than a younger person into your eighties. That's because older workers make fewer mistakes, have fewer absences, and are absent less often. They've also got wisdom: They have an eye for efficiency, knowing where their efforts can make the most difference.

If retirement makes little sense today, it's going to make even less sense tomorrow and on into the new economic age. Are you aware of nutrition and the benefits of exercise? If so, you'll be living longer than average. Have you quit in your head and realized your work is just a job? Then you'll actually find work less frustrating, since you're not placing unreasonable demands on it. Are you a college graduate? Then you're more educated than the average worker from the next generation and you'll be in even greater demand. Are you already an information worker? Then, far from there being a decline in your performance as you age, there will be an improvement—you'll actually be getting better at what you do as you get older. Why, for heaven's sake, would you want to retire? The only possible answer is there's no alternative. And that's wrong. There is another way.

FROM LEMMING TO EPIC HERO

The best metaphor I can think of for today's pursuit of retirement is of a mass of lemmings busily struggling up a steep cliff and then jumping off the cliff into the abyss. I'm suggesting that you switch your role model from a mouselike rodent that mindlessly follows the crowd to oblivion to the hero of one of the seminal epics of Western civilization—Ulysses.[2]

---

[2]I wish I could claim credit for this analogy, but I can't. It was originally promoted by a Canadian scholar named A. B. MacLeish and it was brought to my attention by Lydia Bronte, author of an excellent book entitled *The Longevity Factor*.

Rather than viewing your life as finite, as a climb to an arbitrary fixed point—at age sixty-five—at which you stop, approach life as an adventure. Like Ulysses you're on a journey, a trip over hills and through valleys with no known ending other than death. Don't accept someone else's judgment as to when your trip should end. Do your own navigation and make your own decisions on your journey to the new economic age.

You need to shift to a more flexible view of work and career, one that abandons the ultimatum of retirement—a false choice between full-time and no time. You can already see the beginnings of the shift to more options in trends toward flex-time, telecommuting, job sharing, part-time professionals, and project-length employment. Those are the early trends you and your peers will be turning into mass movements as we move into the third millennium.

Similarly you need to shift to a less rigid approach to earned income. No longer can you look at your earned income as continually increasing up until age sixty-five, at which point it will stop entirely. From now on you need to approach earned income as you do unearned income. It may grow, it may be stagnant, or it may decrease, all depending on market conditions and your own choices. Savings and investments, rather than being parts of a fixed formula that results in a specific amount at a specific time (the day you retire), should be used to generate unearned income that can supplement your now-protean earned income.

ROLE MODELS

If you're looking for role models for this new approach, look east to Japan. Even though the official retirement age there was set more than eighty years ago at fifty-five (when life expectancy was forty-three), the Japanese have in practice adopted a very Ulyssean approach to their lives—one that, with some adaptation, could work here.

While they haven't scrapped that absurd fifty-five marker—they're very attached to their traditions—they have gotten around it. Most Japanese workers continue on the job long after they reach fifty-five, but as "temporary workers." That doesn't necessarily mean they work shorter hours, though that is one option. Instead, for most it means giving up seniority and promotions and accepting equivalent cuts in their income. If they decide to leave their job, they are usually welcome to return to the company in another position later on. In other words, rather than being forced over the cliff after having reached the top, they can gradually climb back down the hill.

BECOMING A ULYSSEAN ADULT

Giving up retirement allows you to chart your own course through the new economic age. I know. You're excited by this newfound freedom, but you're also frightened by the lack of fixed rungs on a life ladder. Well, just because there are no rungs on a ladder doesn't mean there aren't guidelines you can apply. Here are some tips for savvy navigation. (Once again, I'll touch on specifics in Part Two.)

1. You're on your own path.

There's no longer a predetermined path. You're on a voyage of discovery that could take you from project to project, employer to employer, employment to entrepreneurship, industry to industry, perhaps even career to career.

2. The only finish line is death.

Just as the path you take is up in the air, so is your time line. The only finish point you should worry about anymore is death. Up until then you can do whatever the market and your skills will let you.

3. You're not a job chronology.

Just as you're no longer your job, your career is no longer just a chronological listing of where you've worked and what titles you've held. You are a constantly expanding package of skills and abilities that can be applied to solve a host of problems or tackle a range of projects, large or small, short-term or long-term.

4. Just grow your money.

Throw away all those frightening tables and formulas that tell you how much you have to be investing and at what rate of return in order to retire comfortably at age sixty-five. There's no more rote pattern. This isn't a race. No one is measuring you. Instead you've got a fairly simple goal: grow your wealth as much as you can, as quickly as you can, within your own comfort range.

5. Rethink risk.

But you should definitely rethink that comfort range. Most folks have based their risk/reward analyses on retiring at age sixty-five. If you're a boomer and you're not retiring, you've got lots more time to recover from stock market setbacks—perhaps as many as twenty more years. That means you should stick primarily with equity investments (stock mutual funds, for example) far longer than those traditional charts and formulas say. Don't take your foot off the gas too soon.

6. Keep a liquid reserve.

If you're going to keep the pedal to the metal, you'll need some backup. In the twenty-first century anyone looking to practice sound money management will need to have access to enough cash to cover six months' worth of expenses in order to overcome detours along their chosen routes.

7. Cover your income, not your life.

At the same time you'll need to have adequate insurance protection for when minor detours turn into serious redirections. That means maintaining the best health insurance coverage possible, and most important of all, having the maximum disability protection. Almost all my clients start off having more life insurance and less disability insurance than they need. I'll wager you're no different. The longer you work and the longer you live, the bigger a mistake that becomes.

8. Pile up the pensions.

Finally, make sure you max out on every retirement savings and investment opportunity you've got. Even though you've no intention of hanging up your wingtip shoes, there are incredible tax advantages to filling up your IRAs, Keoghs, SEPs, or 401(k)s. There are going to be so few ways left to shelter income in the twenty-first century that you've got to take advantage of every one, regardless of what it's called.

AN ADDED BONUS

Giving up the pursuit of retirement has a great many practical and psychological advantages. But it also has an added spiritual bonus: By eliminating the finish line, life stops being a race. With all of us on our own path there's no way your progress can be compared to anyone else's. No one—not your parents, your friends, or *Money* magazine—can look at your life and say you're not as far along as you should be. More important, you can stop measuring yourself against an arbitrary standard and feeling inadequate for not meeting the grade. You're on your own unique self-charted journey. Where it ends only God knows, so until then all you can do is keep rowing.

THE STORY OF RICK DARROW

Most of my clients are young enough that retirement is more an abstraction than a reality, so giving up the idea is often more a relief to them than an actual sacrifice. But for Rick Darrow it was pretty traumatic.

When I first met Rick he was sixty and one of America's most well-respected fee-only financial planners. I'd interviewed him for an article I'd written and we'd struck up a friendship. He first came to me as a client when he wanted to discuss the drafting of a partnership agreement. Rick was planning to retire in five years and figured that the best way to do that would be to take on a partner who could start taking over the business, and then buy Rick out when he turned sixty-five. He had found someone he thought he could work with, had reached a tentative understanding, and wanted my help in formalizing the arrangement. Outwardly, he seemed happy with the idea.

I pointed out that for the next couple of years Rick's income would drop. After all, the business would be supporting two instead of just one, and until the billings picked up, Rick would have less to take home. That didn't sit too well. Rick wasn't a spendthrift, but he did like to live well: He owned a lovely, book-lined two-bedroom apartment on Manhattan's Upper West Side, dined out at least three times a week, had a cozy vacation cottage on the Rhode Island coast, and took yearly trips to London for the theater.

Then, as we started going over the details of the agreement, Rick began acting uncharacteristically stubborn, arguing over even the most minor points. It was clear to me that in the process of considering a buyout, Rick suddenly realized how much he loved his business. He had built it up from nothing and had a real emotional commitment to it and his clients. He loved helping people and managing money. But wouldn't he love being retired more? I asked. He said nothing. What did he plan on doing when he retired? I asked. He said he hadn't thought about it. Why then, I asked, was he going through all this? What else could he do? he asked.

When I first told Rick my own theories on retirement, he looked at me like I was crazy. Steeped in the world of retirement planning, Rick had never given a second thought to the alternatives. Over the course of the next two months he and I went over all the possibilities open to him. I helped him use the same analytical approach he brought to others' problems to tackle his own. The idea of retirement became less enticing as he realized there was no reason he had to stop doing what he loved just because he turned sixty-five.

Today at age sixty-six, Rick is as hard at work as ever before, with the full intention of remaining that way as long as he wants. All thoughts of taking on a partner are gone. He is now actually building up his practice so it's positioned to carry him, and his clients, well into the next century. Part of that repositioning, by the way, involves encouraging his clients to look at alternatives to traditional retirement, and planning for lifelong employment.

OVERCOMING THE RETIREMENT COMPLEX

Part of that planning, for Rick's clients and for you, is being prepared to buck the system. Just as there's a powerful military-industrial complex, there's a powerful retirement complex, one both Rick and I used to belong to. It includes everyone in the financial services industry, which markets most of its products and services as ways to ensure a good retirement. It includes politicians and lobbyists who can continue to deliver pork to constituents as long as they accept the idea of retirement. And it includes all those corporations that use retirement as a way to pare their workforces and grow their profits. This powerful confluence of interest groups isn't going to give up their control over your life without a fight. You're going to need the courage to buck what, at least for the moment, is the conventional wisdom.

But if anyone can do it, it's you. After all, yours is the generation that got the vote at eighteen, ended a war, and elected the first among you to run for president. Destroying the false god of retirement could in the long run be your generation's greatest contribution to society.

The retirement complex has produced a society ill at ease, full of contradictions, and unsuited for the next century. Isn't there something wrong with a society that criticizes people with limited skills who collect welfare rather than work, while applauding when its potentially most valuable contributors spend their days on the golf course?

Die Broke

5

If you'd have told me two years ago that a client like Craig McKay would provide me with the final crucial element in a new twenty-first-century financial philosophy, I'd have said you were crazy.

When new clients call for an appointment, I tell Kim, my assistant, to ask them to bring in a net worth statement. Kim explains that this is a shortcut so I can get a quick but clear picture of their financial status and not waste their time getting the answers to mundane questions. In order to get a snapshot of their lifestyles, I have Kim instruct them to include estimates of the worth of their personal property, and to bring along a list of their monthly income and expenses. Once she makes an appointment, Kim comes in to give me a preliminary briefing—she's a very good judge of character, even after just a brief telephone conversation.

After setting up the meeting with Craig, she told me he was interested in buying a parcel of commercial real estate. I asked what he was like. Kim thought for a moment and then said, "Confident." That was a polite understatement.

Look up the word *yuppie* in the dictionary and you'll see Craig's picture. At thirty-four he's owner of his own multimedia Internet design firm that specializes in designing Web pages for corporate America. Basically he helps staid, buttoned-down businesses look like they're on the cutting edge. Craig has never met a consumer product he didn't like. And he can afford to indulge his whims. Single, with an income of more than $300,000, he lives alone with his toys and a closet full of black clothes in a converted loft one floor above his business in New York City's Flatiron district.

Craig told me he was thinking about buying the building in which his home and business were located and wanted some advice. In the two minutes it took for me to glance at the numbers he'd brought with him, Craig both called his office on his cell phone and checked his beeper. One line on his net worth statement jumped out at me—a line in the asset column read "Inheritance, $400,000." I looked up, extended my hand, and offered my condolences. "Oh, my parents aren't dead yet," he said, "that's just an estimate."

THE INHERITANCE OBSESSION

While Craig's callous audacity was unique, his sense of entitlement to his parents' estate was not. For the past two or three years I've heard more and more of my clients half joke about their inheritance, using it as a segue into a serious discussion of how to shelter their parents' assets. After just a couple of minutes it's clear they're just as concerned with preserving the estate for their own eventual use as they are with helping their folks.

I think you can trace all this back to a rash of stories that appeared in the press back in 1993. That was when a couple of Cornell University economists, Robert Avery and Michael Rendall, published a study postulating that baby boomers would receive the largest collective inheritance in history—about $10 trillion—and that this massive patrimony would reach far deeper into American society than any previous generational transfer of wealth. Inheritance was going middle class.

The media jumped on the story and the financial services industry took notice. The retirement complex I described in the previous chapter got to work once more. Brokerage firms expanded their trust subsidiaries and begin soliciting the middle class in addition to their usual upper-crust clientele. Insurance companies started pushing second-to-die policies, which are designed—among other things—to pay estate taxes, and long-term care policies, which also serve to keep estates out of Uncle Sam's hands. What's particularly disturbing is that many of these products are being marketed to the likely recipients of bequests, not the givers.

Financial advisers have begun fashioning themselves as "inheritance counselors," encouraging clients to take a proprietary role in their parents' financial lives. Attorneys are beginning to specialize in "Medicare planning," offering advice on how to artificially impoverish parents so they qualify for government assistance without using up their assets.

I can understand what has driven boomers to these lengths. After being squeezed by rising living costs, soaring college tuition, stagnant wages, and shrinking real estate values, a big inheritance looks like the answer to your prayers. But when you look at the whole issue objectively, it looks shabby, doubtful, ruinous, and vestigial.

First, you've got to remember that you're not entitled to your parents' money. Whatever case you can make for there being a generational debt owed by the silent generation to the baby boomers (and believe me, a demographic case can be made), that doesn't translate into a personal debt your parents owe you.

Second, despite the Ivy League pedigree of the theory's two prophets, there's no guarantee you're actually going to get such a big generational inheritance.

Third, even if does happen, it's not necessarily something good, either for your folks, for you, or for society.

And fourth, but most important, the concept underlying inheritance is an unhealthy relic of the past. In your abandonment of it are the seeds to an entirely new, healthier, and more holistic view of money: a practical *and* spiritually rewarding financial philosophy for you to take into the new economic world.

INHERITANCE ISN'T AN ENTITLEMENT

Inheritance has been around for as long as humans had something of value to pass along to their children. In preindustrial America inheritance most often took the form of something tangible: a farm, some land, a set of tools, a family business, silverware, or furniture. (That was because only the wealthy few had any intangible assets.) The passing of these assets from one generation to another wasn't simply a gift—it was part of an intergenerational contract. The oldest son of a farmer would gradually assume more and more of the work as the father aged, knowing the farm would be his when the father died, as long as he continued to take care of his mother and then passed the

farm on to his oldest son. A daughter might receive the family silverware or furniture with the proviso that they were to be cherished
and then passed on to future generations. A younger son might get a
set of tools or even books, with the understanding that they would
be put to good use and, once again, passed on to subsequent generations. Assets came to you as the result of hard work, ambition, or
virtue.

In the industrial era we shifted to a more mobile, urban society in
which there were fewer such tangible assets. Families no longer had
things to pass along. And whatever intangible assets they might have
squirreled away probably vanished in the Great Depression. For most
of America, inheritance stopped being a practical part of the family
contract and became an idle fantasy of sudden wealth. Television
shows like *The Millionaire* (in which every week an average Joe was
handed a check for $1 million from an anonymous benefactor) and
characters like Little Lord Fauntleroy and Charles Foster Kane became
part of our collective unconscious. Inheritance was something from the
world of fiction.

Ronald Reagan changed all that. It wasn't just him, of course. As
I've mentioned before, your parents' generation was able to accumulate wealth to an unprecedented degree thanks to a unique combination of economic, demographic, and political forces. It was the "Great
Communicator," however, who made it possible for them to potentially pass on that wealth. His 1981 tax cuts chopped by two-thirds
the number of estates subject to tax—and sliced taxes on the rest.
After his bill was signed into law, a savvy couple could leave their kids
$1.2 million tax free. By the end of the 1980s the number of families
who could potentially leave estates had doubled.

But a piece of the puzzle is missing: The contractual nature of
inheritance has disappeared. Our view of inheritance has been transformed, thanks partly to all those fictional accounts of money
descending like manna from heaven, and partly to its nature shifting from tangible to intangible assets. Treasury bills don't carry
with them the same moral road map as the family farm. For inheritance to work it has got to be part of a contract. In shouldn't be an
entitlement. It must be earned. When it comes for no other reason
than an accident of birth, it's problematic, as I'll explain later in this
chapter.

THE POT OF GOLD MAY BE EMPTY

Of course, the whole question may be moot. All the inheritance hype is based on a pretty shaky set of numbers. To their credit, Avery and Rendall admitted the shortcomings of their figures. But the media and financial services industry, in their rush for headlines and profits, brushed them aside.

Most obviously, those inheritances were calculated in 1989 dollars, so decades of inflation weren't taken into account.

Gifts to charity or family, which could deplete estates, also weren't considered. A quarter of all college tuition prepayment plans, and nearly all for children under twelve, are being paid for by grandparents, according to a recent study. And the National Association of Realtors notes that the number of first-time home buyers getting money from grandparents is rising dramatically. Your folks may bypass you entirely and simply give the money to your kids.

The Cornell economists didn't address the impact the rising cost of end-of-life health care would have on the estates of boomers' parents. Understandably a family does all that's possible to alleviate a dying person's pain and suffering. And also understandably, a physician—taught to preserve life at all costs—pushes to perform every procedure that could possibly postpone the inevitable. The resulting huge expenditure is now so common it has a name: "the million-dollar death." Couple that with the cost of nursing home or in-home care prior to the final days of life and the continuing advances in longevity and you've got a potentially huge drain on those estates.

Changes in the spending patterns of older Americans weren't factored into the numbers. In the 1960s the average eighty-year-old spent only $.65 for every $1.00 spent by the average thirty-year-old. Now, that prototypical octogenarian is outspending his grandson by $1.16 for every $1.00. While rising medical costs account for part of this, consumption by older Americans is up in every category. Those "We're spending our kids' inheritance" bumper stickers aren't a joke.

Finally, even if those pots of gold survive all these factors, there's always the long arm of Uncle Sam. While Republicans are famous for their hatred of estate taxes, the Congressional Budget Office has noted that a windfall of some $80 billion could come to federal coffers by cutting the personal estate exemption in half (to $300,000) and applying capital gains tax to estates. That's an awfully attractive chunk of money, especially if the alternative is cutting Social Security or Medicare.

Add all this together and you'll see why I'm telling my clients to forget about inheriting any money from their folks. There are no panaceas in life. Despite all the hype, inheritance remains what it has been for years: a fantasy. You've got a better chance of winning the Publishers Clearing House Sweepstakes than inheriting great wealth.

PATRIMONY IS PROBLEMATIC

I don't believe that's something to mourn. You see, inheritance, even the expectation of inheritance, is inefficient and actually harmful to families, the giver, the recipient, and society. And while your own feelings about inheriting money may not matter, I think you should also give up the idea of passing money on to your own children.

Inheritance is a terribly inefficient way to pass wealth to others. Estate taxes are among the highest the IRS levies, ranging up to 55 percent, depending on size. Then there's state tax. And if the estate is primarily in a qualified retirement plan—not an uncommon occurrence—the bite can even soar as high as 70 to 85 percent.

The division of estates has always been the cause of family fights. While there is a traditional societal pattern for the disposition of tangible assets (oldest son gets the farm), there's no such consensus about splitting intangible assets. The two most common approaches—need-based division or equal division, regardless of need—both can lead to animosity.

The expectation of an inheritance changes the dynamics between family members. Suddenly, every dollar spent by the parent, whether on a new dining room set or a month-long vacation in France, is a dollar coming out of the child's pocket. That's a horrible situation for both parties to be in. The child is put in the position of being hurt by the parents' pursuit of happiness and pleasure. And the parent is forced to choose quality of death over quality of life. This can lead to an endless cycle of guilt.

It has long been believed that inheriting money actually erodes an individual's work ethic. That belief has even been backed up by some interesting studies. One shows that almost 20 percent of people who receive inheritances of $150,000 or more drop out of the workforce; another shows that those who simply expect an inheritance spend more and save less than those who have no such expectation.

If you believe, as I do, that the increasing division of America into two groups, the haves and the have-nots, is bad, then inheritance is clearly bad for society. Most of those who receive very large inheritances already have incomes more than double the median family income. Basically, inheritance helps the rich get richer.

Finally, inheritance is soul killing. Think of the effect on your child's psyche of having to rely on inheritance for his financial future, of having to wait for a loved one to die so he can finally come into his own. Just ask Prince Charles.

DYING BROKE MEANS LIVING WELL

If I've convinced you to forget about counting on an inheritance from your parents, or hoping to leave one to your own children, that's just the first half of the battle.

Inheritance isn't just a financial transfer between generations. The underlying belief behind inheritance is that assets are meant to be maintained and preserved, even beyond the life of the owner. It's a view that your financial life is separate from your corporeal life . . . sort of like a corporation whose job it was to accrue, maintain, grow, and pass along intangible assets. Inheritance is the ultimate expression of a philosophy of personal finance, a philosophy designed for a world in which jobs were secure, real estate values climbed, credit cards were wonderful tools, and retirement was an idyllic reward.

Following the rules of this philosophy has led you to your current state of fear and frustration. That's because it's an incredibly inefficient approach to money. It leads to unnecessary sacrifices in the here and now that far outweigh any future benefits. It encourages the mistaken belief that money has an intrinsic value of its own rather than just being a tool. It fosters family conflicts. It forces you to live your life by a strict and arbitrary schedule. Simply put: It's an outdated philosophy, one designed for your parents' industrial age, not your own information age.

The most important step is next. It requires taking your new awareness of the nature of inheritance, turning it on its head, and using it as a pattern for your own financial life from now on. You've got to treat your assets as resources to be used while you're alive rather than treasures to be hoarded for use after you're dead. You've got to forget about trying to build up an estate of your own and aim to die broke.

Free from the burden of having to preserve an estate, you can use your accumulated wealth to help your family and improve your own life. You'll be able to give money to your children while it can still do the most good. Rather than them spending it on a cruise when they're sixty, they will be able to start a business when they're forty. You can pass along funds for them to acquire twenty-first-century skills. You'll get the joy of being thanked for your gifts as well. You'll also be able to enjoy your own life. Abandoning the idea of building up an estate, not using your credit cards, is the way you'll be able to get over to Ireland while you're still young enough to climb Croagh Patrick.

The old philosophy of personal finance encouraged you to live above your means in your early years, and then make up for it by living beneath your means when you're older. The Die Broke philosophy says you should live fully up to, but not beyond, your means for your entire life.

You are not a corporation—you are a human being. Your money shouldn't outlive you. You should exit life as you came into it: penniless. Your assets are resources to be used, for your own benefit and for the benefit of those you love. Every dollar that's left in your bank account after you die is a dollar you wasted. Use your resources to help people now when you know they need it, when it will do the most good, rather than hoping they'll be helped when you're dead. The last check you write should be to your undertaker . . . and it should bounce. Your priority should be the way you live, not the way you'll die. Dying broke means living well.

ROLE MODELS: JOHN AND WENDY KOWALSKI

It would be easy for me to offer up as role models any of the extraordinarily wealthy people, ranging from Andrew Carnegie to Warren Buffett, who have sworn off inheritance. But I don't want you to think that this is just a philosophy for the rich. That's why I suggest you model yourself after John and Wendy Kowalski.

The Kowalskis came to me earlier this year for help in drafting their wills. John is a seventy-three-year-old retired bus driver and Wendy is a seventy-year-old retired executive secretary. Since their retirements they'd been living on their Social Security payments and pensions. Even though they'd never made more than $60,000 a year, they had built up quite a nice nest egg. They owned their own apartment in a once lovely but now declining section of New York City. They'd been frugal all their lives and, thanks to the very generous pension/savings plan offered by Wendy's former employer, had been able to put away almost $225,000. But even with this solid foundation they were anxious.

John and Wendy were preoccupied with the welfare of their forty-one-year-old daughter, Rachel, and her fifteen-year-old son, Dylan. Rachel was divorced and she had been having a hard time of it financially. John and Wendy wanted to preserve as much of their wealth as possible so it could be passed on to Rachel and Dylan. In effect, they were depriving themselves during their lifetimes in order to provide for their daughter after their deaths.

What struck me first was their living conditions. While the building itself was well cared for, it didn't have an elevator . . . and their two-bedroom apartment was on the third floor. With their increasing problems navigating the stairs, they were near prisoners. Even when they did make it downstairs, they didn't find themselves in an idyllic setting. The once solidly middle-class neighborhood had been slipping for years, and street crime was now a constant presence.

I tried to explain how they could afford to get another, more accessible apartment in a better neighborhood, but Wendy cut me off instantly. What about Rachel and Dylan? she asked. And besides, she added, we wouldn't fit in anywhere else. John and Wendy are an interracial couple. Wendy was afraid that, as a black woman, she wouldn't be accepted in a more upscale neighborhood.

Calmly and clearly I explained to John and Wendy my belief that they should plan to "die broke." I showed them how much they could do for Rachel and Dylan now, while still doing things for themselves. I told them how my parents had taken out a mortgage in their eighties to buy a new home.

Today John and Wendy are actually living rather than just existing. They've bought a new apartment—it's smaller but in a much better part of town and has many more amenities. They're making regular gifts to Dylan in the form of deposits to a college fund. And together, the four of them have gone on a vacation to the Caribbean to see the town where Wendy was born. John now jokes that all he wants to have left when he dies is a quarter so he can call me to say good-bye. Perhaps more important is the change that has come over Wendy. By opening herself up to the possibility of a new approach to her financial life, she has been able to overcome many of the fears, both financial and social, that had inhibited her in the past. Both she and John are now truly living.

A PROGRAM FOR DYING BROKE

I know, you're far younger than John and Wendy. You're not yet worried about preserving your estate . . . you're worried about building one. Even so, you should still focus on living well and dying broke. (A much fuller discussion of the whole process of dying broke appears in chapter 9. But for now, I just want to show you that it's not as difficult as you might think.)

In your early years you should aim to build up as much wealth as you can, first, by paying cash and saving. Those savings should be used to create a six-month emergency fund, because you know your job is by its very nature insecure.

But at the same time don't grow your savings at the expense of your own or your family's real quality of life. That doesn't mean spending on a new stereo system when your current one still works, or buying your son a new pair of Air Jordans every two months. Remember you've got to follow the precepts I outlined in chapter 3. However, it could mean taking that much-needed family vacation, or providing the money for your son to spend a semester at hockey camp in Sweden. My feeling is that if you spend on experiences and education rather than entertainment, you can't go wrong.

Your other funds should be invested for long-term growth—after all, you're going to be living a long time. But now, your goal isn't to build up a nest egg for retirement but to create a pool of money that can be drawn on when your income drops or when you wish to do something for yourself or others.

Then, when you enter your sixties, you should begin putting these elements in place, which will enable you to die broke while guaranteeing you don't outlive your assets—things like annuities and reverse mortgages. (Once again, more specific information on these topics is provided in Part Two.)

Insure Your Streams of Income

As I mentioned earlier in the book, term life insurance is valuable, but strictly as a way to protect yourself against the early loss of a spouse's income. If you haven't gotten some already, do so now. Once you can take care of the potential loss of income through your savings, you can let the policy lapse.

Disability insurance is especially crucial to your safety net, since you're going to be relying on earned income for most of your life. Get a good policy as early as you can and keep it as long as you can.

Take Your Own Pulse

Assuming you've already listened to me and have put your small term life insurance and solid disability insurance policies in place, your next step is to explore your various medical insurance options. The titanic (and growing) cost of medical care is perhaps the single greatest threat to your assets. If you want to be able to use your money while you're alive, yet not outlive it, you've got to make sure that any catastrophic medical bills will be covered by someone else. That means maintaining good major medical coverage before and after you reach age sixty-five, through some combination of private insurance and eventually Medicare and Medigap.

You may also want to explore long-term care insurance. However, for reasons I'll outline in chapter 48, I'm more than a little hesitant about your buying it right away if you're younger than sixty-five years old.

When you do reach your sixties, even though you won't be retiring you probably will find your income declining, by design or default. Since you want to get maximum benefit from your assets, without exhausting them before your death, you need to start looking at ways to provide guaranteed incomes. You do that by turning the assets and wealth you've acquired into guaranteed streams of income.

Take Out Some Longevity Insurance

The single most important financial tool for dying broke is the annuity—it serves as a form of longevity insurance. While there is a dizzying array of options, the basic idea is that you give an insurance company a lump sum of money and it in return promises to pay you (and then, if you wish, a surviving spouse) a predetermined income for the rest of your life (or lives). In effect you're shifting the risk of out-living your money to the insurance company. Most folks will end up opting for an immediate annuity that offers income from the moment it's purchased.

Once you cut through all the options, they're no more difficult to shop for than term life insurance policies. You pick out the insurers who have had a high rating (AAA) for ten years or more—this isn't the kind of contract to sign with a shaky or new organization. Then you just compare their quoted monthly incomes per $1,000 of investment.

If you have a good disability policy in place, have sound major medical and hospitalization coverage, and are committed to dying broke, there isn't a problem with tying up your assets in this kind of irrevocable deal. (Of course, there are annuity products that will let you tap into their cash value . . . but that access comes at a price—a reduced income.)

Get Paid to Live in Your House

If you followed my advice and bought your second home first, you're living in another asset that can be turned into a guaranteed stream of income. A reverse mortgage is a loan secured by the equity in your home, which would otherwise pass into your estate at death. You don't borrow a fixed amount. Instead, the lender gives you a monthly payment for as long as you live, if you stay in the home. The income you receive is tax free, since it's actually a loan. All the fees and interest aren't paid until the loan is settled upon your death. At that time the home is sold to settle the loan. The bank may take half the profit, if there is any. If there isn't, it swallows the loss. Meanwhile you've been paid an income to live in your own house.

Get a Charity to Pay You

There are lots of charities and nonprofit foundations now offering gift plans similar to annuities and reverse mortgages. You hand over a lump sum or title to your home to the charity and it guarantees to pay you a specified income. You also get a heck of a tax deduction in the process and you'll be alive to attend that testimonial dinner in your honor.

Finally, in your eighties you can start making arrangements to ensure that there won't be anything left in the bank when you finally die, but that all your bills are still covered.

Start Giving It Away

There's no limit on noncash gifts. You can give your daughter a new Mercedes every year, and as long as someone pays the sales tax, the IRS couldn't care less. But when it comes to cash gifts the IRS suddenly gets interested. Under current tax law an individual can make a tax-free cash gift to another individual of $10,000 a year. That means a couple can give each of their children or grandchildren $20,000 in cash a year. If your child is part of a couple, and you wanted to, you could also both give your child's partner $10,000 a year. That means you and your spouse could give your married children as much as $40,000 a year in cash. You can even give away more tax free, if you apply the money to your one-time $600,000 estate tax exclusion. That way you get the benefit, not your estate. In addition, any funds paid directly to an educational institution or medical facility for someone else's education or care is tax exempt.

Take Out a Whole Death Policy

You don't even have to worry about keeping money around to pay for your funeral or to clean up your debts. Take out a small whole life policy that will cover those bills and you'll be able to spend every last penny you've got. (Term coverage actually becomes more expensive than whole life after you reach a certain age.) This approach is far more efficient that prepaying for funerals or taking out credit life insurance.

THE STORY OF CATHERINE AND DAVID GENET

I first met the Genets when I was working as the on-air personal finance expert for CNBC. A husband-and-wife production team, they were being interviewed about their latest special, a roundtable discussion series on the world's religions that was airing on public television. We struck up a conversation in the green room, and when I told them about my belief that people should aim to die broke, they looked at each other, laughed, and said I was exactly who they were looking for.

Two weeks later and Anthony was ushering them into my office. David seems younger than his age—forty-four—perhaps because he has longish hair, a beard and mustache, and seems to always dress in blue jeans, sweater, and sneakers. He looks and acts like he would be more at home on a college campus than on the streets of New York. Catherine, on the other hand, actually tries to look and act older than her thirty-five years. Her hair is short and fashionably severe, her manner—at least at first—is very businesslike, her garb would fit right in on Wall Street.

Eventually I learned that this remarkable dichotomy was due to David's handling the "creative" end of the business while Catherine dealt with the financial and political matters. He was out working with cameramen and grips; she was soliciting funds in various boardrooms. Despite their different appearances they were of one mind when it came to money and their lifestyles.

David and Catherine had been remarkably successful . . . far more successful that they ever thought they'd be. They met at a metro-area film school—David was teaching, Catherine was a student—and fell in love. Realizing that their chosen field—documentary filmmaking—wasn't traditionally a path to riches, they'd been prepared to lead a simple and frugal life. In the early 1980s they'd bought a one-bedroom apartment on the Upper West Side of Manhattan.

But thanks to their own skill and a lucky break, their moderately successful production business hit it big. A very well known and well respected television personality approached them to work on a series about mythology. It struck a chord with the public, and the good press and profits struck a complementary chord in the film business. Suddenly they were in demand. They had enough money to have a child—which they did: a lovely little girl named Sydney. They had enough money to actually start saving.

When they met me earlier this year, Sydney was five and they were in the process of rethinking their whole approach to their lives and their finances. I spoke with them for more than an hour and discussed my ideas about paying cash, not retiring, and dying broke. They asked if they could come back for a further discussion after they had a chance to think things over.

Two weeks later they returned with the outlines of a life plan they wanted my help in implementing. Their idea was to move to a farmhouse in the foothills of the Catskill Mountains, about three hours by car from New York City. This would be their home for the rest of their lives. They thought this would let them offer Sydney the best of both worlds—the security, natural beauty, and community of the country, along with the excitement, diversity, and culture of the city. Needless to say, they too wanted to get the best of both these worlds.

All of their efforts, and mine, from that point on, have been designed to make sure they can accomplish this. They've bought their farmhouse. They're continuing to live within their means. They've each taken out enough term life insurance to replace their incomes for three years. In another two years they'll have enough saved and invested to cut back on that cushion (and their premiums). They both have sizable disability policies. Rather than thinking about a "college fund" or a "retirement fund," or worrying about building up an estate for Sydney, their goal is to lead "a simple but intellectually stimulating life" and to invest what they can aggressively so they'll have no problem turning it into a sufficient unearned income to replace drops in their earned income as they get older.

THE ULTIMATE ADDED BONUS

Dying broke means abandoning impossible searches (jobs that are secure, pay well, and are fulfilling), forsaking counterproductive financial practices (the use of credit and the failure to save), eliminating arbitrary deadlines (like retirement at age sixty-five), and giving up hubristic dreams of immortality (building and passing along estates). In return, your money will be far more efficient.

Rather than trying to force old-world practices on a new world, you'll be following rules that fit the circumstances of your life in the twenty-first century. That means far fewer frustrations and a far greater chance of being successful.

Instead of living above your means when you're young, and below your means when you're old, you'll live fully up to your means, but not beyond them, for your entire life. That's clearly a healthier and more holistic way to live.

But the ultimate added bonus is something far more wonderful than all these, a contentment about yourself, a happiness about your life, a peace of mind that I can only call . . . serenity. To find your bliss, just turn the page.

Choosing Your Own Clothes   6

When I first started developing the Die Broke philosophy, I was looking for nothing more than solutions to my clients' immediate problems. They were like ships who'd lost their rudders in a violent hurricane. Finding their lives apparently out of control, despite following all the rules they'd been told would lead them to success, they were desperate for a new compass that would let them reassert their control over the direction of their lives. They wanted answers and solutions, a new map to follow in this stormy new world.

And that's what I gave them, and have now given you: four new axioms to follow that will let you take back control of your life. Quit today. Pay cash. Don't retire. Die broke. Follow those four precepts and you'll be able to steer through all the turbulence surrounding the turn of the century and enter the new millennium on the right course.

However, there's more to it than that. Yes, if you adopt the Die Broke philosophy you'll eliminate your fears and frustration and find a path to career and financial success. But that's only to be expected, since you're following rules custom-fitted to you and your circumstances rather than continuing to apply outdated rules that you and the world have outgrown. What's incredible, at least to me, is that these four principles are actually keys to a hidden treasure.

I've touched on some of the added emotional bonuses of following these new concepts in each of the previous four chapters. But there's more to it than that. Following these axioms enables you to lead a more rewarding spiritual life as well. They give you the chance for real peace of mind, true serenity. That's because they're based on healthier values. They provide the chance to choose your own path, and they allow you to abandon the fruitless pursuit of perfection.

HEALTHIER VALUES FOR THE NEW ECONOMIC WORLD

When you actually examine them closely, the old rules you've been following are based on some fairly deleterious values. Taken collectively, they were a very unhealthy philosophy.

By embracing the single-minded climb up those now-rotted rungs on the corporate ladder, you were saying that what others thought of you was more important than what you thought of yourself; you were saying that your value as a human being was tied to the position or title you held in some bureaucracy. By accepting that you had to dedicate yourself to this climb, you were saying your work was the most important element in your life, more important even than your family or your soul. And by buying into the idea that you had to keep on climbing until you either reached the top or fell off, you were saying that the only rung that mattered was the top one. Anything and everything else just wasn't good enough.

If you used credit cards and borrowed to buy the latest luxuries or satisfy an impulsive want, you were saying that something acquired is just as good as something earned, that patience was foolish rather than a virtue, that immediate gratification wasn't quick enough. If you bought a home with the idea of making a profit on it, you were giving up the idea of "home" and saying the place you and your family live in was just one more commodity. If you intended to continually sell and buy real estate through your life, you were saying that appearances were worth more than community and that dollars meant more than roots.

By pursuing full retirement at age sixty-five or younger, you were saying that work was a burden to be rid of as soon as possible and that physical stamina and strength were more important than experience and wisdom. When you bought into the retirement complex, you were saying that those sixty-five years and older are incapable of contributing to society.

Finally, by counting on an inheritance from your parents, you were saying that their primary focus in life should be your comfort, that the quality of your life was more important than the quality of theirs, and that the greatest gift they had to give you was cash. By trying to build up an estate for your own children, you were saying that wealth was the greatest gift you could give them. At its most basic, buying into the concept of inheritance meant choosing money over love.

I'm no theologian or ethicist. As a lawyer, some would say I'm actually at the opposite end of the spectrum. But I can't help but think that the misguided values underlying the rules we've all followed in the past contributed in some way to the declining moral fabric in our society. Even if you don't share that sense, it has got to be clear to you that abandoning these pernicious values will help you feel better about yourself and your place in the world.

CHOOSING YOUR OWN PATH

Die Broke does more than just help you give up values that are bad for you. It replaces them with something you've never really had before: choice.

Each of the rules of the past comes with an implicit goal, whether it's the top rung of the corporate ladder, having the most toys, full retirement at age sixty-five, or dying rich. When you were handed these rules, you were also handed these goals and told they were your aims in life. You had no choice in the matter. That's why I always refer to them as "rules."

If you're like most of my clients, there's a constant tape loop playing inside your head, telling you what you must do in order to be successful, desirable, happy. At first it may sound like your father or boss or wife, but if you listen closely you'll find it's your own voice, filtered through all those goals that society has dumped on you. When you give up the pursuit of goals others have foisted on you, when you stop trying to achieve what others want, when you stop letting others lead your life and take the reins in your own hands, you'll find those tapes will go silent.

By following the Die Broke philosophy, you have total choice over your goals. I'm really offering you axioms rather than rules. Every job "is just a job," so you're free to quit and then pick and choose another one that's best for you. You can buy whatever you want as long as you "pay cash." If you "don't retire," you can continue working full-time, go back to school, work part-time, or start a business—just so long as you do *something,* you can do *anything.* And when you choose to Die Broke, you're also given the freedom to spend your wealth throughout your life however you see fit, just as long as it's all used up when you die.

Follow the Die Broke philosophy and the new economic world will be just as liberating for you as the New World was to the immigrants of a century earlier. They came to America and found freedom of speech and freedom of religion. You'll come into the new economic world and find freedom of choice. After having had to wear the clothes your parents had picked out for you all these years, you can now finally choose your own. Free from living the kind of life that has been forced upon you, you can finally start to lead your own life.

What could be more spiritually rewarding than finally getting the opportunity to be yourself?

ABANDONING THE PURSUIT OF PERFECTION

Have you found that you're never satisfied with what you achieve? I'm amazed by how many of my clients—arguably among the most successful people in America—are dissatisfied with themselves and their lives. They're trapped in one of the great Catch-22s of capitalism. No matter how rich they are, there's always someone richer. No matter how powerful their computer, there's always one that's more powerful. No matter how successful they are at their profession, there's always someone who's more successful. They're convinced that life is a zero-sum game: that there's one winner and everyone else is a loser. They're convinced the perfect job or home or car is out there, if only they can find it.

I think this self-defeating chase after perfection is just a symptom of following the old world's rules in pursuit of someone else's goals.

When you're told to keep climbing the ladder until you get to the top rung, or fall off into the abyss, you're being taught that only perfection is good enough.

When you're being convinced that there's a new car or exercise machine or sneaker you have to buy because it's better than all the rest, you're being seduced into constantly spending on the perfect possession—whether you have the money or not.

When you're told to save 50 percent of your salary to pay for your retirement, your daughter's college tuition, and her future inheritance, even though 97 percent of your income goes to paying your bills, you're being pushed to become the perfect saver.

Even if you achieve these goals, they're not satisfying. In response you always try to do more, to get more, to be better, in the hope that somehow, sometime, you'll finally be satisfied. You keep on striving, but you get no closer to happiness.

I think that's because they're not your goals. By their very nature, the goals society has dumped on you can never be satisfying. Chasing after them has turned you into a modern-day Sisyphus, forever pushing that boulder up the hill.

If you follow the Die Broke philosophy, you'll finally be setting your own goals. And you know what? When you achieve them you'll be satisfied. I'm not suggesting you will or even should stop striving to improve yourself and your life. All I'm saying is that if you set achievable goals and meet them, you'll be free to set other achievable goals. Life will become a process of attaining what you set out for rather than striving and never getting there.

Follow principles designed for you and the time you're living in. Pursue goals you've chosen for yourself. Do the best you can with the resources available. If there's a secret formula for achieving happiness, for reaching serenity, that's it.

Helping Your Parents Die Broke

7

Don't expect your parents to understand your decision to die broke. No amount of discussion—calm or heated—and no explanation—however well reasoned and documented—will get them to accept this program.

That's not because they're dense or foolish. It's because they're too heavily invested, both psychologically and financially, in the old way of looking at things. Remember, by and large the old rules worked for them, so they assume they should work for you. That's why they taught them to you in the first place. You may be saying "the old rules no longer work," but they're hearing: "The rules you lived by and taught me are wrong."

And if they can't accept your decision to die broke, they're certainly not going to be convinced they should die broke as well ... even though they should. Go right ahead and tell them that you don't need an inheritance from them. Stress that they should spend all their money on themselves while they're alive. Most likely they'll smile, thank you, and go right on doing what they're doing.

Assuming they're comfortable in retirement,[3] your parents' two

---

[3] I know that's an awfully big assumption to make. But it's hard to address the alternative in any kind of objective fashion. Should you cut back on your own lifestyle to help your parents if they are struggling financially? Should you cut back on spending on your children to help your parents? What if you have siblings? What if they can't help, but you can? I'm afraid I have no easy answers to these very disturbing questions. I suppose it's really a matter of personal choice and depends on your rela-

major fears are running out of money or seeing the money they've struggled to save their entire lives taken away by the government. They won't buy into a program designed to improve the quality of their current life at the expense of their estate—most are determined to leave an inheritance even if it means making do with less. What they might buy into is a program that ensures they retain their dignity and quality of life for as long as they live, and then makes sure that whatever money is left is passed on to their family rather than the state. So that's the program you're going to sell them. Don't call it Die Broke. Call it Live Well.

MAINTAINING QUALITY OF LIFE AND DIGNITY

The Live Well program is designed to avoid the most dangerous senior citizen financial disaster: rapid impoverishment due to health care costs, followed by a lessened quality of life, which can only be improved by outside financial support.

The all-too-typical scenario is that your aged parent, living alone and far from you, suffers an injury or illness that doesn't kill her but that renders her unable to take care of herself. Assuming she's over sixty-five, her Medicare (see chapter 50) and Medigap (see chapter 51) insurance policies will cover a hundred days in a skilled nursing facility, and some part-time or intermittent home health care. What Medicare and Medigap won't cover is custodial care or long-term skilled care. And of course, those are just the areas where coverage is most needed.[4]

In all honesty, if a senior citizen needs a high level of skilled care, the odds are they're apt to be hospitalized or near death. In either case it's not a long-term situation. For most people the problem is long-term custodial care: Your parent can no longer safely go from her bed to her chair to the bathroom; or she can't seem to keep her medication schedule straight; or she seems to have given up on eating. She needs

tionships with your parents and your children. My first instinct is to say that you shouldn't divert money from your children to your parents. But I don't know if I'm basing that on anything other than choosing the future over the past. I do know it's not a sufficient answer, but all I can tell you is that every situation is unique, there's no set answer or pattern, and all you can do is your best.

[4]These are also just the areas long-term care insurance should address. But as you'll see if you read chapter 48, there are a great many problems with these policies. Few are both affordable and good. If your parent qualifies for good coverage, and can afford the steep premium it's apt to carry, long-term care insurance is a viable alternative to the Live Well program. But until the industry is cleaned up and premiums come down, I think the best defense for most older Americans is to follow the kind of asset reallocation program outlined in this chapter.

someone to help her get through the day safely, not a registered nurse.

The huge bills for these kinds of custodial services, whether in the home (up to $200 a day) or in an institution (up to $6,000 a month), can quickly drain your parent's assets until she is poor enough to qualify for Medicaid (see chapter 49), at which point the government starts picking up all the bills. Since you're not concerned with an inheritance, you'd think the story could end there. But unfortunately, it doesn't.

Personal Spending Is the Problem Area

Personal spending by Medicare recipients is severely limited by government regulation. Each state has its own rules, but all leave individuals in what I believe is a pitiful financial position. Let me use New York State's rules as an example. A Medicaid recipient can receive no more than $520 a month in income if she resides in the community, and no more than a $50-per-month personal needs allowance if she resides in an institution. Regardless of where she lives, she's allowed to have only $4,500 in personal resources (not counting her home, household goods, furniture and dishes, and one car), $1,500 of which is supposed to pay for her burial.

It's pretty obvious that $520 a month isn't going to provide for much of a life in most American communities. Even if your parent is able to take advantage of all the senior services and programs in her community (meals on wheels, tax reductions, adult day care, etc.), she's still going to have trouble maintaining a decent quality of life on $520 a month. Will she be able to have her hair done regularly? Can she buy new clothing as needed? What about paying for cable television? Will she have the money to go out for lunch with friends? Can she afford to have flowers planted in the yard? How is she going to pay her long-distance telephone bill? If she's institutionalized, that $50-a-month allowance will cover even less. And that total of $4,500 she'll have in the bank may not cover the entire cost of her funeral/burial/cemetery bill, let alone provide for anything while she's alive. Where will the rest of the money come from to help her maintain some dignity and quality of life? Her family.

Assuming you *can* do something, it probably won't be as much as you, or your parent, would like. You may have enough problems trying to keep a roof over your head, let alone keeping one over your parent's head too. Then there are your children to think of. Besides, it's humiliating for your parent to have to ask you to pay for her new housedress or hair-dressing appointment. The Live Well program is designed to avoid this scenario. Forget about preserving the estate: Live Well seeks to preserve an individual's assets so they can maintain their own quality of life and dignity and not have to rely on their family's money.

PROTECTING ASSETS FROM MEDICAID

As I'm sure you've figured out, the key to the Live Well program is the shielding of assets from Medicaid. There are two distinct methods of protecting assets from Medicaid: artificial impoverishment and asset reallocation.

The Problem with Artificial Impoverishment

Artificial impoverishment involves a parent gradually transferring assets to her children so that, on paper at least, she appears poor enough to qualify for Medicaid. She then relies on the tender mercies of her children to provide for her quality of life. That's the problem: She's handing her life savings over to you, relying on your verbal promise of fealty. I don't doubt your loyalty or that of your spouse or child should you die. But your parent might. Even if it's just an irrational fear, it could be enough to keep her from taking the action. Especially if you're the one who has proposed the transfer in the first place.

If there was no other alternative, I'd accept artificial impoverishment as a necessary evil for society—no more heinous than income tax avoidance and a required risk for seniors—and urge you to press your parent to make the transfers. However, there is another way to go: asset reallocation.

Asset Reallocation and Medicaid Trusts

Certain types of assets are not included in determining Medicaid eligibility. The most obvious are those I mentioned earlier: a home, household goods and furnishings, and a car. But there are others, most notably annuities that don't allow access to the principal. Your parent can shield some of her assets from Medicaid while ensuring her quality of life by paying down her mortgage or buying an annuity (see chapter 11). She can obtain an income that Medicaid won't go after by taking out a reverse mortgage (see chapter 62). Most effective of all is the establishment of a trust.

Let me start by saying I'm not an estate expert. This is a very arcane and complex area of the law. If you and your parents pursue this option, you definitely need to enlist the help of a specialist. That disclaimer aside, let me explain the basics. If your parent or parents sign their assets over to a trust, as far as the law is concerned they no longer own them. As long as the trust was set up more than thirty months prior to her application for Medicaid, and is not under her control, the assets in the trust no longer count in determining her eligibility.

A trust like this can be set up in a variety of ways. It could begin as a revocable trust with your parents themselves as trustees; basically they'd be paying themselves an income from the trust. The trust could change upon one of them entering a nursing home, so that the maximum incomes allowed under Medicaid are paid to both spouses. Additional income (which could be used to maintain both spouses' quality of life) could be paid to another trustee (namely you). The trust could change again if a sole surviving spouse enters a nursing home. At that point it could become an irrevocable trust with you and an outside party—perhaps your parent's attorney—as trustees, paying the maximum Medicaid income to your parent and the rest to you so it can be used to maintain your parent's quality of life, circumventing Medicaid's restrictions on income.

I think a trust is the way to go. Sure, it will cost your parents some money to set up (about $2,000 to $2,500 if they use an attorney who specializes in this area of the law, as they should). But it provides a legitimate, legally defined structure and process for an otherwise messy business. You'll recall that one of the reasons I'm against inheritance is that it tends to poison family relations. Well, Medicaid planning can do the same thing. If your parent signs over her assets to you directly, there's no legally binding guarantee that you're going to follow her wishes. She may worry that if you die, your spouse or child won't feel the same loyalty to her that you did. I think the way to mitigate these potential problems, and still ensure your parent's quality of life, is for you and a second nonfamily trustee to be legally bound by the dictates of a trust to act in the manner your parent wishes. In my experience, this provides the final level of security many parents need in order to comfortably shield their assets. For many seniors it's easier to put their trust in a trust than a child, a grandchild, or an in-law.

BRINGING UP THE ISSUE

How do you bring this issue up to your parents? Hopefully you won't have to. You'd be surprised how often these kinds of issues are raised when retirees get together to talk. If your parent is already living in a senior-oriented environment, she'll probably come to you one day to talk about her "nursing home nightmare." That can provide you with an opportunity to once again state your disinterest in an inheritance, voice your concerns over long-term care insurance and artificial impoverishment, and suggest the trust option. What's essential is that you present this as information you've learned or that you're examining for your own needs. Suggest she contact an estate attorney on her own. Offer help if she needs it, but don't push the issue. This is her decision, not yours.

If your parent isn't proactive financially, you may feel the urge to bring the topic up on your own. I'd suggest you sit down with her at a quiet moment and break the ice by describing your own emergency measures, such as your living will and durable power of attorney for health care. Explain that you want to make sure she's aware of your wishes. This will probably lead her to express her own wishes, if she hasn't already. Urge her to formally document those wishes as you have. And suggest that, while she's doing that, she might want to think about setting up a Medicaid trust. Reiterate your lack of interest in her estate, then launch into your sales pitch. Offer to help her find her own lawyer—don't suggest your own. Explain that you'll help as much as she'd like. Then drop the issue.

Don't Keep Pushing

It has been my experience that aggressively pushing parents to divest themselves of their assets is counterproductive. If she wasn't suspicious of your motives at first, she will be the third time you ask her if she has called the lawyer yet. Bring the topic up, offer to help, and then let it go. Perhaps it will take some kind of crisis for her to get the message. Perhaps she'll never get it. Whatever the case, it's out of your hands.

If your parent never does anything about shielding her assets, and heaven forbid must one day hand them all over to a nursing home rather than you, you can rest assured that her most basic needs will in fact be met. The money will not be wasted. You and the rest of the family will do the best you can for your parent, both emotionally and financially. And that's all you can do. No one can legitimately ask for more. You'll have fulfilled your filial duty by previously suggesting alternatives. Who knows, by the time your parents needs to deal with this issue the long-term care insurance business may have been cleaned up, making the whole question of Medicaid planning moot. Let's hope so.

Helping Your Children to Die Broke

8

You have *chosen* to die broke, knowing that decision will have a dramatic effect on your life. It will also have a dramatic effect on the lives of your children . . . and they had no say in the matter.

Don't get me wrong. I believe your decision will have a very positive long-term impact on your children, instilling in them a healthier attitude toward money in specific and life in general. However, it could require some painful short-term attitude and lifestyle adjustments for older children.

PARENTHOOD AND MONEY

Before I get too far into this topic I need to address those of you who haven't yet had children. My advice is to consider all the ramifications of becoming a parent, including the financial.

There are libraries filled with books extolling the virtues of having children. And personally, as the father of four and now the grandfather of nine, I can attest to the profound joy I've felt as the result of being a parent. But I can also attest to the financial burden of parenthood.

Just as I'm suggesting you abandon the old rules about work and personal finance, I urge you to forget the traditional dictates about reproducing. Having children isn't an obligation, responsibility, or duty for anyone. What it should be is a joy. Children are not long-term-care insurance policies, guarantees of your immortality, the repositories of your family's genetic essence, or flag bearers for the continuation of an ethnic identity. They are independent human beings with free will. I think the best way to ensure that's the case is to make birthing (or adopting) a conscious act, not a reflex. That means examining your hopes and dreams about your present and future. It also means examining your finances.

Parenthood: Historically an Economic Choice

Don't let anyone tell you money has nothing to do with having children. In the agricultural age families had lots of children in order to boost their finances. Children were needed to help work the farm or, in urban areas, to bring in added incomes. Prior to private pensions and government programs children *were* social security. All the kids would work the farm with you until they reached adulthood. Number one son would then stick around and take over the hard work and support of your wife when you no longer could, in exchange for knowing the farm would become his when you died. At that time, the value of children was economic, not emotional. It wasn't uncommon for children who died young to be buried in rudimentary, nearly unmarked graves. Today we give our pets a better send-off.

Then, in the industrial age, children stopped having economic value and instead became "priceless." While the earliest factories could rely on children as a source for unskilled cheap labor, as manufacturing became more complex, greater skills were needed. This coincided with a rise in immigration. These new arrivals provided a cheap, yet more skilled labor pool. With child labor no longer essential it was easier for reformers to enact legal prohibitions against it. In rural America, advances in agricultural technology made child labor unnecessary. In response, people began having fewer children. Advances in medicine enabled more of those children to survive. With fewer children around, and with those few more likely to live into adulthood, parents' emotional attachment to children grew. But even with this new emotional focus, there remained an economic element to parenthood: Children became precious, but costly. More than 20 percent of the women of childbearing age during the Depression remained child-free. That's the highest percentage in American history. Projections are that almost as many baby boom women will remain child-free.

Parenthood: A Cost/Benefit Analysis

So what are the financial ramifications of having children today? Well, the best estimates I've come across are that a lower-income family (less than $30,000 in annual income) will spend about $150,000 on a child from birth to age eighteen; a middle-income family (between $30,000 and $50,000 in annual income) will spend around $210,000; and a high-income family (more than $50,000 in annual income) will spend almost $300,000.

On the other hand, take it from a father: The joys of parenthood can truly be priceless. No one ever has enough money to have children, yet most people who do survive financially and get great emotional compensation. I'm not saying you shouldn't have children or you should have children. It's too personal and complex an issue for even me to offer an opinion either way. What I *am* saying is that historically, the economic impact of children has always played a role in the decision to reproduce, subconsciously or not. I'm simply suggesting you consciously take it into consideration.

THE MAGIC OF MONEY

Choosing to have a child doesn't end the role money will play in the parent-child relationship. In some ways it's just the first act.

Money is one of the most remarkable concepts developed by the human mind. In order for it to serve as a universal medium of exchange, it has no intrinsic value of its own. That means it's a completely plastic substance, able to turn itself into anything and everything. But that also means it can serve as a blank slate onto which we can project our own fears and dreams.

In our democratic/free market society money is the way we measure the value of everything and everyone, including ourselves. One of the wonderful things about the United States is that, theoretically, as a nation we don't judge you by who your parents were, where you were born, or what you look like: You are free to rise or fall on your own merits. But that leaves society with only one way to measure your value: money.

Money's Role in the Parent-Child Relationship

Since society measures us by our money, we end up measuring ourselves and others that way too. Admit it. Don't you look at your income and wealth not just as a tool but as a way to measure your status? Well, so does your child. We also use money to measure how much others think of us. You look to the boss to give you a bonus as proof of your value to the firm. Your son looks to you for a new pair of Air Jordans.

Money provides not just a way to measure ourselves and others but a way to control other people. Have enough money and you are independent. Don't have enough and you're dependent. Your child is dependent on you, not just for care and protection but for cash. All parents and kids are somewhat aware of this. Some use it. The parent who rewards desired behavior with money and the kid who acts a certain way in order to get money are both accepting money as a means of control.

The impact of money on your family life is inescapable. However, as Die Brokers, both you and your spouse will have gone a long way to mitigating any negative role it plays in your relationship. By viewing your assets as means to an end rather than a ticket to immortality, you'll both have adopted a much healthier view of money. Similarly, by swearing off any claim to an inheritance from your parents and encouraging them to use rather than hoard *their* assets (see chapter 7), you'll have done all you can to separate money from your relationship with them. The next step is to minimize money's role in your relationship with your children by teaching them to Die Broke.

TEACHING YOUR KIDS TO DIE BROKE

Obviously, I don't mean you should enforce your responses to today's economic circumstances on your four-year-old daughter. That would eventually put her in the same boat you were in prior to picking up this book: drawing on her parents' rules to deal with a whole new game. Since it's unlikely her economic world will be the same as yours, your goal should be to give her the attitudes she'll need to develop her own rules. Healthy attitudes toward money are the best legacies you can leave. They're worth more than sheepskins from Harvard or all the Tickle Me Elmo dolls ever made because they can help in every situation confronted throughout life. In effect you'll be giving your child the tools she needs to take charge of her life, just as you're now taking charge of your own. The earlier you start, the better. But don't fret if your child is already a teen; she still has time to learn. After all, you didn't start until you picked up this book.

Allowances as Teaching Tools

As early as possible (say, ages three to five) start letting your child handle money. Have her hand over a dollar bill to pay for the newspaper or pack of chewing gum, and let her hand the change back to you. Try to convey to her that money is the universal medium of exchange; that everyone, regardless of their job, gets paid money, which they can use to buy whatever they need.

Once your child starts going to school, give her an allowance. Present it at the same time on the same day every week, and let her decide what "little luxuries" to spend it on. Don't link the allowance to chores: Those are part of being a family member. Don't link it to grades either: Doing your best at school should be expected. Finally, don't link it to behavior either. Anger, love, family responsibilities, and schoolwork should all have nothing to do with money.

This early allowance should be just enough to pay for things like the occasional comic book or toy. You should still pick up the tab for everything else. If you're in doubt about how much to pay, ask the parents of your child's friends. Talk it over with your child. It's better to pay her too little and then raise it than to pay too much: You *want* her to be forced to make choices.

When your child nears ten years old, you can start broadening what her allowance is supposed to cover. Consider adding enough so she's responsible for buying gifts for other family members, or perhaps give her enough to pay for one monthly outing: say, a movie and a lunch at McDonald's.

When your daughter reaches twelve or thirteen, let her sit in on family budget discussions. Try going from a weekly to a monthly allowance, perhaps expanding it to take care of all her normal entertainment. If your child shows some financial responsibility, think about creating a separate clothing allowance for her. Don't shy away from giving advances, just make sure it really is an advance, not an extra payment: She won't learn responsibility if she doesn't have to make some sacrifices. Help her open up a savings account. You should be able to find a sympathetic local bank (probably a credit union or savings and loan) that will waive the minimum balance fees for accounts controlled by minors. If your young teen needs more cash, consider paying her for doing odd jobs around the house. These shouldn't be part of her normal chore list but tasks you would have paid someone else to do anyway, like clearing out the garage or wash-ing the car.

At around fifteen, part-time jobs can now come into the picture. Don't worry about a paper route taking away from her schoolwork. Most studies show the opposite to be true: Kids with part-time jobs often do better in school since they learn how to manage their time and set priorities. Besides, she's going to need that extra money for her tuition.

HELPING YOUR CHILD WITH COLLEGE

Every parent wants to be able to foot the bill for a child's four years at Harvard. However, few baby boomers are even going to be able to cover the whole tab for a sheepskin from State U., let alone one of the Ivies. For most, the numbers simply won't add up.[5]

College tuition is going up at an incredible rate. In the year 2001, projections are that a bachelor's degree from a public university will cost $38,000, while a diploma from a private school will cost $102,000. And those numbers are just tuition. You'll have to also add in ever-increasing costs for books, room and board, transportation, and entertainment.

Sure, your parents probably helped you out with college. But they were in a much different situation. They gave birth to you in their twenties, so tuition bills showed up when they were in their prime earning years. Their incomes were growing faster than tuition bills. They had federally subsidized loan programs they could tap into. They had secure jobs, private pensions, and homes that were soaring in value.

You, on the other hand, gave birth in your thirties, so tuition bills are likely to show up just when your job gets shaky. Your income is flat (or shrinking) while tuition is soaring. Government loan programs are being cut, and the scarce resources are (understandably) being focused on the truly needy. Your job is insecure, you've no private pen-

---

[5]The math is just as harrowing for those who'd like to send their child to private primary or sec-ondary schools. I hate to see you spend money on private school tuition since, if you're a homeowner, you're already paying for your young child's education in the form of school taxes. Financially, private schools just don't make sense, so this is strictly a lifestyle decision. That means paying the tuition from your stream of income rather than through loans. If you can pare down your spending in other areas, or increase your income, to cover the cost of private school tuition, fine. Otherwise, stick with the public schools that you're already paying for through your taxes.

sion, and your home's value is just about keeping pace with inflation. There's no comparison. Unless you're doing very well, you simply won't have the resources to pick up as much of the cost of your child's college education as your parents did of your education.

Setting Aside 6 Percent

Instead of striving to pick up as much of the bill as possible, just plan on allocating up to 6 percent of your savings and income to your son's college education.

Why 6 percent? That's the amount the federal government *says* you should contribute in its loan programs. Most colleges use the same number in their financial aid calculations. In other words, the government and your child's college will assume you'll be contributing that much for your child's education when they decide how much help to provide him. If you don't provide that much, he'll have to borrow it on his own through a nonsubsidized loan program. Since he's already likely to be borrowing a great deal of money—most financial aid today is in the form of loans, not grants—I think that's too much to ask.

Obviously, since you're a Die Broker and won't be practicing serial investing (house fund becomes college fund becomes retirement fund), the money will need to come from either your general non-tax-deferred savings program or your stream of income.

If you don't have enough, I think you should simply borrow it through one of the private nonsubsidized loan programs available for parents. Most will lend you most or all of the money you need at relatively reasonable interest rates and with long repayment schedules. Here are four of the largest of these lenders:

- **The Education Resources Institute**, (800) 255-8374, the nation's largest private educational lender, will lend up to the total cost of a college education and provide up to twenty-five years for repayment. Terms vary and are dictated by the program's sponsor banks.
- **The New England Loan Marketing Association**, (800) 634-9308, offers loans of from $2,000 to the full cost of a college education, less financial aid. Interest rates are usually 2 to 4 percent above prime. There's also an initial fee of 5 percent of the amount of the loan. Repayment can be as long as twenty years.
- **The College Board**, (800) 874-9390, has an Extra Credit Loan

Program that covers all costs less financial aid for up to four years and gives up to fifteen years for repayment. Its Extra Time Loan Program allows parents to borrow a year at a time, with repayment over ten years beginning after graduation. Interest rates are 4.5 percent higher than the ninety-day Treasury bill. Call for more information.

- **The College Resource Center**, (800) 477-4977, will loan a maximum of $50,000. There is an application fee of 3 percent of the value of the loan. Interest rates can be as low as prime plus 2.5 percent. The minimum monthly payment is $100 a month, or 2 percent of the outstanding balance, whichever is greater.

Don't Feel Guilty About Your Limitations

I don't think you should strip your financial resources bare in order to send your child to college. As a Die Broker you'll have spent on your child throughout his life, and will continue to do so during and after he graduates college. By fully insuring yourself and continuing to work as long as you can, you'll be guaranteeing you'll never be a financial burden on him. If you can provide the 6 percent out of your savings and income, do it. If you can't, borrow it. In either case, don't feel guilty you didn't do more: You've done the best you could with the cards you were dealt—no one can ask for more.

What's essential is that you're honest and open with your child about your limited means. As soon as he reaches his midteens, tell him what you can and can't do. That will give him and you plenty of time to plan accordingly. Don't minimize the importance of such discussions. Many sociologists believe the underlying cause of many of today's most serious family problems is the discrepancy between reality and expectations. If your child knows from an early age that your financial contribution to his college tuition bills will be limited, he can either make the necessary adjustments in his expectations or mentally prepare himself to make any needed sacrifices.

Don't feel bad about showing your child that he may need to make sacrifices in order to achieve his dreams. When your child realizes and accepts that choices in life are indeed limited by financial resources, he'll have developed a healthy attitude toward money—and that should have been your primary goal since the day you handed him his first allowance.

IS COLLEGE WORTHWHILE?

I'd be remiss if I didn't address one more topic: I think the often over-looked first step in college planning is to decide whether or not college is even justified. It's ludicrous for a family to spend or borrow about $100,000 without first examining whether it's a necessary expense. Some educational theorists suggest that only 25 percent of those enrolled in college are actually interested in school.

I've long felt that young people interested in pursuing technical careers are better served by vocational and apprenticeship programs than four years of a liberal arts education. Similarly, those thinking of a creative career—actor, writer, artist—could use those four years to work on their art rather than take Economics 101. Of course, children thinking of pursuing a professional or managerial path will definitely need one, if not more, degrees. If your child isn't sure what path he'd like to follow, I think going to a local community college makes the most sense, both educationally and financially.

The Die Broke Plan   9

Every philosophy needs to have a plan of action if it's to make the transition from intellectual exercise to pragmatic approach. Die Broke is no different.

But there *is* a distinct difference between my Die Broke plan and that offered by traditional financial planners and advisers: Mine has no time frames or age guides.

That's because *my* plan treats each and every Die Broker as a unique human being. It would be hypocritical for me to offer you a philosophy that preaches individual freedom and then give you an age- or time-specific plan to enact it. It would also be a mistake.

Traditional financial plans are all tied to a specific date: your sixty-fifth birthday when you are supposed to retire. The Die Broke philosophy, on the other hand, rejects retirement. It views life as a journey, with its own ups and downs, rather than a climb up a cliff and a jump off the ledge at age sixty-five. Instead of being tied to a specific date assigned by society, my plan is tied to your personal accomplishment of certain objectives and to discernible shifts in your personal income. These accomplishments and shifts will come at different times for different people.

I also want everyone to be able to experience the freedom of dying broke. That means my plan has to be accessible to people of all ages and stages in life. I think it is. If you have accomplished the objectives or met the criteria for a particular phase, you can move on to the next, regardless of your age or circumstances. If you haven't accomplished the early objectives, go back and do so before moving on to the next phase, again, regardless of your age. And if you haven't met the criteria to move into a new phase, don't, whatever your age.

Obviously this plan is just an outline for your life's journey. Every person is unique, and so your particular plan will obviously vary somewhat. As an outline, it's also by its very nature somewhat general. Don't worry: In the second part of this book I'll get into more specific advice about the topics touched on in the plan and some others that Die Brokers will need to approach differently than traditionalists.

I'm sure all this talk of objectives, criteria, and phases has gotten you a little confused. Rather than digress further into explanations, let me cut to the chase and offer you the Die Broke plan[6] for your life's journey.

PHASE ONE: ESTABLISHING YOUR BASE CAMP

The bad news is that by choosing to live fully up to your means you are taking some risks that those who live beneath their means are not. The good news is that by adequately preparing for your journey you can eliminate all those risks. So before you can start dying broke you've got to establish a base camp fully stocked with all you need.

Start by having enough cash aside to pay your bills for three months. This will be your emergency cash reserve in case you're terminated or become ill. This money should be put in three laddered **certificates of deposit**. This takes precedence over everything else, since no one's job is safe anymore.

Next take out sufficient **disability insurance** and **life insurance**. Your chances of becoming disabled at an early age are much higher than dying, so the disability coverage should come first.

Reexamine your **health insurance** coverage, making sure you're either getting coverage worth the high price you're paying or not spending more than you need.

Develop a new **résumé** and start **job hunting** . . . now. It's never

---

[6] I know, I promised to stop digressing and here I am making you jump down to a footnote. This won't take more than a minute, though. Throughout the rest of the text you'll see that some words are in boldfaced type. This indicates that there's a separate entry providing more information on that specific topic in the second half of this book.

too early or too late to realize "it's just a job" and to start looking for another one that will pay you more money. Constant job hunting is part of a twenty-first-century safety net.

With your cash reserve established, your insurance protection in place, and your job hunting under way, take a look at your **credit card** debt. Get rid of it. Start paying cash instead.

Take a look at all your expenses and cut back where possible. At first, those savings will go toward your new insurance premiums, but after living by the Pay Cash maxim for a little while, you'll start accumulating some extra money. Put this in a **money market** account—you'll need it for phase two.

If you're about to get married, consider a **prenuptial agreement**. If you plan on living together permanently, take steps to formalize your **domestic partnership**. In either case, draft a **durable power of attorney for health care** and a **living will**. While you and your partner are at the lawyer's office, have your **wills** drafted as well.

If you have children, start teaching them to Die Broke as soon as they start learning the alphabet. If you have a child who may not ever be able to support him or herself fully, take out **second-to-die insurance** to take care of him or her when both you and your spouse are gone.

While you and your spouse are dealing with all these other pleasant topics, you might as well also write down and sign a letter outlining what kind of **funerals** you'd both want. You don't have to worry about paying for them just yet—simply memorialize your wishes.

Move on to Phase Two only after you've completely stocked your base camp and have accumulated some cash in that money market account.

PHASE TWO: THE OUTBOUND LEG

Start by finding yourself a good **financial planner**—he or she will serve as your guide on the rest of your journey. Explain your Die Broke philosophy to the planner and discuss an **asset allocation** philosophy that fits your age and risk aversion, keeping in mind that you won't be retiring and you're likely to live a lot longer than previous generations. As a Die Broker you'll probably lean toward **stocks,** using **mutual funds** to mitigate some risk. Even though you won't be retiring, exploit every opportunity you have to invest through tax-deferred **pensions.** Save and invest as much money as you can. Don't worry, you'll be able to start enjoying it in just a few years.

For instance, start thinking about **home ownership**. What kind of home would you like to live in for the rest of your life? Buy a home when you can afford one that at least comes close to your dreams—don't compromise just to get a tax deduction. Once you're a homeowner, take out adequate **homeowner's insurance** and, if necessary, separate **flood insurance** or **earthquake insurance**. Think about **umbrella liability insurance** as well.

Speak to your parents about their dying broke. At the very least, help them set up a Medicaid trust. Keep teaching your kids about how to Die Broke, and start talking to them about college plans and tuition bills. If they think university is in their future, start considering where you'll come up with the 6 percent of your qualified assets you'll need to give them for college. (Remember: You can always take out loans for it.) Help them to start coming up with their own share, and to investigate loan and aid plans.

With those new-home expenses and possible college loans in the future you'll have plenty of motivation to keep right on job hunting in an effort to increase your earned income. In fact, you won't be ready for Phase Three until you feel like you've reached your peak earning potential.

Obviously you're not going to know for certain when this will happen. But if you're an employee you'll probably get a good idea based on your knowledge of your industry and profession. Sure, you may continue to get income increases, either through raises or taking other jobs, but after a certain point they're not likely to be as substantial as in the past. You'll probably be able to sense when you've just about maxed out.

If you're self-employed, it will be more difficult to tell because the signs are apt to be internal. Do you feel yourself losing interest or energy? Have your billings leveled off and you no longer find that troublesome? Does the idea of starting another business or branching off in a new direction make you excited or angry? If the first two items are true, you may not have reached your peak. If the last item is true, you probably have.

PHASE THREE: ENJOYING THE VIEW

When Die Brokers reach their peak earnings, they shouldn't forget to enjoy the view. This is the turnaround point on your life's journey, but don't hurry past it. Keep on putting some money away in your invest-ment portfolio, perhaps slightly adjusting to a more aggressive asset allocation formula. But don't be afraid to spend some money too.

Now is the time to take those family vacations to Europe. Consider buying a **summer, weekend, or vacation home**. Maybe you can truly make your home fit your dreams by using a **home equity loan** to finance **home improvements, renovations, or additions**. Perhaps you start **gifting** and help your child buy a home or start a business. If the timing isn't right for such sizable cash gifts, at least consider some experiential spending: Help your daughter and son-in-law come with you on vacation to the Virgin Islands, pay their airfares to come home for the holidays, or offer to pick up the cost of child care for them to go on their own vacation. The choice is yours. Remember that you're a Die Broker. Be prudent, but don't sacrifice quality of life or joy.

And don't forget to keep job hunting. That's especially important now, since if you notice that your value on the market is not just stag-nant but has begun dropping, it's time to move on to Phase Four.

PHASE FOUR: GETTING HELP FOR THE RETURN LEG

Now is when a Die Broker's years of saving and investing really pays off. Unlike traditionalists who will be looking to conserve their assets, you'll start turning them into lifelong income streams. With the help of your financial planner, set up a planned gradual shift of your money into **annuities**. These will provide you with unearned income to com-pensate for the drop in your earned income, allowing you to maintain your lifestyle.

By all means keep on working as long as you can. But do take advantage of all the programs you become eligible for when you turn sixty-five. Sign up for **Medicare**. Turn your existing health insurance into a **Medigap** plan. Contact **Social Security**.

Now is also the time to investigate **long-term care insurance** policies and to think about prepaying for your own funeral.

Reexamine the gifting issue. If you can now afford cash gifts, make them. If not, just stick with your other contributions to your kids' lives.

When you sense that you'd like to or need to stop working com-pletely, even if it's to perhaps volunteer part-time instead, you're ready for Phase Five.

PHASE FIVE: THE HOME STRETCH

With no earned income coming in, it's time to ensure that you Die Broke and get all you possibly can from your assets while you're alive to enjoy them.

Look at **charitable remainder trusts** as a way to fully annuitize your savings and investments. Take out a **reverse mortgage** to ensure you get the most benefit from all that home equity you've built up. And, of course, continue your gifting and spending, making sure that you'll leave behind only enough to pay your bills. If you haven't yet, this is the time to make those annual cash gifts to your children or to help with your grandchild's college tuition bills. If you haven't pre-paid for your funeral, take out a whole life insurance policy for just enough to cover the costs. With that last obligation taken care of, you can kick back and enjoy all the time you have left.

SOME PARTING THOUGHTS

When tailoring this general outline to your own life, it will help to keep three things in mind.

First, one of the secrets to being able to Die Broke successfully is to share the risks you're taking with others. That's why I'm a big believer in insuring whenever possible and investing through mutual funds. If you find yourself facing a risk I haven't specifically addressed in this book, before taking it on, look to see if there's a way for you to share it with others.

Second, as a Die Broker you should always focus on your personal income statement rather than your balance sheet. While traditionalists fixate on their net worth, you should be watching your income, your expenses, and your cash flow. Die Brokers grow their assets in order to be able to eventually turn them into larger streams of unearned income, not simply to increase their net worth. When a Die Broker dies, his net worth should be zero.

Finally, remember that each of us takes a different path in our life, but as Die Brokers we all want to end up in the same place. Life is not a race or a contest. You shouldn't worry about how you measure up against others, only about how you measure up against yourself. All you can do is your best, and that's all you owe yourself or your loved ones. Every Die Broker gets dealt a different hand in life. Just play your cards the best you can. The goal is for each of us on our final day to look back on our life, appreciate the time we had, and have no regrets; we were true to ourselves. Our loved ones will remember us for who we were and what we did for them and with them while we were alive. Our legacies will be intangible, but valuable beyond measure.

Part II

Putting Theory into Practice

INTRODUCTION TO PART TWO

Accepting and understanding a theory is one thing. Putting it into practice is another. That's especially true when the theory is a revolutionary one like Die Broke. There are lots of wonderful encyclopedias of personal finance out there . . . but they're all based on the old rules. If you were my client, I could tell you to just call me when you had a question. But you're my reader, not my client. I can't just turn your financial world upside down and then let you loose in the world without a lot more practical advice. That's where Part Two of this book comes in.

It's an alphabetical examination of sixty-three different career and financial subjects. I don't claim that it's comprehensive. I've primarily addressed topics that are approached differently, or topics that take on an added importance, when you choose to follow the Die Broke philosophy. If a subject isn't covered here, just follow the best mainstream advice.[1] For example, you won't see chapters on investing in commodities, options, futures, derivatives, and precious metals here. That's because my advice would be no different than that offered by every other responsible personal finance adviser: forget about them unless you're a professional investor.

Similarly, some of my chapters may not be as comprehensive as the

[1] To me, that means reading *Consumer Reports* and Jane Bryant Quinn's newspaper columns.

entries in other personal finance books. For instance, I won't be spending pages and pages telling you how to apply for a mortgage. That information is available from lots of other good books (including a couple of my own), so there's no need for me to cover it here. Instead, in these pages I'll offer you the Die Broke perspective on mortgages, which you can then bring to the background information you've gathered elsewhere. Of course, in those important areas where there isn't a lot of good information available elsewhere—such as annuities and reverse mortgages—I'll be more comprehensive.

Each of these chapters is treated as if it were a telephone conversation—albeit one-sided—between you and me. You've called me and asked, "Stephen, what do you think I should do about life insurance?" for example. The chapter is my answer. Since I bill by the hour I've tried to keep all of them tight. If you have any more questions, just give me a call.

Accountants 10

Some people, because of their personality or their training, see the world as being one-dimensional. For instance, I've a friend who's a dentist. He's single, and my wife and I are always trying to match him up with someone. But whenever we introduce him to a woman and later ask what he thought of her, he always says something like: "She has a terrible overbite." He doesn't see a person; he sees a set of teeth. That's the problem with most accountants, except they're fixated on taxes rather than teeth.

I think it's essential all of us have a savvy, innovative accountant on our team of professionals to ensure we take maximum advantage of all our tax avoidance opportunities. I'm also a firm believer in hiring someone who's a CPA because they're—pardon the pun—professionally accountable. (Not only have CPAs passed some tough exams, but they're members of the American Institute of Certified Public Accountants and are held to that organization's high standards of behavior and continuing education.) But I'm opposed to using an accountant as your investment adviser.[2]

While it's important that tax issues be considered when putting together a personal financial plan, it's not the only issue. And for Die Brokers it's not on the top of the list.

---

[2]Or as your business consultant for that matter, unless he also has an MBA.

Die Brokers concentrate on turning assets into the maximum possible streams of income rather than preserving investment principals and keeping them out of the tax man's hands. That's a concept alien to most accountants. CPAs are schooled in asset protection. They spend most of their time making sure assets can move from one generation to the next with as little tax impact as possible. Well, as a Die Broker you don't want to preserve your assets—you want to use them. You're not worried about estate taxes since you're not going to have an estate.

By all means find yourself a good CPA. Call her with your tax questions. Listen to her advice on record keeping and filing issues. But when she offers investment advice, just smile politely (after all, unlike insurance brokers who offer investment advice, she means well and isn't trying to enrich herself) and say you need to speak with your financial planner (see chapter 31). If she persists, give her your planner's telephone number.

Annuities 11

Annuities have always lived on the opposite extremes of the traditional personal finance world. One type—the fixed annuity—is seen as a prudish kind of retirement plan favored by rich old maiden aunts. The other type—the variable annuity—is viewed as an aggressive tax avoidance technique for mercurial investors. But in the Die Broke world annuities take center stage. That's because the single-premium fixed immediate annuity is our magic bullet.

I generally get one of two responses from clients when I tell them about my Die Broke philosophy. Some, because they lack imagination, are very fearful, or are natural conformists, refuse to get past their reflexive aversion to the concept and shut their minds totally. Others, because they're open to new ideas, are frustrated with their current state, or are natural nonconformists, accept the concept with one reservation—"How can I keep from outliving my money?" That's where our magic bullet comes in: For the Die Broker, annuities are, first and foremost, longevity insurance.

ALL ABOUT ANNUITIES

An annuity is simply a contract that guarantees a lifetime income. Generally it's an agreement between an individual and an insurance company, although other institutions, including charities and corporations, enter into annuity agreements.

Varieties of Annuities

Annuities are further defined by the nature of their income, premium, and payouts. If the amount of the income is established at the time the contract is signed, it's called a **fixed annuity**. If the amount of the income is determined by the performance of an underlying investment portfolio, it's called a **variable annuity**. In a **single-premium annuity** an individual makes just one lump-sum payment to the insurer. In a **periodic payment annuity** an individual makes a series of smaller payments for a predetermined length of time and at set intervals, say monthly for thirty years. **Immediate annuities** start paying an income immediately (actually thirty days) after the total premium is paid. **Deferred annuities** don't start paying out until some predetermined point is reached—say, age sixty-five.[3]

String these definitions together and you get a nearly total understanding of the product. For instance, a single-premium immediate fixed annuity is one in which you make one payment to the insurer, who promises to immediately start paying you a fixed amount. On the other hand, a periodic payment deferred variable annuity would require you to make a series of payments to an insurer who promises to pay you an income, of an amount to be determined, at a date sometime in the future.

Finally, there are also options on how long the income from an annuity is actually paid. A **single life** annuity pays an income only as long as the person who bought it lives. A **life with period certain** annuity pays an income either for as long as the person who bought it lives, or a set number of years, whichever is longer. If the person dies before the period certain expires, his heir(s) get the income for the remaining years. A **joint and survivor** annuity pays an income for as long as both the person who bought it and his named beneficiary (or beneficiaries) live. You get the highest return on a single life annuity, since it will pay out the shortest length of time, and the lowest for a

---

[3]There are also a couple of common annuities defined by their tax status. Neither are really germane to Die Brokers, but they're so common and so often confused that I thought it important I describe them. A tax-*deductible* annuity is a retirement plan like an IRA or SEP, commonly offered to teachers and those who work for nonprofit agencies. It is basically a pension you fund, partly or entirely, with your own pretax dollars. A tax-*deferred* annuity, on the other hand, is a tax shelter funded with an individual's after-tax dollars. The growth of the annuity isn't subject to taxes until you take the income out of it, and then you only pay taxes on the money you actually withdraw. While there are some other uses for these instruments, they are most often sold as tax shelters.

joint and survivor annuity, since it will pay out for the longest length of time.

The Advantages and Disadvantages of Annuities

Annuities have three distinct advantages for Die Brokers:

- Annuities are the only financial products in the world that can definitely provide a **lifetime income**. It's possible to outlive the income from every other investment, regardless of how conservative or risky it may be. Buy an annuity and you can rest assured you will never outlive your money—they truly are longevity insurance.
- Fixed annuities provide you with a **guaranteed income**. The stock market can turn bullish or bearish, interest rates can climb or plummet, but the income from a fixed annuity will never change. If you buy an annuity that promises to pay a 12 percent return, it will continue to do so even if interest rates fall dramatically.
- The income paid out of an annuity is **partly tax free**. That's because a portion of each payment is considered repayment of the money you put in, not income. The older you are when you buy the annuity, the larger the portion of the payment that is tax free.

Of course, nothing's perfect, not even our magic bullet. Here are the downsides to annuities:

- They are **irrevocable**. Once you hand over your money you can't get it back for any reason. The exceptions to the rule are some new products that will let individuals get back a percentage of their money for a period of time in order to pay for medical emergencies.
- While the income may be guaranteed it **might not keep pace with inflation**. What was a nice monthly income in 2000 may not stretch as far in 2010 if those were ten years of high inflation. Fixed incomes are always mixed blessings.
- An annuity is **only as certain as the financial solvency of the insurer** that issued it. When you buy an annuity, you're counting on the insurer being around to pay that income as long as you're around to collect it.

One oft-cited downside of annuities is the risk that you could die soon after buying one, not collect that much in income, and have the bulk of the money end up in the insurer's hands rather than your heir's. However, for a Die Broker who's planning on spending everything, that's not an issue; it's just the same kind of risk you assume when you buy almost any insurance product. In addition, Die Brokers have the opportunity to easily mitigate the other potential downsides.

Simply by making sure you have adequate home, auto, liability, and health insurance and, when it makes sense, long-term care insurance, you're providing all the protection from financial disaster you need. If you've got a sound insurance package, you'll never need the money for an emergency, so the irrevocable nature of annuities won't be a problem.

The inflation risk attached to annuities can be lessened by following a savvy purchase strategy. I'll describe this strategy fully in a moment, but for now it can be summed up as: buying only as much income as you need, as late as you possibly can.

Finally, the risk of insurer insolvency can be mitigated by researching the financial health of insurers and buying annuities only from those that are judged highly. Again, more on that in a bit.

THE DIE BROKER'S ANNUITY STRATEGY OF CHOICE
By following a simple six-step strategy, Die Brokers can take maximum advantage of annuities while minimizing potential problems.

Buy Only Single-Premium Immediate Fixed Annuities
These are the annuity equivalent of straight term life insurance: plain vanilla products. They offer all the features you need with none of the frills and complications that could make comparison shopping difficult. If you focus on just single-premium immediate fixed annuities, you'll find it very simple to compare rates.

Buy Them As Late As You Possibly Can
The older you are when you buy an annuity, the higher the rate of return it will offer and the larger the portion of the income that will be tax free.[4] For a Die Broker the time to start thinking about buying an annuity is when you can see that simple earned income may no longer be enough to maintain your lifestyle.

---

[4]Unlike the actuarial tables used for life insurance policies, those used for annuities do not take gender into account. In addition, the specific medical condition of the individual(s) has no bearing on the rates paid. If you're buying a joint and survivor annuity, the rate will be based on the age of the younger person.

Since you're not going to retire, your earned income will continue past age sixty-five. But even though it's not stopping entirely, it's safe to assume it will eventually drop below the peak levels you experienced in your fifties and early sixties, either intentionally or unintentionally. While the exact timing of when you buy your first annuity will depend on your own unique circumstances, as a general rule most Die Brokers enter the annuity market when they're about seventy. By then most have a good idea of what their post-sixty-five income and expenses will be.

A oft-cited rule of thumb is that the yield on an annuity will increase around 2/10 of 1 percent for every year you delay buying it.

Buy Only As Much As You Need at the Time

Just because you see your earned income beginning to drop at age seventy doesn't mean you should turn your entire investment portfolio into an immediate annuity right away. Since the rate of return on an annuity is locked in when you buy it, you could be dooming yourself to a lifetime of below-market interest. As long as you don't need the income, you can do better investing it in equities.

A more sensible approach is to start by taking only a portion of your nonqualified savings (those moneys not in IRAs, SEPs, or 401[k] plans) and buy just enough of an income to compensate for the drop in your earned income. Then, when you once again see your income dropping below the level you'd like, buy yet another annuity, locking it in at the then-current rate. In this way, you keep from locking all your money in at what might turn out to be a low rate. Because you waited and got a few years older, you'll automatically get a better deal and you'll have helped offset the impact inflation will have on your income. As your earned income continues to naturally decline, just keep annuitizing your savings and investments (both nonqualified and qualified) until finally you're invested entirely in fixed annuities.

There's nothing to fear about eventually being entirely invested in annuities—in effect, giving away all your principal. The reasons traditional financial advisers tell people to shy away from tapping into their principal is to preserve their estate and to ensure they don't outlive their money. As Die Brokers we want to get the maximum use from, rather than preserve, our estates. And since we've bought annuities, we can't possibly outlive our money.

Buy Them from Only High-Rated Insurers

There's no getting around the fact that when you buy an annuity, you're counting on the insurer being solvent longer than you live. While state insurance funds may step in to make good on claims against failed insurers, that's not something you want to rely on. Instead, make it your business to personally check the health of every insurer you're shopping.

A. M. Best is the rating service that rates more insurers than any of the other firms, so I'd start with them. Write down the list of insurers you're thinking of buying an annuity from and call (908) 439-2200. You'll receive a Best ID number for each of the insurers you're interested in. Then call Best's automated ranking line at (900) 420-0400. You'll be prompted to enter the ID numbers to receive the latest Best rating of the insurers. It will cost you $2.50 per minute to use this automated service.

I wouldn't stop there, however. Every rating firm has its own criteria. Play it safe and make sure more than one of the rating services gives your insurer high marks. The second call I'd place would be to Weiss Research at (800) 289-9222. For a fee of $15 it will provide you with an oral report on a company. Obviously, ask for reports only on insurers that you've already learned Best rates highly.

Now you'll have a list of insurers rated highly by two services. As a final check, call the three other firms that rate insurers: Moody's at (212) 553-0377; Standard & Poor's at (212) 208-1527; and Duff & Phelps at (312) 368-3157. They all provide one free quote over the telephone. Ask each for a rating of one of the insurers you've found were highly rated by both Best and Weiss. That will give you three independent judgments on three of your candidates.

If you've more than three candidates, or aren't satisfied with just three judgments, check all the candidates by using Standard & Poor's ratings on the Insurance News Network Website at http://www.insure.com. If you don't have Internet access, you can find books listing Moody's and Standard & Poor's ratings in the reference section of a good library.

Don't let a half of a percentage point sway you into buying an annuity from an insurer that isn't given top marks. That additional return will be worthless if the insurer goes belly-up. Stick with companies rated A or better.

Shop Around Before You Buy

Do not, I repeat, do not, take the easy way out when shopping for an annuity. While single-premium fixed immediate annuities are plain vanilla products, there are price differences. Every insurer has its own actuarial table, investment projection table, and desired profitability. That means their individual annuity products will very likely offer different incomes to the same person.

Couples Should Opt for Joint and Survivor Annuities

Just because one of you succeeds in dying broke doesn't mean the other should thereafter live broke. If you have a life partner, I urge you to buy a joint and survivor annuity, which will continue to pay an income as long as one of the two of you is alive. (Federal law requires this option be offered to everyone purchasing an annuity, and that spouses sign a waiver if it's not selected.) Granted, this will result in a lower income than if you took out a single-life or life with period certain. However, you can lessen the effect somewhat by electing that the survivor gets either two-thirds or one-half of the benefit rather than the exact same income. Just make sure you figure out the actual drop in expenses after the death of one spouse before you select one of these options.

THE CHARITABLE OPTION

Insurance companies aren't the only institutions offering annuities. The most interesting alternative is to purchase a charitable gift annuity. Rather than giving the lump sum (or series of payments) to an insurer, you give it to a charity, which in exchange promises to pay you (or you and your survivor) a lifetime income, starting either immediately or when you turn sixty-five. The most obvious advantage of charitable gift annuities is that they offer a tax deduction as well as income. A portion of the lump sum is considered a charitable contribution, which can be deducted on your taxes immediately. That can provide a substantial increase in the buying power of whatever income you receive. That could also compensate for having to fund an annuity with qualified dollars that, having been withdrawn, are now subject to high taxes. Of course, you also get the joy of giving to a service organization rather than to an insurance company. And since you're making the gift while you're alive, you'll get to be there when they name the building after you.

The most significant disadvantage to charitable gift annuities is that you're relying on the continued financial solvency of a charity rather than an insurance company. There's no A. M. Best or Weiss for charities, so there's no way you can make that kind of judgment. Instead, you need to rely on the regulations of the insurance fund in the state in which the charity is based. New York State, for example, has very strict guidelines on how much a charity that offers annuities must keep in reserve, and how it invests that reserve money. Other states are less stringent. Some offer no protection. Therefore, when you shop for a charitable gift annuity, you not only have to shop based on the financial return and your feelings about the charity's mission but also on the policies of the charity's home state. Don't rely on the word of a fund-raiser; pick up the telephone and call the state's insurance department and get the information directly from the source.

Asset Allocation 12

Nearly every personal finance book and magazine article offers some handy little asset allocation formula, designed to make sure you have the right mix of equity, debt, and cash in your portfolio, based on you age and risk aversion. There are brokerage firms who have made their names with computerized asset allocation programs into which their clients' vital statistics are be entered and which then spit out a "personalized allocation formula." I think this is all utter nonsense.

I've spent half this book railing against the blind acceptance of general rules based on the past. I'm not about to start promulgating such rules of my own. All of the four adages I've suggested you adopt—it's just a job, pay cash, don't retire, and die broke—offer the freedom to make your *own* specific choices based on your circumstances, needs, and wants. The same goes for asset allocation. I can no more tell you exactly what percentage of your savings you should have in aggressive growth mutual funds or corporate bond funds than I can tell you how you should spend your money now that you're not building up an estate for your children. If you want to spend it on European vacations, that's up to you. Similarly, if you want to put 75 percent of your money into a global health sciences fund, that's your choice as well. This book is about freeing you from chains, not forging new ones.

All that said, I think there are three *general* factors you need to consider in developing, along with your financial planner, your Die Broke portfolio.

You Are Going to Live a Long Time

Life expectancy is increasing dramatically. Take care of yourself and you could easily live well into your eighties. Most standard asset allocation formulas, however, seem to assume you'll be dead—or forced onto Medicaid—in your early seventies. They tell you to start shifting your assets away from equities as early as your forties. In effect, they stunt your financial growth just when it's finally picking up steam. Based on our new longer life spans, I don't believe a Die Broker should even think about decreasing his or her equity position until the mid-fifties. And then I think it should be done by shifting not from equity to debt but from very aggressive equities to less aggressive equities—for instance, shifting your stake in a sector fund into an index fund.

Everyone should have some debt instruments in their portfolio throughout their lives, but if you intend to grow enough money to live rich into your eighties, you can't rely on bonds. View them as another strand in your safety net—an extension of that three-month cash reserve you've put in certificates of deposit—not the whole net. As a Die Broker your major protection comes from your intelligent use of leverage. Your insurance package—all those premiums you're paying for good life, health, disability, auto, homeowners', liability, and perhaps long-term care coverage—is your real protection. You get more security for each dollar through buying insurance than by keeping a sizable cash holding.

You Are Not Going to Stop Working at Age Sixty-five

Almost every one of those traditional asset allocation packages assumes that earned income will come to a sudden, permanent halt at age sixty-five. For you that's not true. As a Die Broker you're not planning on jumping off the retirement cliff. Instead, you intend to continue working—in one form or another—and therefore continue to bring in earned income past age sixty-five. That income may be the same as you earned before, less, or perhaps even more; you won't know until you get there. But you do know you'll be bringing home some kind of a paycheck. Once again, that decreases the need for shifting equity investments into debt instruments the day you blow out your sixty-fifth birthday candle.

The traditional asset allocation formulas assume you'll have no earned income after age sixty-five and that whatever pensions you're earning won't be sufficient to totally replace the buying power of your salary. That's why they suggest shifting from growth to income-generating investments. With an earned income you won't need to be so hasty. You'll be able to wait perhaps until you're seventy before you start relying on your nest egg for income, and at that point you'll probably find it more efficient to shift from equities into annuities rather than debt instruments. By doing that you not only generate as much income but guarantee you won't outlive it.

You Are Not Interested in Financial Immortality

Traditional asset allocation formulas are based on doing everything possible to preserve assets for the next generation. That's why they advocate putting assets in very secure debt instruments as you get older, generally at the expense of growth and income. As a Die Broker you've no interest in financial immortality. You've decided to instead live fully up to your means, using your money for yourself and others while you're alive. That allows you to choose annuities, charitable remainder trusts, and reverse mortgages—techniques that use rather than protect principal—instead of debt instruments to provide income. By forgoing financial immortality you can ensure lifelong incomes.

A Pattern Rather Than a Formula

There's no set asset allocation formula for Die Brokers. Instead, there's a basic pattern. Grow your wealth through equities. Keep just enough of a cash/debt instrument reserve that, together with your insurance package, you have sufficient protection. As you reach the age when your earned income starts to slow, begin shifting from equities to annuities in order to compensate. Continue to steadily shift from equities to annuities as you get older, eventually adding other techniques, including charitable remainder trusts and reverse mortgages, to finally totally convert your assets into income. At that point you're ready to Die Broke.

Automated Teller Machines and Cards 13

When was the last time you wrote a check to cash? If you're like most of my clients, it has been close to two decades. That's because in the past twenty years ATMs have become ubiquitous. Not only are they at every bank, but you can find these twenty-first-century one-armed bandits at convenience stores, malls, rest stops on the interstate, even hospitals.

I'll admit there are times these machines can be lifesavers—especially for people who have sworn off credit cards and always pay cash. They're also the best way to get funds overseas.[5] Used judiciously they're good emergency tools—like cellular telephones in a car. But just like those cell phones, it's awfully hard not to abuse them.

I've found that most of my clients can't identify where 30 percent of their cash goes each month. That's because, thanks to ATMs, it has become so easy for them to get cash anywhere at any time. Before ATMs were everywhere, people used to make a special weekly trip to the bank to withdraw a predetermined amount of cash. Sure, it was a

[5]While I hate to admit it, ATMs really are the best sources for cash overseas. There are now more than 175,000 ATMs overseas that belong to the Cirrus or Plus electronic funds networks. The local currency you get is changed into dollars at the wholesale rate. You can get the addresses of ATMs overseas by calling Cirrus at (800) 424-7787 or pulling up the Plus ATM locator at the Visa home page at http://www.visa.com. Two warnings: make sure you know the numbers, not just letters of your PIN because many overseas keypads are numeric only; and find out the transaction fee for overseas ATM use.

pain to have to go to the bank on your lunch hour and wait on a long line to get your money. But that pain made you focus on your cash needs. You didn't want to have to go through that "torment" more than once a week, so you made sure you knew how much cash you needed for the next seven days. And then, when you were out and about, you were more hesitant to spend that cash on something unplanned, since you didn't want to go back to the bank again.

With an ATM card you don't have to wait on lines; you don't have to worry about when the bank is open; in many cases you don't even need to go to the bank. This convenience has made it much easier for you to spend your money. You've been anesthetized to the pain of spending.

Let me explain. You're out at night and, after a movie, decide you want to get coffee and desert. Unfortunately, you don't have enough cash. Not to worry, there's an ATM machine around the corner. You slide your card in, key your PIN number, and the choices come up. One is a wonderful "fast cash" option that lets you take $100 from your checking account without pressing any further buttons. Since your friends are waiting for you, that's the one you select. Besides, you think you're actually saving yourself money by taking out $100 rather than the $20 you need. Since this isn't a machine from your own bank, you're going to get hit for a $1 service charge. If you took out only $20, that would be a 5 percent fee, but since you're taking out $100, it's only a 1 percent fee. Besides, the money won't go to waste. Pleased at your financial acumen, you pocket the cash and head over to Starbucks.

Believe me, I'm no masochist. But a little pain is good for you if it's associated with spending your hard-earned and increasingly rare cash. Not only has that ATM led you to spend money you didn't plan to, but it has also convinced you to withdraw more than you needed. And with those crisp $20 bills in your wallet, and another $100 just one push button away, you're going to be a lot more cavalier about where that money goes.

My suggestion is that from now on you take your ATM card out of your wallet and leave it at home. You don't have to put it in the same inaccessible location as your remaining credit card (see chapter 22), but it should be someplace out of the way—you should have to think about taking it with you. That way, if you do have a legitimate need for it—let's say you're going on a trip—you'll know where to find it. I actually keep mine inside my travel kit.

What do you do for cash? Well, go back to the way it used to be. Figure out how much cash you *need* for the week and make a special trip to the bank to withdraw it from one of your accounts. Do not, I repeat, do not, factor in any extra emergency money. That's what your charge card is for (see chapter 19). If you have to go without the occasional cafe latte that's okay: Caffeine isn't good for you anyway.

Automobile Insurance **14**

The only thing in the world that can make riding the bus look good to a teenager is a quote for auto insurance.

Not only is auto insurance very expensive, but the business is so tightly run and regulated that you have little choice about what you're spending your money on. Many states require motor vehicles to be insured with certain minimum coverages. If you lease your car, the lessor will have certain minimum insurance requirements. If you borrowed to buy your car, the lender will have its minimum requirements too. In other words, there's not much room to maneuver.

Because of that, I want to concentrate on those few money opportunities rather than waste lots of space on background information that is both boring and useless. So, let me see if I can sum up auto insurance in one short paragraph:

You live in either a "fault" or a "no-fault" state. In a fault state, the person deemed to be at fault in an accident (or his insurer) is liable for the damages and injuries of the other party or parties. In a no-fault state each person (or his insurer) is responsible for his own damages and injuries.

Okay, on to ways to save money.

Trim Coverage to Just the Essential Elements

Auto insurance policies can have up to ten separate elements. The first way to cut your costs is eliminate the nonessential elements and pare down the others. However, keep in mind that your state may mandate certain coverages and amounts, making it impossible or foolish to trim as much as you'd like.[6]

- **Liability for bodily injury** pays if you hurt someone in an accident. You want enough coverage here to pay for the highest legal judgment you could be required to pay. That means having coverage equal to your net worth, but no more.
- **Liability for property damage** pays if you damage another person's property in an accident. You really need enough here only to cover the fair market value of the average car in your area. In a rural community $15,000 might be more than enough. In a wealthy suburb you might need more.
- **Medical payment coverage** pays the medical (or funeral) bills of someone injured in your car regardless of who caused the accident. Here's an area you can definitely cut back. An injured individual's health insurance will pay for their care, so the only thing you need this coverage to do is pay their deductible. If they don't have health insurance or it isn't sufficient, they can sue you . . . and that will be taken care of by your liability coverage.
- **Personal injury protection** pays your own medical (or funeral) bills and possibly a percentage of lost wages. If you have good health (see chapter 35) and disability (see chapter 25) insurance, you can trim this back to a minimal amount—just enough to pick up otherwise unreimbursed bills.
- **Collision coverage** pays for repairs to your own car after an accident, regardless of who caused it. Since an insurer will pay for repairs only up to a car's book value, there's no point in having collision coverage on older cars. If you have a new car, you can lower the cost of collision protection by opting for a higher deductible— say, $500 or $1,000 rather than $100 or $250.
- **Comprehensive coverage** pays for random damages to your car and the theft of items from your car. Once again, payments are limited to the book value, so I urge you not to keep comprehensive coverage on an older car. On newer cars you can increase your deductible to trim costs, say, from $100 to $500. Check your

---

[6]The classic example of this is New York State's requirement that the first $50,000 in bills for your own medical care for injuries from an auto accident must be paid by your no-fault auto insurance policy rather than your health insurance policy.

homeowners' policy to see whether it already covers you for thefts from your car.

- **Windshield coverage** pays for a replacement windshield, regardless of the cause of damage, usually without a deductible. This is cheap, remarkably efficient coverage that's well worth keeping.
- **Towing and service reimbursement** pays for the cost of towing your car after an accident or breakdown, and perhaps the labor required to make repairs. Even though it's cheap, forget about this coverage and join AAA instead. You'll get the same service plus other benefits and all the free maps and guidebooks you'll ever need.
- **Rental car reimbursement** pays a small daily stipend so you can rent a car while your vehicle is being repaired. If you truly need your car to make a living, this is worthwhile. Otherwise it's just an unnecessary frill.
- **Uninsured and underinsured motorist coverage** pays your medical bills and perhaps a percentage of your lost wages if you're injured in a hit-and-run accident, by an uninsured driver who's at fault, or by a driver who's at fault but whose insurance isn't sufficient to meet all your bills. If you own top-quality life (see chapter 45), health (see chapter 35), and disability (see chapter 25) policies, you don't need this coverage.

Don't Drive an "Expensive" Car

Insurance companies keep track of how much it costs to repair different cars, how often they're stolen, and how often they're in accidents, and charge accordingly. When it's time for you to buy or lease a new car, ask your local insurance broker for a list of cars to avoid.

Move

Rates for the same driver and the same car in different locations vary dramatically. For example, you could save $1,500 a year by moving from the New York City metro area to another part of the state.

Look for Package Deals

You can generally get discounted rates by insuring more than one car with the same insurer, or by buying your auto, homeowners' (see chapter 38), renter's (see chapter 59), and umbrella liability (see chapter 71) policies from the same company.

Take Advantage of Your Lifestyle

Your auto insurance bills should be lower if you don't use your car for commuting, or park it in a garage or off the street. If you do drive to work, start carpooling and your bill will go down.

Minimize Your Teen's Access to the Car

Do not let your teen have her own car—unless of course she's paying the insurance bill. Instead, let her share a car with either you or your spouse, making sure she uses it less than 50 percent of the time. Ship your teen off to a college more than a hundred miles from your home and your rates will drop.

Take Advantage of Safety Discounts

Discounts are available for drivers who pass defensive driving courses, take driver education, or who get good grades, and for cars with air bags, automatic seat belts, antilock brakes, and antitheft devices.

Pay the Bill in Full

Paying in installments or quarterly adds to your costs. If you can manage it, pay the bill in full when it arrives.

Comparison Shop

Finally, shop around for the best deal. Rates vary widely among insurers. A company that offers a comparatively low rate in Philadelphia may charge a comparatively high rate in Pittsburgh or even Shamokin. Start by calling GEICO at (800) 841-3000. It sells by telephone and mail rather than through agents, and is always among the lower-priced insurers in an area. If you qualify,[7] call USAA at (800) 531-8080. It's also usually among the most affordable carriers, though it's more selective. With those quotes in hand, contact a good local insurance broker and ask him to beat them.

---

[7]USAA will sell auto insurance to the families of: commissioned or warrant officers of the Army, Navy, Air Force, Marine Corps, Coast Guard, National Oceanic and Atmospheric Administration, Public Health Service, and U.S. Information Agency; foreign service officers of the U.S. State Department; and special agents of the FBI and Treasury Department.

One Last Tip

If you're ever having trouble getting auto insurance due to your driving record or age, head over to the Department of Motor Vehicles. When you get there, look next door or around the corner for an insurance broker's office. I can almost guarantee you that guy is an expert at insuring problem drivers quickly.

Automobile Loans

15

If you've ignored my advice (see chapter 44) and have decided to take out an auto loan, do yourself a favor and at least shop around: In metro areas interest rates can vary by as much as 4 percent.

Auto dealers generally offer the best deals only when they're having a hard time selling cars; when sales go up, so do their interest rates. In addition, dealers usually require a 10 to 20 percent down payment, though they might accept your trade-in car as an alternative. Of institutional lenders, credit unions usually offer better rates than savings and loans and banks—yet another reason to become a member. Some may not even require a down payment.

Steer clear of variable-rate auto loans. While they'll start out lower than fixed-rate loans, there's no ceiling or cap on how high they can rise.

Make sure you compare loans by annual percentage rates (APRs), since upfront fees and one-time charges can result in a loan with a lower interest rate actually costing you more.

Finally, please don't use a home equity loan or line of credit to buy a car. I know it will let you write off the loan payments. But still, you're using a productive asset (your home is at least keeping pace with inflation) to buy a nonproductive asset (your car will depreciate dramatically the moment you leave the lot). Your home equity is a valuable tool you shouldn't squander. It should be used to finance investments or increase your income, not get you a set of wheels. If you're looking for a way to make your monthly payments lower, just lease instead (see chapter 44).

Banks

16

Are you old enough to remember when people used to know their bankers? I am. When I first started in business in what was then a sleepy town on Long Island, I took an office opposite the local bank. I arrived that first day just around 8:00 A.M. As I went to open the door to my office I saw the bank president doing the same across the street. He waved and smiled. Later that day he came over to welcome me to the area and to solicit my business. Amazing how times have changed. Today, the number one concern for people selecting a bank is how many ATMs the bank has and where those machines are located.

But as a Die Broker you have a chance to buck the trend. The last thing you should care about is ATMs. You're going to make one trip a week to your bank, and you'll deal with human beings. Ubiquitous ATMs are actually a drawback, representing needless temptation. What you want is a bank, like that old institution across the street from my first office, that knows who you are and treats you like a customer. Luckily such institutions still exist, and they offer some added bonuses as well. They're called credit unions.

Credit unions are nonprofit, federally insured and regulated[8] institutions that provide banking and financial services to their members. While some limit their services to employees of a particular company—say, a major university—or to members of a select group—like

---

[8]Ninety percent of credit unions are federally insured.

teachers—others are open to anyone in the community who applies. Due to their small size and nonprofit nature, most treat their depositors like valued customers. They may not have their own ATMs, but that shouldn't bother a Die Broker. They may not return your canceled checks, but fewer and fewer commercial banks are bothering with that either. What they do offer are longer hours, lower fees, better interest rates, more liberal lending policies, a higher sense of community responsibility, and better customer service. What more could you ask?

You can find credit unions in your area either by checking your local telephone directory (under credit unions, not banks) or by logging on to the Credit Union National Association's (CUNA) Website at http://www.cuna.org. The site has a database of its member credit unions that is searchable by state. If you're into techno-banking you can also search through a list of credit unions that have an on-line presence at htpp://www.commonbond.com/cu.html.

Bonds

17

You probably don't need me to tell you what a bond is. If you do, you're reading the wrong book. What you need from me is advice on how taking the Die Broke approach puts a different spin on the information you already know.

Having already read my thoughts on asset allocation (see chapter 12), you know I believe that right now a Die Broker should put the bulk of his or her savings in equity-based mutual funds and keep them there for as long as possible. But that doesn't mean you should forget about bonds.

For years it was tough to convince middle-class investors to put their money in the stock market. But thanks to mutual funds and the bull market of the 1990s, it now seems that everyone is in equities. While that's good in the long term, it may not be good in the short term. All the enthusiasm and excitement generated by the recent bullish market has, I'm afraid, glossed over the fact that stocks can be, in the short and medium terms, quite erratic (see chapter 67). I've found that far too many of my clients have grown so used to getting yields of 10 percent and more on their stock investments that they're viewing bonds with disdain. That's a big mistake.

While bonds don't offer the meteoric climbs of stocks, they're also not as prone to dramatic drops. Sure, if you had seventy-plus years to invest you could rely almost entirely on stocks, secure in the notion that over that time period they have outperformed all other investments. But that stellar performance has not been consistent. There have been decades when bonds have matched or even outperformed stocks. And even with your increased longevity and your rejection of retirement, you still must look at your life in decades, not centuries.

If you can invest money in secure bonds or a bond fund (government-issued or AAA-rated) and get yourself a rate of return of around 7 percent, that's nothing to sneeze at. Granted, if you're trying to grow your money over two or three decades, I wouldn't want all my money in bonds. But I wouldn't want all my money in equities either.

Don't make the increasingly common mistake of comparing the returns from stocks to the returns from bonds. That's comparing apples and oranges. Bonds will never offer the growth rates of the best-performing stocks. But stocks will never offer the security and certainty of the best-performing bonds. Of course, nothing is for certain. Bonds can fall in value if interest rates rise.

Certificates of Deposit   **18**

When your mother tells you she just bought a new CD, she's probably referring to a recently purchased certificate of deposit, not *Anthology 3* from the Beatles.

Certificates of deposit are the most conservative investment anyone can make—they're one step above a piggy bank. They are cash deposits that you promise to keep in the bank[9] for an agreed period of time—generally one, two, three, or six months, or one, two, or five years. In return for your promise to keep the money on deposit, at the end of the agreed period of time you get all your money back, plus an agreed rate of interest, set at the time you buy.

The advantages of certificates of deposit are: your money is federally insured up to a total of $100,000; they're very easy to buy (some banks let you buy them over the telephone); it's easy to compare them (just look at the yields); their yields are greater than on regular savings or interest checking accounts; you know exactly how much you'll end up with when the investment is over; you'll pay no charges if you buy them directly from a bank; they can be used as collateral for loans; and your interest won't go down regardless of changing economic conditions.

---

[9]Brokers also sell certificates of deposit, but since they charge commissions (banks don't) you generally don't get as a good a yield as you would from a bank.

Conversely, the disadvantages are: your interest won't go up either; you'll pay large penalties if you need to withdraw the money before the agreed time; when it comes time to reinvest, the rates may have dropped; and the interest you earn is taxable income.

As an investment vehicle, certificates of deposit are far too conservative for Die Brokers, since you're looking for either more growth or greater income, depending on your stage in life. They're also not a very convenient way to accumulate your savings prior to investment, since you can't make deposits or withdraw the money to make another investment whenever you want. However, they're the perfect vehicle for every Die Broker's financial foundation: your three-month cash reserve.

I've explained earlier that, since no job or business is secure today, everyone (even non–Die Brokers) should establish a cash reserve sufficient to pay their expenses for three months. If you kept that money in your regular checking account, it would be too easy to tap into it for a nonemergency. Besides, you wouldn't even get enough interest on it to keep pace with inflation.

The best place for this reserve is in a set of three certificates of deposit with staggered maturities, one month apart. Even if you lost your job tomorrow you wouldn't need the entire three-month reserve all at once. Using the money in your wallet, your checking account, your severance, and—if necessary—a charge card, you can last one month without an income. At that point you could cash in your first certificate of deposit and you'd have enough money to cover the next month's worth of expenses. By the time that money ran out you could cash in the second certificate. When that money ran out you could cash in the third, if you hadn't yet lined up another job.

Set the system up all at once as soon as you have sufficient funds set aside. Find the local bank that generally offers the best rates—since you're going to be rolling these over all the time, feel free to trade a little bit of interest for added convenience. Divide your cash reserve into three equal portions and purchase three certificates of deposit: one thirty-day, one sixty-day, and one ninety-day. From that point on, as soon as each comes due, simply roll it over into a ninety-day certificate, letting the interest accumulate so your cash reserve keeps pace with inflation.

Charge Cards   **19**

Years ago, a charge card like the American Express card was a status symbol. In the past decade, with the surge in credit card use they've became sort of old-fashioned . . . even retro. Well, it's time for them to make a comeback.

A charge card offers the Die Broker four outstanding features:

- It provides basically **unlimited purchasing power** in case you're faced with an emergency.
- It gives you **thirty days of interest-free credit**—just long enough to transfer funds to pay the bill or to get reimbursed for business expenses.
- It provides **consumer protection** in case you've had a problem when ordering goods through the mail, over the phone, or on-line.
- It **lets you do those things that, in effect, require plastic**—buy airplane tickets, check into a hotel, rent a car—without forcing you to borrow.

Of course, to take advantage of those features you're going to have to pay an annual fee. But if you stick with the simplest type of charge card—an American Express green card, for example—you can keep that annual fee to less than $50. That's a pretty fair price for all the potential help it can give you.

However, don't fall into the ego trap and opt for any of the higher-priced cards, like the Gold or Platinum versions. Sure they offer added "perquisites," but I don't think they're worth the added cost. Why do you need an annual itemized list of your charges? Just keep your important receipts. Almost all those other "special" travel services are available to anyone who slips the hotel concierge five bucks.

Get yourself and your spouse American Express green cards if you don't have them already. If you have one or more gold or platinum cards, call American Express customer service at (800) 327-2177 right now (they're available twenty-four hours a day, seven days a week) and tell them you want to shift your account to a green card.

By the way, don't let them talk you into an Optima card—that's the American Express credit card. While it has in the past offered lower interest rates than Visa and MasterCard, it's still anathema to a Die Broker.

Charitable Remainder Trusts   **20**

I'm now going to let you in on one of the secrets of the very wealthy—sometimes you can make more money by giving something away than by keeping it. Case in point: the charitable remainder trust.

The charitable remainder trust is one of the secret wonders of capitalism. Don't let its name scare you off. Far from being solely a device for wealthy philanthropists, it can be an incredible income-generating tool for any Die Broker who owns an asset that has appreciated a great deal and isn't generating sufficient income, or who could simply use a substantial tax break. Let me explain how they work.

Say you own a piece of property, a stock portfolio, or a business that has dramatically increased in value since you purchased it. Perhaps you bought a rental property for a song that's now worth a small fortune. Or maybe your cousin Jeff talked you into buying a block of Microsoft stock back before Bill Gates owned the universe. Or maybe the business you started from scratch twenty years ago is now a growing concern. For argument's sake and to make the magic of this technique more obvious, let's say this asset is worth $1 million. (I know that you don't have an asset worth close to that much. Don't worry: the math works just about the same for any other amount; only the tax savings aren't as dramatic.)

As a Die Broker you believe you should live up to, not beneath your means, whether that involves spending on yourself or on your loved ones. Even though you're still working, your earned income has dropped. You could use some more to keep up your lifestyle and to continue helping out your kids. You've got this asset worth $1 million, but it's generating only a 2 percent income for you. If you sell it you'll be required to pay capital gains tax based on how much it has appreciated. If it started being worth almost nothing and is now worth $1 million, you'll end up keeping only about $650,000 after the federal, state, and local governments get their cuts. Take that $650,000 and invest it in something that pays a decent rate, say 7 percent, and you'll end up with an annual income of only $45,500 from your $1 million asset. (If you weren't a Die Broker and wanted to pass this asset along to your kids, that $650,000 would be subject to around a 50 percent estate tax bite, leaving your heirs with $325,000—a nice sum only if you don't remember the original asset was worth $1,000,000.)

Okay, now let's see what would happen if instead of selling the asset, you gave it away, using your own charitable remainder trust. You take your asset and give it to a trust that you create with a little help from your lawyer, The trust, not you, sells the asset for $1 million. You instruct the trust to pay you a guaranteed income of 7 percent a year by investing the money. You also instruct the trust to hand the money over to a charity (named or unnamed) when you die. Now, since you don't have to pay capital gains taxes, you're earning 7 percent of $1 million, or $70,000, rather than 7 percent of $650,000, or $45,500.

In addition, since you've given the asset to a charity, you're entitled to a tax deduction. The IRS, using actuarial tables and income projections, will estimate the income the trust will pay you from its $1,000,000 asset while you're alive. This amount is subtracted from the asset's value, and the result is the projected "remainder," which will be left by the trust to charity. Say the IRS determines that your lifelong benefit from the asset is equal to 50 percent of its value; that means the remainder is 50 percent, and results in a $500,000 income tax deductible charitable contribution. That could result in a $175,000 tax savings.

By giving the $1 million asset away rather than selling it, you not only have increased your income from $45,500 to $70,000 but have also gotten a $175,000 tax savings in the process. And you'll be the man of the year at the charity's annual dinner-dance since you've given them $1 million (they won't have to pay capital gains either). You're happy. The charity is happy. For Uncle Sam it's a wash: He has lost out on some capital gains and estate tax revenue, but that's theoretically offset by all the good the charity will do with that $1 million. It's your heirs who appear to have lost out. Sure, that $325,000 inheritance wasn't a big share of $1 million, but it's better than nothing, which is what they'll get when you die if the asset is given to a charity.

But as a Die Broker, you know that inheritance isn't the only way to help your children. Sure, you could use that extra income and those tax savings to travel the world. But you could also use them to help your son set up a business, or to help your granddaughter go to medical school.[10] So even your heirs haven't necessarily lost out. Incredibly, everyone has done better by your giving an asset away rather than selling it.

---

[10]If you weren't a Die Broker you could take that $175,000 tax savings and use the money to buy a second-to-die life insurance policy on you and your spouse so your kids could still end up with a $1 million inheritance, even though you'd given the asset away to a charity.

Checking Accounts 21

Die Brokers should use checking accounts for two purposes only: paying bills and getting cash. No checking account pays enough interest for it to be a worthwhile place to temporarily store your savings. Use a money market account for that instead (see chapter 52). Keep just enough money in your checking account to pay your bills and keep from incurring added fees, but no more.

Instead of worrying about how much interest a checking account pays, focus on the fees it charges. As a Die Broker you'll probably be writing more checks than most people—that means you should do all you can to avoid accounts with per-check charges. Similarly, you can avoid paying anything extra for overdraft protection if you simply balance your checkbook every time you get a statement. It's ludicrous to pay more for special checks or those sold by your bank; get the cheapest ones you can from a discount check-supply house. Finally, don't shy away from a low-cost credit union checking account just because they don't return your canceled checks. More and more banks are doing away with that practice anyway to save money.

Credit Cards

22

How much cash do you have in your wallet? I bet you have no idea.

How can you be so blissfully ignorant of the contents of your pockets? You've got credit cards in your wallet. You never worry about not having enough cash because you've got your magic plastic cards. If you're like most of my clients, you've got at least one Visa card and one MasterCard, maybe an Optima Card and Discover Card, a couple of gasoline company cards, and lots of store cards—Bloomingdale's, Eddie Bauer, Staples, Macy's, Sears, probably one for every shop you go to regularly.

You carry enough cash to pay for those few things you buy that cost less than, say, $15: your morning newspaper, the cup of coffee you drink on the way to work, maybe a sandwich if you decide to work at your desk. For everything else, plastic takes the place of cash.

Having read Part One of this book, you know you're paying a high price for this convenience . . . too high a price in my opinion. According to the American Bankruptcy Institute, more than 90 percent of personal bankruptcies are the result of excessive credit card debt. Outstanding credit card debt has doubled in less than five years to $500 billion, and service on that debt is a higher percentage of income than it has been for two decades. Not surprisingly, delinquency rates are also higher than they have been for two decades. So how come the average American is still receiving twenty card offers a year, many of them for preapproved cards?

New Economic Age Battleground

Credit cards have become the basis for economic success in the current consumption-based society. They make borrowing and spending easy and painless. And anything that helps you spend your money is good for the national economy. At least that has been the message.

I think it's insane for you to keep following this message, however. What has been good for the consumer products companies and the financial services industry and bankruptcy lawyers hasn't been good for you. Your ability to grow your net worth, by saving and investing, is being hamstrung by consumer debt.

But you can't expect those benefiting from your debt to help you clear it up. Not only are the consumer products companies and banks actively pushing credit cards, but Wall Street has gotten into the act too. Over the past two decades those ingenious Wall Streeters have figured out that they can bundle credit card loans into bonds and sell them to investors. This repackaging has become so profitable that, despite the rising delinquency rates, the financial services industry continues to crank out more and more credit cards. It's not just banks anymore; now unions, sports teams, fan clubs, and professional associations are also offering their own cards.

Credit cards are one of the primary battlegrounds on which you have to fight for your economic life. Those forces that are doing well in the current environment will do all they can to keep you locked into the borrow-and-spend lifestyle. So don't expect those new card offers in the mail to slow down anytime soon. In order to get your financial life together for the next millennium you've got to fight and win this war and shift to a save-and-invest lifestyle. Your first battle is to abandon the use of credit cards.

I know, like any addict—and let's face it, you're addicted to the convenience of credit card use—you don't see how you can kick the habit. Well, that's where the rest of this chapter comes in: It's a six-step program for kicking the credit card habit.

1. Just say no.

Right now, before you do anything else, remove every single credit card from the wallets of both you and your spouse. That includes Visas, MasterCards, Optimas, gasoline cards, and store cards. If you have pay-as-you-go charge cards, like American Express or Diners Club, keep one in your wallets (see chapter 19). If you've Visa- or MasterCard-branded debit cards that automatically deduct purchases from your checking account, you can hold on to one as well. They're good for emergency use in those places that may not take American Express or Diners Club (see chapter 23). Put the rest of your cards somewhere safe yet inconvenient: a fireproof box where you store your insurance policies; a safe-deposit box at the bank; or maybe the box in the basement where you keep old tax records. From this moment on you're going to just say no to credit and "pay cash" for everything you buy.

2. Determine your needs.

Make a rough estimate of how much hard currency you and your spouse individually need to get through a week. Include all those little purchases you both make like newspapers, coffee, and lunches at your desk. If one or both of you drive to and from work and usually fill up your cars using a credit card, include enough cash to pay for the weekly fuel. Total the numbers and withdraw that much cash from your checking account and put it in your wallets. If you don't have debit cards, pull one or two checks from your checkbook and put them in your wallets as well. Now you're both fully protected sans credit cards: You've each got cash, a debit card or blank check, and a charge card.

3. Calculate the damage.

With the offending cards safely out of reach, sit down and figure out the damage they've done to your financial life. List every single credit card you and your spouse possess. Take the most recent statement from each and note the interest rate, outstanding balance, and minimum payment. Total up the individual outstanding balances to come up with a grand total of your credit card debt.

4. Consolidate at a lower interest rate.

Credit cards kill, not only by making spending pain-free but by charging outrageous interest rates, usually from 17 to 21 percent. Your goal is to take all your high-interest credit card debts and consolidate them into one, lower-interest debt.

You can turn this debt into a tax deductible one by taking out a home equity loan or line of credit and using it to pay off your credit card debt. However, do yourself a favor and don't opt for one of those lines of credit that gives you a credit card rather than a checkbook. After all, the last thing you need is further temptation (see chapter 36). And, think twice about refinancing an asset that you could use as a stream of income later if it was fully paid for (see chapter 62).

If it's neither possible nor savvy for you to transfer your credit card debt to mortgage debt, look for one new, low-interest credit card that will offer you enough of a credit line to consolidate all your other credit card debts.

There are probably two or three preapproved credit card offers arriving in your mailbox each week. Rather than instantly tossing them out, take a close look at them. One of the most common sales pitches they use today is a teaser rate: an incredibly low rate for a short period of time. If you know you can transfer and then pay off your entire outstanding credit card debt within that period of time, jump at one of these offers.

If you don't get any good teaser offers in the mail, explore low-interest credit cards on your own. Contact the BankCard Holders of America, 524 Branch Drive, Salem, VA 24153; (540) 389-5445. For $4 they'll send you a list of banks offering low-rate credit cards. You can get similar information from Ram Research, (800) 344-7744; http://www. ramresearch.com.

However, be aware that the cards with the lowest rates usually require pristine credit ratings. Since applying for credit cards and being turned down could further adversely affect your credit rating, my suggestion is to call each potential lender and get at least some sense of your likelihood of being approved for enough credit to pay off your other cards.

As long as you're making telephone calls, contact the bank that issued the card on which you're carrying the biggest balance. Tell the customer service representative of the much lower interest rate you've either found or been offered, and of your intent to shift your debt. It's possible they'll match the rate for a long enough period of time for you to pay it off completely. Hey, it can't hurt to try.

I'm not crazy about debt consolidation loans (see chapter 24) and would urge you to avoid them unless you truly cannot meet the minimum monthly payments on your credit cards.

5.   Dig yourself out.

Now that you've got one huge credit card bill to take care of rather than ten, you've got to pay it off as quickly as possible. Forget about that "minimum monthly payment." If that's all you're going to pay, you'll be carrying this debt to your grave. I want you to die broke, not in debt.

One way of paying the debt down quickly is to take the total outstanding debt, divide it by the number of months you've got of low interest, and make that your monthly payment. For example: If you've got a $12,000 debt with a guaranteed low rate of 5.9 percent for twelve months, divide the $12,000 by twelve months and pay $1,000 each month. If you can afford to pay a little more, tack the monthly interest charge onto your payment too. If not, you'll be left with a having to make a thirteenth payment.

Another technique is to take any "found" money and immediately use it to pay down your debt. Get a bonus from work? Apply it to your debt rather than a new television. Did your parents send you a check for your birthday? Apply it to the debt rather than buying a new outfit.

Finally, realize that the single most important thing you can do financially is pay off credit card debt. If you were unable to lower that high interest rate you're currently paying, funnel all your available funds, even those earmarked for savings and investments, to paying off the debt. It's better to pay off a 19 percent debt than it is to earn 12 percent interest.

6.   Start fresh.

Okay, the credit card monkey is finally off your back. How do you keep clean from now on?

Start by locking up that low-interest-rate card you've just paid off. The only time it should be used is in cases of dire emergency; instances when you cannot possibly pay off a bill within, say, thirty days, even by tapping into your liquid savings.

At the beginning of each week, go to the bank and withdraw enough cash to pay for all your regular anticipated purchases. Don't provide yourself with any "discretionary funds" or "mad money." You don't need it, and besides, if it's in your pocket you'll spend it.

Keep a charge card or a Visa- or MasterCard-branded debit card in your wallet for times when you don't have sufficient cash. The former are preferable since, in effect, they provide you with thirty-day interest-free loans (albeit ones that must be paid in full after those thirty days). The latter deduct the funds from your account immediately, but are useful for those times when a merchant won't accept your charge card.

Don't worry about the charge or debit card enabling you to go on a spending spree. In my experience that may happen for the first month of your new regimen. You may well see that new compact disk on Monday and buy it; run across a sweater that's on sale at The Gap the next Wednesday; and decide to go out for Thai on the following Friday. But when the bill rolls in at the end of the month and you've got to pay it off—in full—or when your bank statement comes and you see those spending sprees deducted from your checking account balance, you'll quickly realize those purchases were for real.

Take one check from your checkbook and keep it in your wallet. That way you'll be able to get emergency cash, if needed, by writing a check to cash. (I'm totally against ATM cards—see chapter 13.)

Armed with cash, one charge card, a single blank check, and the desire to pay cash, you're fully equipped to deal with anything you might face, from day-to-day purchases to a major emergency.

Debit Cards 23

How times change. In the old economic world, debit cards were ple-
beian tools for people who couldn't *get* credit. In the new world they're
a device for savvy individuals who don't *want* to use their credit.

Debit cards look just like credit cards, carrying either a Visa or
MasterCard logo. They are accepted everywhere that takes the equivalent credit card. The difference is that rather than automatically
extending credit to you when you make a purchase, they debit a desig-
nated bank account for the price of the purchase.

While they don't provide as much spending deterrence as writing a
check—there's nothing like physically writing the amount three
times—they're an excellent complement to your pay cash arsenal. If
you don't have sufficient cash for a necessary purchase, and the merchant won't accept your charge card (see chapter 19) or personal check,
slap down your debit card.

The main downside to debit cards is that the money is instanta-
neously deducted from your account so you lose interest from the
moment you make a purchase.[11] That's why I'd rather see you use a

[11]Another downside is that if your debit card is lost or stolen you have greater liability than if your
credit or charge card is stolen. You are responsible for a maximum of $50—if you report a loss or
fraudulent charges within two or four days. If you wait any longer you could be responsible for up to
$500. If you're totally oblivious and don't bother reporting the loss or fraudulent charges for from 60
to 90 days, subsequent losses could be entirely your responsibility. Of course, if you waited that long
to report a problem you *deserve* to foot the bill.

charge card, which will let you earn another thirty days' worth of interest on that money. But if you can't, you can't. If you're forced to use a debit card, just remember to save the receipt and log the deduction in your checkbook register as soon as you can.

Most banks will provide you with a debit card linked to one or more of your accounts for no charge. Unfortunately, these debit cards can also be used at ATMs to withdraw cash or transfer funds electronically (see chapter 13). Still, as long as you can ignore that temptation, they belong in your wallet for those times when "they won't take American Express."

Debt Consolidation Loans 24

I'm not crazy about debt consolidation loans. They're not without their uses, but I don't think they're right for Die Brokers. Let me explain.

The way most debt consolidation loans work is that the lender provides you with a lump sum of money that you then must use to pay off your outstanding credit card balances. You then must pay off this one large loan rather than a series of smaller ones. The loan may be unsecured or secured, depending on the amount borrowed, your credit history, and whether or not you have any assets.

The advantage of debt consolidation loans is that the one monthly payment is lower than the total of all your individual credit card payments. That obviously makes it easier on your cash flow.

The disadvantage is that you'll be paying this loan off for a long time, whether you want to or not. The interest on your debt consolidation loan is probably as high, if not higher, than the interest you were paying to the credit card companies. The reason your monthly payment is lower is that the lender has structured the loan so it stretches out for a much longer term than the credit card loans. And to ensure it makes the maximum profit, the lender will probably penalize you heavily if you try to pay the loan off ahead of schedule. You've still got the same amount of high- (or even higher-) interest debt. In the long run you'll actually be paying more than you would have if you had kept the balances on the credit cards. All you'll have gotten in exchange is a more affordable monthly payment.

For folks who have gotten in over their heads, and who, even after cutting their spending to the bone, simply cannot meet their monthly payments, a debt consolidation loan can be a worthwhile life preserver. However, for a Die Broker who's able to make those monthly payments, but realizes his spending is out of control and is holding him back from investing for his future, they're foolish. Rather than helping you dig yourself out of debt, consolidation loans cement you in place; you're no longer desperately struggling to keep your head above water, but you're no closer to the surface either.

Die Brokers should instead follow the advice I outlined in chapters 3 and 22: Stop using plastic, consolidate all your credit card debt into one lower-interest credit card loan, and pay it off as soon as you possibly can.

Disability Insurance

25

I'm sure you're already familiar with the argument: Your chances of becoming disabled at a young age, temporarily or permanently, are far greater than your chances of dying early; therefore, you need disability insurance much more than you do life insurance. It makes perfect sense. It's totally rational. And it's an opinion shared by everyone in the personal finance industry. Yet few people follow up on the advice. Why?

It's more than just an academic question for me for a couple of reasons. First, I contracted tuberculosis in my mid-forties. I was unable to work for about eighteen months. The only things that kept my family afloat financially were my wife's income and my disability insurance payments. So, I've firsthand knowledge of the importance of this protection.

Second, in encouraging you not to retire and to Die Broke I'm telling you to rely on your stream of income even more than the average person does. Stream of income is, quite literally, the lifeblood of the Die Broke lifestyle. Without it, you'll not only die broke, you'll live broke. When you decide to quit today and realize your job is nothing more than that, a job, you protect yourself somewhat. After all, someone who knows "it's just a job" will have an easier time getting reemployed than someone who's looking for work that's "meaningful." But the right attitude alone won't compensate for a head injury, or being laid up after a heart attack, or contracting tuberculosis. You need disability insurance too. For a Die Broker the single most crucial financial step is to make sure your income is insured. I can't stress that too highly.

That brings me back to the essential question: Knowing all the facts, why don't more people take out disability coverage? After talking to lots of otherwise intelligent clients of mine who have ignored my previous urgings to buy disability coverage, I think I've figured out the answer: Disability insurance seems like an expensive luxury to them, and perhaps to you.

I'll admit premiums for disability policies are high when compared to life insurance. But that's just because the chances you'll make a claim at an early age are much higher. Compare the cost of disability to buying your own health insurance and you'll no longer think it's so expensive. Besides, I can help you trim the costs dramatically.

"But," you might say, "I know I'll get sick and I know I'm eventually going to die, so I'll definitely collect on those policies. I don't know I'm going to become disabled, so I may never collect. That makes it a luxury." No more so than homeowners' insurance or auto insurance is a luxury. You don't "know" your house will burn down or that your car will be totaled, yet you insure them both.

"But those polices will pay for minor damage, not just total loss," you could add, grasping for another excuse. So too will disability insurance pay for short-term, temporary, and/or partial disabilities. Depending on the terms of your policy, you could collect benefits if you broke your leg and were able to work only part-time for a month or two.

"If anything happens I can collect workers' compensation and Social Security disability," you may finally rationalize. Unlikely. The former pays only for disabilities that result from on-the-job accidents. I'll wager the most dangerous piece of equipment in your workplace is a stapler. The latter pays only if you're unable to work anywhere, doing anything. If you can bag groceries or answer a telephone, you're not disabled according to Social Security, even if you used to trade commodities or perform neurosurgery.

Hopefully I've at least convinced you to read on. What you'll learn should make it clear that not only can you afford good disability insurance but that you can't afford to be without it.

The secret to being a smart disability insurance shopper is understanding which are the aspects of coverage where you can afford to compromise in order to save money and which are the elements where you shouldn't make concessions.

Your Minimum Needs

There are a few things you definitely need in your disability coverage.

It's essential your insurer defines disability very simply and objectively as a decline in income as the result of sickness or accident. It is, after all, just such a decline in income that you're protecting yourself against. Steer clear of policies that define disability using phrases such as "the main duties of your regular occupation," or "occupation for which you're reasonably suited by education and experience." As you can imagine, such definitions are entirely subjective and it's the insurer who'll be making those judgments.

Insist on a policy that's either "guaranteed renewable" or "guaranteed renewable and noncancelable." Guaranteed renewable means your coverage can't be taken away if you pay your premiums; however, the insurer can raise those premiums. Guaranteed renewable and noncancelable means the insurance can't be taken away and your premiums cannot be increased. Stay away from policies that are "class cancelable." That means the insurer can cancel all polices that fall into some definable group or class, like those covering dentists, those issued in 1995, or those covering people who live in Montana.

Look for policies that pay either "residual" or "recovery" benefits depending on if you're employed or self-employed. Residual benefits are partial payments made to someone who has gone back to work but at less than full-time. Recovery benefits are partial payments to someone who's self-employed who needs time to rebuild a customer or client base back up to the level it was prior to the disability.

Make sure your policy will immediately pay for disabilities resulting from disclosed preexisting conditions, and that you understand what it considers a preexisting condition before you fill out the application. Some insurers consider a bout with high blood pressure as a newborn a preexisting condition for a forty-year-old. Others will overlook a heart attack as recently as two years prior to the application.

Your policy should also be liberal toward intermittent disabilities. Let's say you're disabled in January, get better, and then suffer a relapse in June. A good policy won't require you to go through two waiting periods if the recurrence takes place six months or less after the initial problem.

You also need a policy that waives your premium entirely if you're disabled for more than a brief period. Good policies will require you to pay the premium for just the first three months you're collecting benefits, and then, if you continue to be disabled, will refund those premiums and waive future bills for as long as you're laid up.

These latter two features are especially important for those who are stretching to afford coverage, since, as you'll see in a moment, one way of doing so is to commit to drawing on your savings early on in an emergency.

Finally, make sure you shop around for the insurer that gives the best classification to your occupation. Insurers generally divide all jobs into four or five classes. The top class, which pays the lowest rates, consists of occupations the insurer thinks are the safest and/or the ones to which people are most likely to want to return. Doctors, lawyers, accountants, and other professionals fall into this class. The next one or two classes would have other professionals, white-collar office workers, and some skilled blue-collar workers. The most expensive one or two categories would include unskilled laborers and those whose work is physically dangerous and demanding, such as construction workers or baggage handlers. If your occupation is neither clearly at the very top nor at the very bottom, it pays to shop around and find the insurers that rate it most favorably.

How Much Coverage Do You Really Need?

The ultimate disability coverage would simply replace your income, dollar for dollar. However, such a policy is neither possible nor sensible: not possible, since no insurer will cover 100 percent of your income—you'd have no financial motivation to go back to work; not sensible, since it would be very expensive and actually represent an improvement in your standard of living. Let me explain.

Obviously, the larger a benefit a policy pays the higher its premium, so a lower benefit saves you money and makes coverage more affordable. Not so obvious is the fact that benefits from a disability policy on which *you* pay the premium are nontaxable. Therefore, you only need to, at best, match your take-home pay. Even that's probably too much, however.

If you're disabled and have good medical insurance, you'll actually be spending less money than before: no more commuting costs, fewer lunches out, and lower dry-cleaning bills. Figure out how much less you'll be spending and subtract those numbers from your take-home pay in order to come up with the maximum disability benefit you need.

Set that number aside for a minute and turn to your expenses rather than your income. Sure, it would be great if you could replace your income so you could still afford the same level of discretionary spending as before you were disabled, but that may not be possible. You need to bring in enough income to cover your essential bills; any more than that is a luxury. Remember, your spouse and your kids could help pick up the slack by increasing their incomes. Think of these economies as potential coinsurance payments that are enabling you to afford disability coverage.

Calculate how little you really need to get by. When you go shopping, use that number as your minimum need and the earlier estimate based on your take-home pay as your maximum need.

If you have disability coverage from your employer, you should factor that into the equation as well. However, be careful and check into exactly how much you'd receive. Most employer-provided disability policies issue a very small benefit for a very short period of time, and start paying only long after you've been disabled.

Do not take Social Security or workers' compensation into consideration when figuring out the benefit you'd need. Almost no one qualifies for Social Security disability since its definitions are so restrictive. And a very low percentage of disabilities result from on-the-job accidents or work-related illnesses.

Dealing with Inflation

This is a legitimate worry: Having already factored lifestyle sacrifices into the selection of your benefit, you don't have any wiggle room; and if you're taking this out when you're relatively young, you may need to compensate for thirty years of inflation. There are riders available that will increase your benefit every year to keep pace with the consumer price index. As you might imagine, these cost a fortune. A more affordable approach is to buy a rider that gives you the right to purchase specific amounts of additional benefits at predetermined periods in the future, regardless of your health at that time. These are called either "option to purchase" or "guaranteed increase" riders.

How Long Can You Wait for Your First Check?

Having determined the minimum benefit you need to get by, the next step in savvy shopping is to see how long you could wait for that first check. The time gap between a disabling event and the first benefit check is called the elimination period. The longer you can wait for that first check, the lower your premium.

No one needs coverage that begins paying benefits immediately—that's why no insurer sells it. If you're an employee, you'll probably have some paid sick leave. Even if you're self-employed you could at least partially compensate for a short illness by working weekends and doing without a vacation. The soonest most policies will start paying benefits is thirty days after a disabling illness or accident. The other typical options are sixty days, ninety days, six months, or one year.

Find out how much paid sick leave your employer will provide. If you're fortunate, it will be enough to let you at least pay for that first month of disability. If you were successful in following my advice earlier in this book and have established a cash reserve equal to three months' income, you've got another cushion right there to draw on. By trimming your spending you can probably use that three months of income to pay for four months of expenses. That means employees with decent sick pay and a good cash reserve can readily wait at least five months for benefits to start. Add another month from savings and that allows for a six-month elimination period, which makes for quite affordable premiums. The self-employed—who probably don't have sick pay—and those who haven't been able to establish a cash reserve will need to rely even more on their savings.

Unfortunately you're probably going to need to tap into your savings to one degree or another in order to extend the elimination period and thereby get affordable disability coverage. It's not the end of the world. Besides, if you don't buy insurance and you become disabled, you're going to have to draw on those savings for a lot longer than one to six months.

How Long Do You Need the Coverage to Last?

Let me ask that in another way: For how long were you planning on having an earned income? It makes no sense for a Die Broker to take out disability insurance that doesn't extend up to and beyond age sixty-five, even though it's cheaper. On the other hand, policies that pay a "lifetime premium" are very expensive and don't really make much sense either. After all, you weren't expecting your income to remain the same after age sixty-five anyway. Instead, you need a policy that offers full benefits up to age sixty-five, at which point a "retirement rider" kicks in, providing partial payments from then until death.

Both Spouses Generally Need Coverage

Do you depend on both your incomes? If you do, then you both need disability insurance. It's as simple as that. If you're a two-income couple, you'll then make the unpleasant discovery that women pay more for disability coverage than men. Why? Insurers say that actuarial data shows women are more likely to get disabled then men. Thus far, every state insurance commissioner has accepted this as a valid reason to have gender-specific rates.

Start with a Telephone Call

As soon as you've come up with a list of what you want in a disability policy, give USAA Life Insurance Company (800-531-8000) a call and ask for a price quote. This is a highly rated San Antonio, Texas—based company known for excellent auto and homeowners' policies offered only to present or former military officers and their dependents. USAA offers its life insurance and disability policies direct to the general public, using no agents and therefore, paying no sales commissions. With a quote from USAA in hand, go to your insurance broker (see chapter 41) and ask him or her to beat the price. Before you grab a lower premium, check the health and reputation of the insurer (see chapters 11 and 45).

When All Else Fails: ARDI

If you find you can't afford the level of disability protection you've determined you need, and you're under age fifty, don't immediately start cutting back on the benefits package. Instead, take a look at a new product called an annually renewable disability income (ARDI) policy. These work very much like term life insurance policies. While traditional disability policies have level premiums, the premiums on ARDI policies start out low (25 to 50 percent of what the level premium would be for the same coverage) and increase a small amount every year as you get older and the chances of your becoming disabled increase. The hope is that your income will increase each year along with the premium so it won't ever become a burden. Once you reach your mid-fifties, however, ARDI starts becoming more expensive than level-premium policies, so it might make sense to shift coverage if you're still insurable. ARDI isn't offered by every insurer (the two largest and best known insurers who offer it are Guardian Life and Equitable Life), so you may need to shop around for it. It's worth the effort.

In fact, every sacrifice you make in the quest to get disability insurance is worthwhile. As a Die Broker you are counting on a stream of income, however changeable, being there for you to live on for your entire life. You must do everything you can to ensure that that lifelong flow is never interrupted.

Divorce and Mediation   **26**

Divorce has never been easy. And despite recent changes, such as no-fault divorce, equitable distribution, and community property, it remains an emotionally traumatic thing. That's not all together bad. I'm not convinced that making divorce less emotionally trying won't in some way reduce the emotional strength of the bond. However, there's no reason divorce needs to be as financially devastating.

Separating Money from Love

Thanks to our own deep-seated neuroses, love and money have become linked. That's just as true in romantic relationships as it is in parent-child relationships. I believe that adopting the Die Broke program offers an opportunity to break these harmful links. In chapters 7 and 8 I explained how in helping your parents and children to Die Broke you can eliminate the harm money does to those relationships. The same is true for your marriage. That can be done by treating the financial aspect of your marriage as separate from the emotional element.

A couple that is happily married can do this by making sure both are equal parties to the couple's financial decision making. You don't have to take turns paying the bills, but you both do have to feel that you are equal partners, that there is no discrepancy in power. Couples who marry young and/or who bring no real individual assets to the marriage actually have the advantage of starting with a blank slate on which they can inscribe their own equitable pattern. Couples who marry later and/or who bring sizable individual assets to the marriage can separate the financial and emotional elements of their relationship by drafting a prenuptial agreement (see chapter 56). Already established happy couples who have fallen into unequal habits and patterns can use their joint adoption of the Die Broke philosophy as a chance to start over and (with the help of a financial adviser and perhaps even a marriage counselor) separate their financial and emotional lives. But already established unhappy couples are unlikely to be able to do that. Unfortunately, their chance to separate money from emotion will come only through divorce.

Mediate the Money Relationship and Divorce the Emotional Relationship

Invariably, money is the prime battleground in divorces. (Unless there are issues of abuse involved, when push comes to shove, most couples agree on doing what's best for any minor children when it comes to custody.) That's because money's neutral, mannalike nature lets it become a mirror that reflects all the other emotional issues surrounding the unhealthy relationship. Attorneys can feed this confrontation, and their wallets, by dwelling on money issues. That's why I suggest divorcing couples begin their split with mediation.

I don't handle divorces in my legal practice. However, I do handle mediations.[12] A couple comes to me as an unbiased, financially astute, compassionate third party. They fully disclose their individual and joint financial holdings, as well as their needs and wants. I'm not an advocate of either side. My goal is to reach an equitable split both can accept. I draft a plan that separates their finances. If both agree to the terms of the plan I've come up with, they sign an agreement to that effect, then hire their own individual divorce attorneys to handle the nonfinancial aspects of the split. With the most contentious issue resolved, the two advocates have little left to fight over. The legal aspect of the divorce then moves speedily.

---

[12]I'm far from the only person who handles these kinds of mediations. Any financially savvy attorney who represents the process rather than one party or the other can do the same thing. In addition, there are mediators who specialize in just this kind of situation. You can get a list of such individuals by contacting the American Academy of Family Mediators at (617) 674-2663.

This isn't a perfect system. There are times when one party or both won't accept the mediated financial split. There are other times when one or both attorneys undermine the mediated agreement and try to reopen the money battle. But most often, this mediated approach leads to a speedier, more affordable, and far less contentious divorce.

Domestic Partnerships

Marriage isn't just a religious institution. It's also a financial and legal arrangement.

From a financial-planning perspective, marital status and/or sexual orientation should have no bearing on decision making. A single gay man or lesbian should approach his or her financial life in the same manner as a single heterosexual. Similarly, an unmarried couple, whatever their sexual orientation or marital status, should approach financial decisions the same as a straight or married couple in the same circumstances would. Every individual or couple who wants to Die Broke should follow the program outlined in chapter 9. For example, domestic partners can be named the beneficiaries of each other's life insurance policies and can buy joint-and-survivor annuities.

However, from a legal perspective, domestic partners of every sexual orientation do need to approach things differently. That's because they don't enjoy the same legal privileges as spouses. A domestic partner cannot file a joint tax return, share a health insurance plan,[13] recover damages due to injuries to the other partner, receive survivor benefits, automatically inherit property, obtain residency status for a foreign-born partner, or make medical decisions for an incapacitated partner.

---

[13]A handful of employers, insurers, and municipalities do enable insured persons to extend their health insurance coverage to individuals other than spouses and children. In most of these situations this could be a domestic partner as well as a parent or other person.

Some, but not all, of these discrepancies can be addressed through savvy legal planning.

The first thing a domestic partnership needs to do is find an attorney experienced in their unique needs. Such a lawyer will be able to get around many of these problems. For instance, well-drafted living wills and durable powers of attorney for health care can allow domestic partners to make medical decisions for each other. Partnership agreements can allow domestic partners to jointly own property and other assets and guarantee ownership passes to the surviving partner.

Such maneuvers are neither pleasant nor easy, but they will remain necessary until society accepts a new legal (if not religious) definition of marriage.

Durable Powers of Attorney for Health Care

28

A power of attorney is the legal granting of authority for someone else to do something specific on your behalf; in effect, to act as your proxy. It's most often used for financial transactions and legal matters, such as appointing a broker to trade securities for you or an attorney to sign your name to a contract. A power of attorney is considered "durable" if it remains effective even if the person granting the authority is no longer competent. So, a durable power of attorney for health care (sometimes called a health care proxy) is a document that gives a person you name the authority to make health care decisions for you if you can't.

Durable powers of attorney for health care differ from living wills in that they give the proxy power to make all health-care-related decisions for you whenever you're incapacitated, not just life support decisions when you're terminally ill or injured (see chapter 47). For instance, they can decide if you should have surgery or just therapy, if you should get general or local anesthesia, or if you should be placed in a nursing home. Ultimately, they can also decide if you should be placed on or removed from life support.

Theoretically, if you have a durable power of attorney for health care, you don't need a living will. As long as your proxy knows and agrees to carry out your wishes about life support, that should be sufficient. Practically, however, I recommend you have both. It's very difficult for someone to make those kinds of life-and-death decisions on their own. Even though it's not legally necessary, having a formal living will that documents your wishes will make it easier for your proxy emotionally and psychologically.

Have your durable power of attorney for health care drawn up simultaneously with your living will by the same lawyer. (It shouldn't take more than an hour of her time to draft both documents—often it's done in tandem with other legal work, such as crafting a will.) That way you ensure there are no contradictions. Inconsistencies could be used by overly zealous doctors as a rationale for ignoring both documents.

As a Die Broker it's important you let your health care proxy know that your goal is for your financial and corporeal lives to end at the same time. That way they'll feel no obligation to keep one eye on health care decisions and another on your estate.

One more important note: It's absolutely essential for nonmarried spouses, gay or straight, to have durable powers of attorney for health care naming each other as health care proxies. Most state laws ignore unmarried life partners in their "substituted judgment" statutes, instead passing authority on to parents, children, or siblings. Having done this, you've little to fear, even from the most homophobic of in-laws: The proxy's authority is legally unassailable.

Earthquake Insurance

29

Homeowners' insurance policies generally do not cover losses due to earthquakes. If you live in a region where earthquakes are a fact of life—such as California—or an area that has the potential for a catastrophic quake—such as Tennessee—you definitely need to either obtain separate coverage or add a rider to your policy. After all, your primary purpose in taking out homeowners' coverage is to protect yourself against disaster (see chapter 38), and nothing could be more disastrous to a home than a quake.

Because earthquake damage is so common in California, policies issued there are subject to higher deductibles and premiums. Deductibles in California are generally a minimum of 10 percent of the insured value of the property; so, if your home is insured for $200,000, your deductible is $20,000. Californians can also expect to pay premiums as much as 500 percent higher than residents of other states.

Wherever you live, your premiums for earthquake coverage will also be affected by the structure of your home. Interestingly enough, wooden homes, which you'd expect would be the least durable in a quake, actually cost less to insure than brick or stone houses; apparently they're more flexible and can roll with the punches better.

Estate Planning

30

Since you're planning to Die Broke, you might think you've no need for estate planning. Wrong.

While the Die Broke program can enable you to live fully up to your means while alive, without worrying about outliving your money, it cannot tell you when you will die. This program will help you grow assets throughout your life that can be turned into sources of unearned income at a point when your earned income starts to decrease. However, it cannot guarantee you'll live long enough to reach that point.

I've repeatedly cited studies that show life expectancy is on the rise. Taken as a large group, baby boomers will *indeed* live into their eighties. Using this generalization, as well as the current industrial view of workers sixty-five years old and older, I've suggested you start thinking about annuitizing your assets (shifting from growth-oriented equity investments to income-producing annuities) between ages sixty-five and seventy. Unless you know you're likely to have a shorter life span, that's the most prudent approach.

It's also prudent to take steps to protect your family should you die prematurely. That's why you have life insurance. But you need to supplement that financial protection with some legal protection as well, namely a will (see chapter 72), but probably not a living trust (see chapter 46). A will ensures your loved ones will have full and easy access to the assets you had intended to either live off of or give away had you lived long enough. (It should also ensure your minor children are cared for in the manner you'd like.) Frankly, for a Die Broker this isn't estate planning, it's premature death planning.

Financial Planners   **31**

It seems that nearly everyone these days calls him or herself a financial planner. Stockbrokers, accountants, insurance brokers, and attorneys are all, in increasing numbers, saying they provide financial-planning services. If this keeps up, your plumber will soon be touting his mutual fund expertise. Why is everyone jumping on the financial-planning bandwagon? I'm sure you can guess the answer: money.

Providing financial advice is now big business. Investing is no longer something only the rich do. That's in large part due to the growth of the mutual fund (see chapter 54), an investment instrument that has made balanced, diversified stock and bond investing both easily accessible and affordable. It's also because throughout the early 1990s there was a very long and sustained bull market. Today almost everyone is "in the market," and that makes financial planning a mass-market service.

Stockbrokers who used to rely on servicing the wealthy are now recruiting middle-class customers through community "seminars" and warm and cuddly television spots. Accountants are not only telling their clients they should put money in tax-deferred retirement plans but also offering to set up those plans. Insurance brokers, not satisfied with making money on your life, home, health, disability, auto, and long-term care insurance coverages, now want to sell you tax-deferred annuities as well. There may well be a place for all these individuals in your life . . . however, it's not as investment advisers. That role falls to someone whose sole profession is financial planner.

By using a financial planner you ensure that the advice you receive won't be biased toward one or two particular types of investment instruments. It's in the interest of stockbrokers to steer you toward equities. Insurance brokers make money only if you buy insurance products. And accountants, though they may not have a financial interest in it, are predisposed to focusing on tax avoidance above all else. Only someone with the credentials of a certified financial planner can provide unbiased advice on all these areas. A planner will tell you to buy stocks or mutual funds when that makes sense, annuities when they're the best tool, and tax-free bonds when they're what's needed.

Financial planners make their money in one of three ways: They charge an annual fee based on the size of your portfolio, earn commissions off the sale of whatever you purchase, or charge an hourly fee for their services. I believe a true professional should offer the same quality of advice to clients whatever their net worth—that's why I'd suggest you steer clear of planners who base their fees on the size of your portfolio. I'm also not crazy about planners who earn their money solely through commissions. While they may not have a bias toward a particular product, they've a vested interest in getting you to buy products that offer the highest commissions. I'd prefer you work with a fee-only planner who charges you a straight hourly fee, just as your attorney and accountant do.

Unfortunately, there aren't that many fee-only planners around. That's because with so many other individuals—like stock and insurance brokers and commission-only planners—offering "free" financial advice, consumers have tended to shy away from planners who charge fees. As a result, most fee-only planners limit their customers to those who have above a certain net worth. Others charge a more affordable hourly fee, but in compensation also take commissions on whatever they sell. Until you have a sufficient net worth to interest a fee-only planner, I think you'll have to be satisfied with someone who both charges a fee and takes commissions.

By the way, the initials CFP after a candidate's name stand for certified financial planner. They indicate a certain level of education as well as adherence to a code of professional conduct and ethics. Though not yet an industrywide standard—there are still many highly educated and scrupulously honest financial planners who aren't CFPs—you can take the accreditation as a final seal of approval for your choice.

The best way to find a good financial planner is through personal recommendations. Ask your attorney and accountant for some names. Speak with friends and relatives whose economic level is similar to your own. You can also call the Institute of Certified Financial Planners—the organization that bestows the CFP accreditation—at (800) 282-7526 and ask for a list of CFPs in your area.

When you have a list of two or three candidates, call each to set up a preliminary interview. If someone won't see you in person or resists answering questions, cross him or her off the list and find another candidate.

In your initial meeting you want to learn:

- How long they've been a planner.
- What is their area of expertise.
- How long they've been with their current firm.
- How long their firm has been in business.
- Whether they work full- or part-time.
- Their educational background.
- Whether they're a CFP.
- The number of clients they have.
- How they continue to keep abreast of changes in the field.
- What is the average size of the portfolios they manage.
- What other services, if any, they provide.
- Whether they have any special investment strategies.
- If they're registered with the SEC.
- How they're compensated.

When you have those preliminaries out of the way, explain your Die Broke philosophy to the planner and ask for his or her thoughts on your approach. Most savvy financial planners will be open, even eager, to work with a Die Broker. That's because your desire to fully exploit your net worth rather than preserve it for the next generation offers them a chance to more fully work their craft. Ask if the planner has any other clients who are Die Brokers.

One sign of a good planner is someone who, after answering your questions, will put a few to you. So be prepared to answer questions like these:

- What are your assets and liabilities?
- What are your monthly expenses?

- What is your income and how secure is your job?
- What benefits does your employer offer?
- Are you married, and do you have children?
- How much insurance coverage do you have, including life, health, property, and disability?
- Do you expect to inherit money at some point in the near or distant future?
- How much risk are you willing to assume?

Before you leave, make sure to get the names of three references whose circumstances, if not philosophies, are like your own. And make sure to call them to check on how responsive, prompt, and professional the planner has been. It's important to realize that these references will be predisposed to giving good reports—that's why the planner gave you their names. So rather than asking for opinions ("Has he done a good job?") ask quantitative questions ("How long does it take for her to return your telephone calls?") whose answers will let you form your own opinions.

All other things being equal, listen to your gut when it comes to choosing a financial planner. If someone strikes you as too smooth or slick, she probably is. If someone strikes you as not knowledgeable enough, he probably isn't. You're not looking for a friend, but you are looking for a trusted confidant, someone you can trust to provide the tactical wisdom to bring your Die Broke strategy to fruition.

Flood Insurance

32

The biggest gap in most people's homeowners' insurance coverage is flood damage. Almost no standard policy covers flooding; a few don't cover water damage of any kind (see chapter 38). That's an awful omission, since the most common significant damage to homes comes from flooding. (Damage from fire and wind is rarer, and not coincidentally, usually covered.)

If you live near the ocean, or along a lake, river, or stream, you clearly need flood insurance. But no private insurer wants to assume these high risks. Thankfully, the federal government has stepped into the picture. Its National Flood Insurance Program provides coverage to residents of communities that have met its standards for flood prevention. While the coverage is somewhat limited, it's quite affordable . . . and it's all you can get.

Each year the National Flood Insurance Program runs notices in the local newspapers of areas it covers just before the most dangerous time of year (spring thaw for inland areas and hurricane season for shoreline communities). You can also call (800) 638-6620 for information all year round. A good local insurance broker (the one who helped you obtain your standard homeowners' coverage will be the most helpful) can provide you with information and guidance.

Funerals

33

Have you ever noticed how the nicest big old house in every small town is always the funeral home? That's because the funeral director is making more money than anyone else in the county.

It just kills me to see all the money that's being spent on funerals. Let's look at the average send-off. First there's the care and dressing of the body. Then there's the casket and perhaps a grave liner. Of course there's the rental of the funeral home for visitations and services. At least one limousine is needed to ferry the mourners to the cemetery where a plot was purchased. There's the check made out to either the clergyman, or his church, to pay for his prayers. You need to pay for the grave to be opened, for the casket be lowered, and for the grave to be filled in. Then, unless you want your loved one spending eternity in an unmarked pile of dirt, there's the headstone, plantings, and maintenance of both. Even without buying "top of the line" the total bill can easily run between $3,000 and $5,000.

This kind of spending is foolish for everyone, but if it's spent on or by a Die Broker, it's simply insane. Why would those who believe money is a tool to be spent in the here and now on themselves and their loved ones want to see it buried in the ground where it's of no use to anyone but the funeral director?

As a Die Broker it's your obligation to yourself, your parents, and your children to make sure this nonsensical funeral spending stops. I think the best way to do that is to dig deep and get to the underlying reasons behind this pattern.

Why do we spend so much more money on funerals than we need to? Setting aside all the ancillary cultural and sociological issues, I think there are two main reasons:

- Those who are alive are making the arrangements; and
- The body is present.

Whenever our loved ones are forced to buy funeral products and services, they consciously or subconsciously feel the need to show the world how much they cared for the deceased. The only way of doing that, other than showing emotion, is by spending money ("showing your final respects"). Their belief is that people will measure their love by the opulence of the funeral. The most scrupulous and ethical of funeral directors won't dissuade people of this notion; the unscrupulous will prey on it. ("After all, this is the last thing you'll be able to do for your father.") If the body of the deceased will be present at the ceremony for all to see, things get even worse. Not only will everyone be able to see the person in "your final gift to them," a casket, but it's as if the person himself was still there, checking to see how much was spent on him. Survivors, caught up in the understandable grief and emotion of the situation, are apt to think that a loved one who spent his whole life clipping coupons and darning socks would really want the $4,500 solid mahogany casket. ("Dad would have wanted to very best.")

The best ways to ensure that this kind of thing doesn't happen in your family is to plan your own funeral in advance and make sure your body won't be part of the proceedings. That means arranging a funeral that involves either direct burial or immediate cremation, followed by a memorial service. Either of these options will eliminate the need for your family to have to go through the ordeal of arranging your funeral. They won't feel the need to literally "pay" their last respects. They won't feel the pressure of having to house your body in a box that demonstrates the depth of their love. They won't wonder what you'd have wanted, since you'll already have spelled it out for them.

In addition to preplanning your funeral, as a Die Broker you need to prepay for it as well—after all, you won't be leaving anything behind to pay the bill. That could mean pricing and purchasing your own funeral package and paying it off in one lump sum or in installments. If you choose this route, make sure you've left no stone unturned and that every possible expense (from limos to headstones and plantings) is either deemed unnecessary or paid for. Make sure that any contract you sign guarantees there will be no further charges for your survivors. Alternatively you could plan and price out the funeral you'd like and pay for it yourself through a life insurance policy. If you take out such a "funeral policy," make sure it has an inflation rider so the benefit keeps pace with the rising costs of funeral goods and services. If you're younger than seventy, it will probably be more affordable to prepay directly with a funeral home. If you're older than seventy it's apt to cost less by financing it on your own by taking out a small whole life policy (at that age term is more expensive).

Besides all the financial savings, I think arranging for this kind of funeral for yourself results in a more dignified and moving event. By taking the odious task off your family's hands, you allow them to focus on their emotions and feelings rather than dollars and cents. And by holding a memorial service without your body present, you enable everyone to focus on your life rather than your death in a place that had special meaning to you, rather than in the nicest big old house in town.

Gifting

34

One of the greatest joys of being a Die Broker is giving financial gifts while you're alive to see them enjoyed and to receive thanks. That doesn't mean you should just start handing out huge checks to all your grandchildren without any planning or forethought. Just as there are ways that giving to charity can be beneficial to all involved (see chapter 20), so too can gifts to children or grandchildren be given in ways that benefit both the giver and the recipient.

Tax-free Gifting

Most people have heard or read that one individual can give another a cash gift worth up to $10,000 each year tax-free. But few people actually understand what that means. Gift taxes are paid by the giver, not the recipient. Gifts of more than $10,000 in cash must be reported the year they are made to the IRS on Form 709, which is filed with your income tax. The tax you owe on the gift is then applied against your lifetime unified gift and estate tax credit of $192,800—the amount of taxes you would owe on an estate worth $600,000. Every taxable gift (gifts of more than $10,000 a year in cash) you make during your lifetime reduces that tax credit.

For a Die Broker that might not be such a bad thing. After all, you're not planning on leaving an estate, so you shouldn't have to worry about estate taxes, right? Not necessarily. You could die before you've had a chance to spend, give away, or annuitize all your assets, leaving a substantial estate behind despite your plans to do otherwise. But if you're married, there would be no estate taxes due, since the money would go to your spouse, not your children. So if you're a Die Broker whose spouse is still alive, and you have the means and desire to make such a sizable cash gift that it becomes taxable, don't worry about it. If you're a single or widowed Die Broker, think twice about making taxable gifts—not just because of the potential estate tax impact but because it's very easy to figure out ways around gift taxes.

Remember that the $10,000 limit is for each discrete pair of individual givers and recipients. That means while you can only give your daughter $10,000 a year tax-free, your wife could also give her $10,000 tax-free.[14] If your daughter is married, you could each give her husband another $10,000 as well. And since there are no tax limits to the gifts one spouse can give another, he can then hand her the $20,000 with no tax ramifications. In effect, you and your spouse can give every one of your married children $40,000 each year without impacting your estate tax credit. If you're single or widowed, you can effectively give every one of your married children $20,000 a year.

You can also make noncash gifts. As long as someone pays the sales tax, the IRS doesn't care if you buy your son a new pickup truck. Similarly, as long as someone pays the Social Security tax, the IRS doesn't care if you pay for a nanny so your daughter can go back to work.

Finally, you can give tax-exempt cash gifts of more than $10,000 if the money is used to pay for college tuition (but not room and board) or hospital bills. The way these qualified transfers, as they're called, work is that you actually make the gift to the college or the hospital in exchange for the understanding that the bills will be considered paid. That means you can still give the beneficiary of this gift another $10,000 tax-free (or more, as we've seen).

Retaining Some Control over Your Gifts

One advantage of making a qualified transfer is you know the money will be put to the use you intended. That can sometimes be

---

[14]If you and your spouse file a joint income tax return, you'll have to file a Form 709 indicating that you gave more than $10,000 in gifts that year. However, all your spouse will have to do is sign the form, indicating that these were two separate gifts, and no taxes will be incurred.

quite important, particularly with gifts being made to minors, perhaps your grandchildren.

The simplest way to give money to a minor is to hand him or her a check. Of course, that gives the child total control over it. That's fine for birthday and Christmas presents, but you don't want to hand your sixteen-year-old grandson a check for $10,000 and simply tell him to put it toward college. Just think of what you would have done with that kind of money at that age. If you put the money in an investment or account that names him as a beneficiary, he wouldn't get it until you died, and you'd be responsible for taxes on the interest it earns. Putting both your names on the account would be worse, since that would mean you would need his signature to access the funds and the money would count as part of your estate if you died, since you made the deposit.

The solution is to use either the Uniform Gifts to Minors Act (UGMA) or the Uniform Transfers to Minors Act (UTMA).[15] You fill out a simple set of forms that your banker or financial planner can help you with, naming a custodian to manage and control the account, until the minor turns eighteen, twenty-one, or even twenty-five. The money is a gift; therefore, the $10,000-a-year limit applies, but so do the ways around it. If you name yourself as custodian and die before the minor gets control of the funds, the money will be considered part of your estate. That's why it usually makes sense to name either your spouse or the child's parent as custodian instead.

Two caveats to consider before using either the UGMA or UTMA. First, since the gift becomes the minor's property, college financial aid officers will expect that a very high percentage of it would be dedicated toward tuition, and would therefore reduce their grant and loan offers accordingly. And second, remember that the child could owe tax on the interest this gift earns. Depending on how much that is, the rate could be as high as what his or her parents are paying.

The Real Limits on Gifting

As you can see, gift taxes really only impact those who are making truly monumental transfers of cash. Unless you're one of those

---

[15]Which you would use depends on which is the law in your state. The UTMA is newer and more flexible, allowing more for the transfer of more complex assets, including real estate.

Microsoft millionaires, the only limitations on your gifting are your needs and wants. Obviously, the choice of how much to spend on yourself and how much to spend on your children and grandchildren is a personal one. But don't make the mistake of viewing the two as mutually exclusive. One of the most wonderful things about money is that you can spend it in ways that will bring joy to everyone.

When my wife and I bought a farm in Connecticut, it was certainly for the two of us. But it was also for our children and grandchildren. There's enough room for all of them to stay the weekend if they'd like. There's a barn in which we've held family weddings and parties. There's a swimming pool around which three (and sometimes four) generations of our family gather on sunny summer Sundays. That farm has turned out to be the best purchase I ever made. It's something that brings joy to our whole family.

Health Insurance 35

Health insurance is one of those subjects where there is so much information (or should I say propaganda) and so many options that a relatively simple decision has become problematic. Let me try to cut through all the noise for you.

First, you and your family need health insurance. The costs of adequate, let alone good, medical care are staggering. As a Die Broker you're relying on your stream of income more than the average person, so huge unexpected doctor and hospital bills could be even more devastating. Therefore, going without coverage isn't even an option.

Your (Limited) Choices

If you are self-employed, or your employer doesn't provide health insurance, you have three options: taking out traditional fee-for-service coverage, joining a health maintenance organization (HMO), or signing up with a preferred provider organization (PPO). If your employer provides coverage, you may have these same three choices, or you may be able to choose only between competing HMOs and/or PPOs.[16]

---

[16]Actually, both the self-employed and employees may have a fourth option: a medical savings account. These accounts were offered as an experiment at the time this book was being written, and may either be abandoned or expanded by the time you read this. In a nutshell, these are joint accounts set up by you and your employer. One or both of you contribute a certain number of dollars (from $1,500 to $2,250 for individual coverage, $3,000 to $4,500 for family coverage) into an account, claiming a yearly tax write-off for the contribution. This money is to be used to pay for rou-

With a fee-for-service plan, you choose your own doctors and hospitals. After you have met a certain deductible on your own, either per person covered or as a family, your benefits kick in. The insurer then pays either a predetermined rate (the reasonable and customary charge) for specific covered services or procedures, or more likely a percentage of that rate, leaving you to pay a coinsurance charge. Coverage is rarely total. Some expenses, such as prescription drugs, may not be covered at all, or not covered as fully as other costs. Other expenses, such as psychological counseling, may be subject to annual ceilings. Fee-for-service plans are available for hospitalization expenses only, for non-hospital expenses only, or for both types of expense.

The advantage of a fee-for-service plan is that you are in total command of your medical fate. You decide what doctor to go to, when, or what hospital to use. Your insurer can require you to get second opinions prior to some procedures, or can limit its reimbursement to "reasonable or customary charges,"[17] but it generally won't stand in the way of you obtaining the care you desire. The disadvantage of a fee-for-service plan, at least for those paying the premiums, is the cost: It is very expensive.

Health maintenance organizations are groups of health care providers and facilities who have banded together in one form or another. In exchange for a premium they provide soup-to-nuts medical coverage, often requiring just a small payment, say $10, per office visit. Rather than having a choice of doctors or hospitals, you select a primary care physician, who then refers you to other member specialists or facilities as needed.

The primary advantage of an HMO is its lower cost. In theory (though not always in practice) it also provides coverage of more preventative care than a fee-for-service plan, since it's in the HMO's inter-

---

tine medical bills. If medical bills run more than the maximum contribution, there's an underlying health plan that kicks in. If medical bills don't exhaust the money, you get to keep it. Basically you're paying for medical bills with pretax dollars and have an incentive to minimize your use of medical care. On first glance medical savings accounts are a good deal for the self-employed, the very healthy, and those who get seriously ill after having fully funded their accounts. Of course, since this is a government-sponsored health care program, it's far from as simple as I've laid it out here. Plans may have different coverage schemes and can invest your funds in any number of ways. Medical savings accounts may save you money, but they won't save you from having to study policies carefully and make hard decisions.

[17]Set regionally, these can vary as much as 40 percent between a city and its suburbs, for instance. All too often they've been used by insurers as a way to keep from paying the full charges.

est for you to stay healthy and not to have to use its services. The disadvantage of an HMO is that it, not you, is in charge of your medical
care. It's the primary care physician who decides whether you need to
see a specialist or not, or need to stay in the hospital for another day or
not, and which specialist you see or in which hospital you stay. It's in
the HMO's financial interest to limit your use of medical services.
This has led to a great deal of controversy. In some cases, HMO
refusals are made on medically sound grounds. In other cases, HMO
refusals seem to be based on financial rather than medical grounds.
And in most cases, it's hard for the layman to be sure. Of course, an
individual covered by an HMO can always go to a nonmember doctor
or hospital. It's just that they may have to cover all, if not most, of the
cost themselves.

Preferred provider organizations (PPOs) represent the middle
ground between fee-for-service plans and HMOs. They usually consist
of a very loosely affiliated group of medical providers in a particular
geographic area. Generally, your premium entitles you to very inexpensive care from any member of the group. You can obtain care from
nonmembers, but it will cost you a great deal more. PPOs are more
expensive than HMOs yet less controlling. On the other hand, they're
cheaper than fee-for-service plans, but more controlling.

Take the Best Coverage You Can Get

What's the best type of coverage? For an individual in search of
state-of-the-art medical care, there's no question that fee-for-service
plans are the best. They provide both high-quality health care and
personal control over your medical care. Granted, under a fee-for-service plan individual doctors and facilities have no motivation to trim
costs—the more tests they run and the more services they perform the
more money they make—and that makes the premiums high. But fee-
for-service policies can be made quite affordable by opting for a high
deductible—in effect, becoming as much of a self-insurer as possible.
Your major concern, after all, is protection from catastrophic costs that
could disrupt your finances.

You can also make fee-for-service coverage more affordable by getting group rather than individual coverage. There are scores of professional associations, trade groups, and social organizations that offer
their members group coverage. There are even artificial groups,

formed by nonprofit health insurers like Blue Cross/Blue Shield, to offer group coverage to the self-employed.

PPOs aren't as good as fee-for-service plans—since they don't offer as much freedom to control your own care—but they are more affordable and, in my opinion, provide better care than HMOs. If even after opting for a high deductible and joining a group you still can't afford fee-for-service coverage, PPOs are your next best choice.

HMOs are your choice of last resort. They are heavily promoted by employers because they're the cheapest type of coverage. However, the savings come at a price for you. HMOs are motivated to trim care back to a minimal level. The best of them give you all the care you need, if not all the care you want. I've found that not even the best of them actually deliver on their promise to provide better preventative care. Of course, if your only choices are HMOs, you're stuck; just make sure you select one that has a point-of-service option. That lets you "go out of group" and still get some reimbursement.

HMOs and PPOs may be great if you're a corporate comptroller looking at the bottom line or a public policy wonk looking at the "big picture." But from a personal perspective, I want my family to get the best care around, and the more of it they can get, the better. When your child is ill and needs a specialist, you don't want to hear about how rising medical costs could bankrupt the country. I'll guarantee you that those employers pushing HMOs on their staff, and those politicians promoting managed care, have fee-for-service plans for themselves and their own families.

Home Equity Loans 36

It's amazing what a difference a name can make. When these loans were called second mortgages they were feared and reviled; the stuff of Depression-era legends. Now called home equity loans, they have become almost a panacea for whatever ails you financially.

People are being advised to take out home equity loans to pay off credit card balances, to pay for their child's college education, and even to start their own businesses. Why? Because these loans are easy to obtain and relatively affordable, and, in many cases, the interest they charge is tax deductible. But for Die Brokers, these loans can be dangerous.

A Die Broker's home equity represents a precious source of potential income through a reverse mortgage (see chapter 62). If that equity is used to pay for things earlier in life, it may not be there when a Die Broker needs it most. After all, traditionalists will probably be hoarding assets for their retirement and estate, leaving them with a potentially larger cushion when they're old. Whether they choose to use it or prefer to preserve it for their heirs is besides the point—it will be there for emergencies. An older Die Broker, on the other hand, will have used much of his wealth during the course of his life, and will have turned most of his accumulated savings into income streams. His home equity represents the final asset to be converted—it's the safety net that becomes an income at the last possible minute, ensuring the maximum stream of income and the minimum residual estate.

I'm not entirely opposed to home equity loans, but I think they should be used for one purpose only: to improve, renovate, or add to the home itself. In that way, the loan proceeds can serve as spiritual and financial investments. By contributing to the joy you get from the home, they will increase the chances of your staying there as long as you live. And by possibly increasing the home's value, they could even increase the size of a future reverse mortgage.

Paying off your credit card balances is an excellent idea (see chapters 3 and 22). You may indeed need to borrow money to help you child out with her college tuition (see chapter 8). And starting your own business could be the smartest move you ever make. However, there are other ways to do these things, ways that don't involve tearing a hole in your safety net. They may cost a bit more, but they're nowhere near as dangerous for a Die Broker.

Home Improvements, Renovations, and Additions

37

The traditional view has been that home improvements and renovations were investments rather than purchases. People were told not to do anything to their house that didn't add more to its value than it cost. Additions such as in-ground pools were considered sunk investments. For Die Brokers that traditional view doesn't hold water.

Die Brokers know that home ownership's primary benefits are spiritual rather than financial. As a result, they're buying homes they intend to live in for the rest of their lives. In fact, they're not even planning on selling them—they'll let the bank who holds their reverse mortgage do that. That means the spiritual and emotional rewards that could come from improvements, renovations, and additions should outweigh the potential for financial gain. If you and your family are going to spend thirty years enjoying swimming in that pool, the emotional and spiritual benefits you'll receive far outweigh the fact that the cost might not be recouped when the house is sold. How can you put a price on those summer afternoons when the whole extended family, children and grandchildren, gathered around the pool?

I believe that any improvement, renovation, or addition that you can afford and that adds to your ability to enjoy or use your home is a worthwhile expenditure. Obviously I wouldn't advocate installing solid-gold bathroom fixtures—but if you can afford to finish the attic or basement, and it means you can work from home, do it. If you can swing the cost of adding a dining room or great room and it means your family will get more pleasure from the home, do it. And if you can pay for an in-ground pool, and having it will mean that your whole family will gather together in the summer for years to come, that's great.

Let the banker who'll be selling your home to pay off your reverse mortgage worry about whether or not a potential buyer will pay for your renovations. You'll have Died Broke by then, after having spent years and years enjoying your home.

Homeowners' Insurance

38

I'll bet you know less about your homeowners' coverage than any other insurance policy you own. You know whether you have term or whole life, what your health insurance deductibles are, and whether or not you've got collision coverage on your car. But do you know if you've got HO-2 or HO-3, if you're insured for replacement cost, or what your standard limits on valuables are? I'd wager the answer to all three questions is no.

Don't feel too bad about it. Most of us buy homeowners' coverage at the worst possible time: right before the closing on our home. You're worried you're buying the wrong house, nervous of making a thirty-year financial commitment, scared you're getting in over your head, and shocked by the amount of money you're about to lay out. Your only concerns about homeowners' insurance are that it meets your lender's criteria and is in place in time for the closing. If you expressed any preference at all to the broker, it was probably for the cheapest premium. You saw homeowners' insurance as an obstacle to be overcome, not an important financial safety net.

Once you're in the house you forget all about the homeowners' policy. Either you automatically pay the premium bills when they show up in the mail or you don't even focus on the cost since it's rolled into your monthly mortgage payment.

Then something happens. Hopefully it's a minor problem, like a window broken by a tree branch or the neighborhood Nolan Ryan. But it could also be a major disaster, like a fire starting in your toaster oven or Hurricane Hugo absconding with your roof. You riffle through your files—if they didn't burn up or get blown to the next state—for your policy. If the broker you bought the policy from was prudent, you're probably relieved when you find it. If he was just a good salesman, you could be devastated . . . emotionally and financially.

Obviously, my advice to all my clients is to make buying homeowners' insurance a conscious, proactive process rather than an unthinking reactive action. That goes double when you're a Die Broker, since insurance rather than savings is your primary safety net, at least until you've accumulated a sizable portfolio.

Whether you're about to buy your first home, or have resolved to review your existing coverage before you're forced to make a claim, insuring your home is a four-step process.

Focus on Three Types of Losses

First, remember that homeowners' insurance policies are actually packages combining three different types of protection: damage to the structure, damage or loss of personal property, and personal liability. Just because your needs are met by, say, the structure protection part of a "standard" policy, that doesn't mean your needs for personal property and liability protection will also be met by that policy. Basic homeowner policies provide the lowest common denominator for all three types of coverage. In order to make sure your needs are truly met you must create a custom package.

HO-3: The Essential Type of Coverage

Your second step is to select a type of coverage. Start by looking at damage to your home itself—that's probably the biggest potential risk you're covering. Your goal is to cover as many risks to the structure as you possibly can. That's why you should look only at HO-3 policies. These cover losses or damage from all risks that aren't specifically excluded. The typical exclusions are earthquakes, floods, sewer backups, and war. If you're in an area prone to earthquakes, you can either take out a rider that will cover tremor damage or get a separate policy (see chapter 29). Likewise, if your house could be in danger from flooding, you can get separate coverage for that from the federal government (see chapter 32). Unfortunately you can't get protection from raw sewage or laser-guided munitions.

With an HO-3 policy your personal property—whether in your home, temporarily outside your home, or with your daughter in college—is protected from seventeen to nineteen different risks, including fire, theft, wind, and burst pipes. That should be sufficient . . . if you've obtained the right levels of coverage.

The same HO-3 policy will also provide liability protection if someone (not a family member) gets injured on your property or elsewhere due to unintentional acts or damage by you, your family, and even your pets. Even intentional acts by children under thirteen and pets are covered. But be aware that if you've got a repeatedly "rambunctious" son or "protective" dog, your policy may not be renewed.

Simply put: Make sure you get an HO-3 policy. Unfortunately, determining the amounts of coverage you need isn't as simple.

You Need Enough Coverage to Do the Job Right

The third step in the process is to figure out how much coverage you need. Once again, let's start with the structure. You need sufficient coverage so that if your home burns to the ground, it will be rebuilt exactly as it was prior to the blaze. The only way to make sure that will happen is to buy "guaranteed replacement cost" coverage. With this coverage the insurer promises to pay whatever it will take to rebuild your home and garage, and even replace your landscaping. While quite costly, I think it's worth it, especially if you do everything else you can to lower your costs. A less expensive alternative would be to initially insure the home for 100 percent of its current replacement cost, and to simultaneously take out automatic inflation protection. Whatever you do, don't skimp by taking out less than 100 percent coverage . . . unless, of course, you'd be satisfied replacing your three-bedroom colonial with a double-wide.

I think you should take the same kind of guaranteed replacement approach when it comes to your personal property. But most standard policies cover your personal property only up to a total of 50 or 75 percent of the face value of the policy—that's far from sufficient. They also have limitations for how much they'll pay for any one type of item—say, no more than $1,500 total for all your jewelry. In addition, standard policies pay only "market value" for your property. That means you'll only get enough to shop at thrift shops, yard sales, and flea markets to refurbish your rooms, refill your closets, and restock your china closet. You need to buy what's called "replacement-cost coverage." If your five-year-old projection television is destroyed, the policy pays you whatever it costs to buy a brand-new one at retail. Once again, this isn't cheap, but it's worth it.

If you have some very valuable possessions, you can consider "scheduling" them. This means they are independently appraised, listed separately in the policy, and have their own premium. However, I think that if you've taken out replacement cost coverage this is necessary only for things like antiques or artwork where the value may not be apparent and the item isn't easily replaceable. Don't worry about insuring things that have extreme sentimental value. There isn't enough money in the world to enable you to replace Grandpa's pocket watch if it's stolen, so don't even try. Keep it in a safe-deposit box instead.

Most policies offer a standard $100,000 in liability coverage. That's far from enough at a time when $1 million personal injury judgments are commonplace. You can generally buy up to $300,000 or $500,000 of coverage for just a slight increase in your premium. I suggest you go even further and take out an umbrella liability policy (see chapter 71). If you obtain your homeowner and auto policies (see chapter 14) from the same insurer, you can often get up to $1 million in additional liability protection for a very reasonable rate. As an added bonus these umbrella polices often cover claims of invasion of privacy, slander, and libel in addition to personal injury suits.

Seven Ways to Save Some Money

Having urged you to take out top-of-the-line homeowners' coverage, I'm setting you up for a sizable bill, one that's probably much higher than you're used to paying. Please don't overreact and compromise your coverage. If you're underinsured, you're just one fire or broken hip away from financial disaster. As a Die Broker you're especially vulnerable since you're spending or giving away a higher percentage of your income than everyone else. Instead of compromising on your coverage, take the fourth step and consider these ways to trim that premium bill:

- **Take out as large a deductible as you possibly can.** The purpose of homeowners' insurance isn't to replace a broken window or a busted toaster, it's to restore your home and its contents in case of catastrophe.
- **Take advantage of safety discounts.** Most insurers offer discounts for homes that have dead-bolt locks, passive alarm systems, smoke and heat detectors, and fire extinguishers.
- **Take advantage of your lifestyle.** Some insurers offer lower rates to nonsmokers. Many offer discounts to people who work at home or are "retired."
- **Don't overinsure.** Make sure you're not insuring elements of your property that can't actually be destroyed or damaged, like the land itself, your foundation, and underground pipes and cables. Similarly, check that you're not insuring personal property that you wouldn't or couldn't replace. There's no sense paying to schedule the sterling-silver tea set Aunt Millie gave you for an engagement gift if you'd never replace it.
- **Look for package deals.** Most insurers that offer homeowners' coverage also offer auto and personal liability policies. Generally you can save money by purchasing a package of two or three policies from the same insurer. As a bonus you'll have some added leverage with the company when it's time to settle claims.
- **Comparison-shop.** Premiums on identical homeowners' insurance policies vary dramatically: There's no single nationwide low-cost provider. I'd suggest you start off by getting price quotes from State Farm and Allstate, two of the larger nationwide insurers. Next, if you qualify,[18] contact USAA, which is known for its low premiums and excellent service, at (800) 531-8080. If you don't qualify for USAA call Amica Mutual, another well-respected small insurer, at (800) 242-6422. Take the three quotes you've obtained to a good local insurance broker (see chapter 41) and ask him to beat those rates. Chances are he'll be able to come up with a local or regional insurer who will cost you less . . . especially if you're buying a home/auto/umbrella liability package. However, before you grab

---

[18]USAA will sell homeowners' insurance to the families of: commissioned or warrant officers of the Army, Navy, Air Force, Marine Corps, Coast Guard, National Oceanic and Atmospheric Administration, Public Health Service, and U.S. Information Agency; foreign service officers of the U.S. State Department; and special agents of the FBI and Treasury Department.

that low bid, just make sure you check their financial health (see chapters 11 and 45).

- **Pay the bill in full**. Finally, if you can afford it, pay the premium bill in full once a year—it's cheaper than paying in installments or quarterly.

Home Ownership   **39**

Even at the cusp of the twenty-first century, with all the economic changes taking place, home ownership remains one of the greatest experiences available to most Americans. It's one of the few things I can think of that provides both spiritual and financial gratification. Of course, the balance between those two has changed. But that's nothing new.

For most of our nation's history home ownership primarily offered spiritual rewards. You were king of your own castle. No landlord could raise your rent, fail to provide heat, or forget to fix the roof. You were free to turn that home into whatever you wanted it to be. You even had a piece of property on which you could plant vegetables or put up a swing set for your kids. As if that wasn't enough, the interest on your mortgage was tax deductible, and the house generally increased in value at a rate higher than inflation. That made owning your own home a good way to save money.

Real Estate Goes Mass Market and Provides a Windfall

However, up until the 1950s not that many people could take advantage of home ownership. It was hard for middle-class people to save up enough money for a down payment, and harder still to find a home that was affordable. That changed with the growth of the suburbs and the GI Bill. Suddenly, affordable homes were being built and the government was willing to help with the financing. Middle-class people began buying homes in record numbers. Still, it was more for spiritual and lifestyle reasons than for the financial benefits. That was soon to change.

When the first wave of those suburban pioneers began reaching retirement age and putting their homes on the market, they received a pleasant shock. People who bought modest homes for $15,000 in 1965 were able to turn around and sell them for $150,000 in 1985. As their friends saw how much hidden wealth they were sitting on—actually, living in—they too put their homes on the market. And rather than prices going down they kept on climbing. By the 1980s they were astronomical. People couldn't afford not to sell, for fear the bubble would burst and they'd "lose" money. More than any other single factor it was this boom in real estate values that enabled your parents' generation to retire comfortably. Unfortunately, the boom exploded in your face.

It was you and your peers who drove real estate values through the roof. Baby boomers grew up in homes owned by their parents. When they got married they wanted to buy homes too. But there were so many more of them looking to buy than there were available homes, even with expanded development, that prices started to climb. It was simple supply and demand. In effect, baby boomers mortgaged their futures to pay for their parents' (and real estate developers') windfalls. Still, most boomers weren't worried. Look at how well their parents had done with real estate. Surely they'd be able to do the same.

The Rise and Fall of Serial House Ownership

Well, some of them were able to . . . for a while. The leading edge of the baby boom generation was able to practice what I call serial house ownership. They bought a starter house or apartment as soon as possible, held on to it for three to five years, sold it for a profit, and stepped up into a more expensive house. If they caught the wave early enough, they might even have been able to sell that second house for another tidy profit and buy an even larger place.

I use the word "house" deliberately. That's just the word these folks used when they came to my office. If you were going to keep buying and selling property, it made sense to view it as a house, since that was a commodity. A home, on the other hand, was something that had permanence, something that had more emotional than financial value.

These leading-edge boomers were able to practice serial house ownership because they were riding the wave of even more baby boomer buyers coming after them. Just as their parents were able to take advantage of them, they were able to take advantage of their younger siblings. Unfortunately, the wave crashed up on the beach at the end of the 1980s.

Just around 1988 the number of potential buyers began shrinking and, not surprisingly, the residential real estate market began crashing. Those who were able to ride the wave into a comfortable retirement or a house they never otherwise could have afforded were happy. Those who caught the wave at the last minute ended up getting swamped. By the early 1990s there were some people who actually owed more on their mortgage than their house was worth. There were even more who simply couldn't afford to sell and were stuck in houses too small for their needs. Again not surprisingly, it was just about this time that home renovation became a hot topic: All those people stuck in houses too small for their needs were watching *This Old House* so they could figure out what to do. The brief era of serial house ownership was over.

Returning Home

Whether you're one of the lucky ones who rode the wave into more house than you ever thought possible, one of the unlucky ones who got swamped in a house too small for your needs, or someone who's just about to test the water for the first time, it's important to understand that home ownership has changed. Actually, it has changed back.

Home ownership is still a wonderful thing, but for the combination of reasons that attracted your parents to it back in the 1950s and 1960s. It today offers primarily spiritual rewards, with the added financial bonuses of mortgage interest deductibility and growth that outpaces inflation. But that's all the growth you can count on today. Not until there's another baby boom will we see the kind of dramatic increases and windfall profits experienced in the 1970s and 1980s. The good part of that is that you can now return to the idea of home.

Today, when young clients come to be to discuss real estate, I tell them to buy their second home first. I tell them to steer clear of "starter houses" they'll eventually outgrow, and instead buy the kind of home they would have stepped up into after selling a starter house. I tell them to plan on buying a house they could be comfortable in for the rest of their lives, because they just might live there that long.

If that means waiting longer to buy, so be it. That will give you more time to save money, more time to make sure your marriage is firm, more time to learn what you like and dislike, more time to separate your needs from your wants. The result of waiting will be a more intelligent buy.

If that means buying further away from their work, that's okay. Today your home is more permanent than your job. In two years you could be working somewhere else, perhaps in an "edge city" development closer to your home. In five years could be telecommuting rather than riding the train. In ten years you could be running your own home-based business.

If that means buying in a less affluent area than the one they grew up in, they shouldn't be upset. They are, in fact, likely to be less affluent than their parents, even if they have two incomes. Trying to pretend otherwise is just going to have a ripple effect on the rest of their lives. Why should they sacrifice today and for the rest of their lives in order to simply appear to be as well off as their parents? That's crazy. Sacrificing quality of life for appearance's sake is spiritual suicide. Remember, dying broke means living fully up to your means, not beyond them.

Today when clients who already own homes come to me for real estate advice, I'm telling them to either renovate their current house so it can be a home they'll be comfortable in for the rest of their lives or, if that's not possible, sell it and buy another home they *will* be happy in for the rest of their lives.

If that means not making as much of a profit as they'd hoped, what's the big deal? They're not in the real estate business. Holding on to the house longer *won't* make the financial loss any less and *will* make the spiritual loss greater.

In the era of serial house ownership people's compromises all revolved around the size and character of the house. They bought smaller and less attractive homes in order to buy sooner or to buy in a particular area. In other words, they placed greater emphasis on the financial benefits of home buying than the emotional. Today the reverse should be true. Buy the house of your dreams, even if you have to wait longer to do so or travel further to get there. You're now buying a home, not just a house, a place where you could spend the rest of your life and be happy.

Income Taxes

40

Because of their proactive approach to personal finance it's easy for a Die Broker to let income taxes become an obsession. Certainly you should do everything you can to avoid them by hiring a savvy CPA (see chapter 10), but please don't make them the center of your financial life.

Tax deductibility is never a reason to buy anything, and it's certainly not a reason to spend more than you would have otherwise. Similarly, don't invest in something just because it offers tax-free income. Every purchase and every investment must make sense on its own.

If you're going to obsess over something, let it be your income. Spend all your time figuring out ways to make more money—and leave it to your accountant to figure out ways of paying less taxes on it.

Insurance Salesmen

41

Insurance salesmen are like funeral directors: You never want to deal with them, but eventually you're going to have to, and when you do, you'd like them to be as sedate and sincere as possible.

I've found that there are two kinds of successful insurance salesmen: those who are experts at selling, and those who are experts at insurance. The former will come to your home and tell you what you need, the latter will have you come to his office and ask you what you need. And, almost universally, the former are agents and the latter are brokers.

Agents work for one particular insurance company (or more than one noncompetitor). Their only required training is in how to sell the products of their company. Brokers work for themselves. They are required to take licensing exams and really do have an understanding of insurance products. While both make their money on sales commissions,[19] brokers offer you a choice of products from various insurers and can provide unbiased, informed opinions. My advice is simple: use a broker, not an agent.

[19]For example, 50 percent or more of the premiums you pay the first couple of years or so after taking out a whole life policy.

Job Hunting

42

Most people view job hunting with a great deal of trepidation and fear. That's because they think that what they do defines who they are as a person and what their value is as a human being. In looking for a new job they're actually looking for a new identity and for someone who will reaffirm their worth. To make the situation even worse, most people don't start looking for a new job until they're either terminated or know their job is in danger. They're bringing that impending sense of doom and desperation along with them on their job search. As a Die Broker, you know better.

You know that "it's just a job" (see chapter 2) and that the most important thing about a job is the income it provides for you. When a Die Broker looks for a new job, he isn't looking for a new identity or for an affirmation of his personal worth, he's looking for more money. And a Die Broker doesn't wait for signs of danger to start looking for a new job. He knows his job is always in danger and so he's always looking for the next job. He practices bifocal vision: simultaneously focusing on both his current job and his future prospects. These attitudes make all the difference in the world. Far from a frightening reactive process, a job search can now be a thrilling, proactive one.

When most people think of a job hunt, they're actually viewing themselves as the prey. When a Die Broker looks for a new position, she is truly the hunter, in charge and in control, beating the bushes for one thing: more money. And ironically, that's really the easiest thing to find out there in the workplace jungle.

Non–Die Brokers generally have subjective, amorphous goals— more opportunities for advancement and greater spiritual rewards, for example. Those don't automatically come with getting a new job. And even if you think they might, you can't be sure until you make the move. If their goal is security, we know they've no hope at all in finding it. The few traditional job searchers whose primary concern is money are those who have already been fired. So rather than being in the position to ask for more, they're desperate for anything, even if it's less.

Die Brokers have a specific, quantifiable goal: more money. That's almost automatic when you leave one job for another. Go to a new company and you're coming in from outside the existing budget. Talk up your skills and abilities and triumphs in a job interview (see chapter 43) and your future boss sees you doing the same for her and the company. You are unlimited potential and the answer to all her prayers. You are the embodiment of her hopes and dreams for the position. She wants to take you from where you are and bring you on board. To do that, she must give you more money than you're already making. And that was your goal in the first place.

Since your goal is so readily accessible, you don't need to waste time on grand strategy. You can stick to refining your hunting tactics.

Look Behind the Right Bushes . . . and Be Prepared for What You'll Find

Most established large domestic companies are cutting, not increasing, staff. That means you should look at new companies, small and medium-sized organizations, and those that are foreign-owned.

Since you'll be looking in new places, you must be prepared to accept new working situations. You might have to work on a team rather than in a department. Your boss might not be the traditional old, white American male. Your staff will probably consist of your computer and your modem. The only time you're likely to have a corner office is if you're a telecommuter and it's the corner of your bedroom. Otherwise you could be at a workstation or working on the road.

Keep Your Constant Hunting a Secret

Obviously, the people you meet with will know you're looking for another job. And since you'll constantly be on the prowl, you're apt to meet with a lot of people. But they're not likely to spread the word. The people you've got to worry about are your coworkers at your present job. If they think it will help them by diminishing your standing, they'll pass their suspicions on to your supervisor. And if she finds out, no amount of explaining the Quit Today approach will help you. Your name could soon be on top of the list of potential layoffs. At the very least you'll be branded as disloyal. That's absurd, since loyalty is a two-way street and your employer won't show any to you, but it's true nevertheless.

Do your best to keep from signaling that you're on the hunt. Don't show up in a suit for an outside interview when you normally wear jeans and sneakers. Find a place outside the office to change. Similarly, don't take lots of sick days, come in late, or leave early. Most people will be happy to schedule meetings either before or after normal business hours. If that's not possible, use your lunch hour. If you must take time off work for a meeting, take the entire day off and try to schedule more than one interview. Obviously, make sure all your job-hunting correspondence and telephone calls are directed to your home. Just make sure your answering machine has a businesslike greeting.

To Hunt Successfully You Have to Be out in the Field

I hope you know you can't rely on help-wanted ads or bulk mailings to find your next job—that's fishing, not hunting. You're throwing your bait out there and hoping something good snaps at it. (Using the Internet is even worse; not only are you fishing rather than hunting, but you're dropping your worm into the Pacific Ocean rather than a lake.) Leave such tactics to all those desperate traditionalists. Similarly, don't rely on employment agencies or headhunters—that would be like depending on someone else to hunt for the food to feed your family. You might get a few scraps thrown your way, but they'll keep the good stuff for themselves.

More than 70 percent of all jobs are filled through personal contacts, so the more frequently you contact people personally, the quicker you'll find a new job. Keep in regular contact with all your personal and business contacts, letting them know you're always interested in meeting with interesting people to "discuss opportunities."

Ask people if you can rent their Rolodex. I may not know anyone who has an opening in television right now, but I could suggest you to talk to my friend Kenny over at CNBC. He may not have or know of any openings either, but he could send you to speak to his friend Dean over at MTV. Step by step, person by person, you're expanding your network. Keep this up and you'll soon be making more money.

Don't worry that networking will limit your search either geographically or to one industry. The concept of six degrees of separation is correct. Almost everyone is linked to almost everyone else by as few as six individuals. When you limit the connection to the workplace, you've probably cut it down to three degrees.

Also, don't feel like you're putting people out by asking them to pass you on to their contacts. There's an unspoken quid pro quo. Somewhere down the line you'll be getting a call from me or Kenny or Dean . . . especially since we're all Die Brokers too.

Don't Hesitate to Hunt in New Forests

When traditionalists shift industries, it's a reactive step. Terminated and unable to find a comparable job in their own industry, since every other company in it is downsizing as well, they turn to another industry they've heard is growing and therefore hiring. Die Brokers, however, look to different industries as a proactive way to expand their horizons and potentially bring home higher incomes. You're not hunting in a new forest out of desperation because there's no more game in the old forest. You're scouting out the new forest because it might offer better game. Since you're not desperate, your chances of actually bagging something are far greater.

Where are the best new places to hunt? Well, you don't need to be a futurist like Faith Popcorn to come up with those answers. Just look at the world around you.

Notice lots of ads for active old folks on television? That's because the over-fifty population will increase 50 percent in the next twenty years, from sixty-five million to ninety-seven million. The number of those over eighty-five is also soon going to reach an all-time high. And most of these folks have money—if they didn't they probably wouldn't be living so long; therefore, businesses catering to older, affluent people will do well.

Look in the mirror. You'll probably find firsthand evidence that the baby boom generation is also turning gray. What kinds of products and services do you find yourself looking at, and thinking about buying, as you get older? Those businesses will also do well in the future.

Are you seeing lots of baby strollers when you walk around town on the weekend? That's because since 1985 the number of children born each year has increased by 100,000 a year. The birth rate in 1990 was actually higher than in 1950. The U.S. Census Bureau estimates that by 2010, the number of minors in the country will have grown around 10 percent. Obviously businesses that cater to children will do well too. So will businesses that cater to working parents. You know what it was like for you and your spouse when your kids were little. Well, it's the same today. About 60 percent of working women today have children under six. By the year 2000 the percentage is projected to rise to 75 percent thanks to the baby boomlet. Right now, more than $13 billion is spent on child-care-related services. That figure is going to grow.

Look around your office—notice that there's no longer a secretarial staff, a shipping department, or an art department? Businesses are farming out all but their core functions, cutting all but the minimum number of staff people. Therefore, any business that provides ancillary services to other businesses is likely to do well.

Have you heard anything about this thing called the Internet? What type of business will take the checkered flag on the information superhighway? To be honest, I don't know—but then again, no one else does either, not even Bill Gates. Still, you can be sure the Internet will make and break more than one industry.

Hunting in a Strange Place

How can you network in an industry in which you have no contacts? Well, obviously the first step is to find out if your contacts have any contacts there. Odds are you'll find a few folks to talk to that way. But in order to really build up your network you'll have to practice what I call backdoor networking.

First, find a college nearby that offers an MBA program. Go to the business school library. Find the reference librarian. Ask him for the names of some trade publications that cover the industry you're interested in. Write down the names, addresses, and telephone numbers of the editors of the leading trade magazines, and of any general business reporters who regularly cover the industry. Alongside the names, write down some notes about a couple of their articles in recent issues. Contact the editors and writers, introducing yourself as someone who's interested in learning more about their industry. Express your admiration for their work, citing the notes you took about their articles. Ask if you can take them to lunch and speak with them about the industry. Trade magazine editors are underappreciated and underpaid. They will tell you everything they know—which is often a great deal—in return for a couple of compliments and a nice meal.

Second, get involved in a professional association. Attend a few meetings, mingle, and ask around for the names of other members of the association who are in the industry you're interested in. As soon as you get a name, call, introduce yourself as a fellow member of the association, and ask for a brief fifteen-minute informational interview, at a time of their convenience. Don't ask if they know of any openings. Instead, just ask for the name of someone else to speak with about the industry. Call the new name and start the process all over again.

This double-barreled backdoor approach should help you build up a network in no time. Keep it active, and you'll soon be part of the industry rather than an outsider looking to get in.

Job Interviews

43

You're a smart, experienced grown-up, so I'm not going to bore you with interviewing advice like dressing appropriately and showing up on time. Just look and act like you are meeting the most important person in the world . . . because you might be. That woman across the desk could be responsible for your stream of income, and for a Die Broker nothing is more important.

Learn About Your Opposite Number

Assuming the interview comes as the result of networking, ask your contact for everything he or she knows about the person. No information is too mundane or obscure. For instance, if you learn she's a butterfly collector, you could drop Nabokov's name. Go on-line and research the company and its place within its industry. If it's a public company, read the three most recent annual reports.

Play Twenty Questions

Next, sit down and draft concise answers to the following ten questions—you can count on being asked at least six of them.

- Why do you want to work here?
- What makes you think you're qualified for this job?
- Why did you leave your last job?
- What are your strengths and weaknesses?

- What are your career and personal goals?
- Where do you see yourself in five years?
- What did you like and dislike about previous jobs?
- How would you characterize your work and management styles?
- Have you ever had to deal with a difficult boss or subordinate?
- What are your greatest personal and professional accomplishments?

Now, draft your own list of ten questions for the interviewer. Not only will asking questions show your enthusiasm, interest, motivation, and preparation, but it will ensure this is a give-and-take rather than an inquisition. Make her sell you on the company—playing a little hard to get will actually improve your chances. Here are ten general questions you can use as the basis for your own more specific list:

- What are the major responsibilities or objectives of this position?
- What would you consider the major challenges facing this position?
- Whom does the person in this position report to and work with?
- How much staff or outside support will be available?
- Has the budget for this team been increasing or decreasing?
- What's the work atmosphere like in this company?
- What happened to the person who previously held the position?
- What would you consider the drawbacks to the position?
- What kind of projects will this team be handling in the future?
- Where do you see the company headed in the next five years?

Don't let antagonistic pressure interviewers bother you. You've still got a job, so you don't need this spot. Besides, interview pressure is just a game to test your responses. Your résumé has already convinced them you can do the job—otherwise, you wouldn't have gotten the interview. This meeting is just a way to confirm what they saw in your résumé and to rank you among all the qualified candidates.

If you're shifting industries, make sure you have a rationale for the transition—your old industry going down the toilet isn't sufficient. You need to demonstrate excitement for this new business. They may ask you to reiterate how your skills and experience are transferable. Don't worry about it. If your résumé didn't make the case effectively, you wouldn't be there. They're just looking for confirmation and reassurance, since hiring someone from outside the industry is always something of a gamble. Be prepared to repeat this information over and over, maybe to two or three different people. They might all need to hear it often enough so they can repeat it to the chairman later that day to justify your being hired.

Die Brokers Don't Forget Their Goal

One of the most common mistakes traditional job hunters make is failing to realize that getting a job is a two-step process: First they've got to convince the interviewer they're the right person for the job, and second they've got to convince the interviewer they deserve big bucks. Traditionalists, desperate for a job or convinced money isn't central to the process, concentrate on the former. If they get the job, they feel they're successful. But for Die Brokers that's only half the battle—and not even the most important half. Remember: Your goal was and continues to be getting more money. If you get a job offer but don't succeed in getting more money, you've failed.

If an interviewer even brings up salary, you can breathe a silent sigh of relief—she definitely wants you to take the job. But don't show your relief or become complacent. You'll never be in as good a position with this company again. Right now, before you're hired, you have unlimited potential. You've never made a mistake or let them down. You're the living embodiment of the employer's dreams.

But simply realizing you're in a powerful position isn't enough. You've got to use it to your advantage.

Who Comes First?

The key to salary negotiating is not being the first to put a specific number on the table. If you lead off, the negotiation will center on decreasing it. If the employer is the first up, the negotiation can be about increasing it. Savvy employers will try to get you to name a figure by asking apparently innocuous, friendly questions like "How much of a salary are you looking for?" Respond with equally innocuous and friendly answers like: "One commensurate with my experience and skills." Then turn the question around, asking, "What salary are you willing to pay the person who takes this position?"

Obviously you can't let this little dance go on all day. If the back-and-forth threatens to get ridiculous, throw a number out there. But make sure it's high enough so you can be forced down and still be happy.

Employers always have a salary range rather than a specific number in mind for an open position. You can assume it's about 20 percent, centered on the salary the last person who held the job was making. For instance, if the last person was making $100,000 when he left, the company might want to pay as little as $90,000 but be willing to go up as high as $110,000. It's also safe to assume the employer would publicize or start off with their top figure.

There's More to Money Than Just Money

While your goal is getting more money, it need not come in the form of salary. It could come from tuition reimbursement, extended vacations, or special insurance coverage, for example. It might be easier for the employer to come up with these other kinds of benefits than it is to increase the salary figure, due to the way the company's budget works. Just make sure you're actually receiving something that's of material, not just psychic, benefit. If it can't be converted into dollars, it shouldn't be valuable to a Die Broker.

Play Hard to Get

A final technique that has worked for many of my clients is to step right up to the brink of acceptance and then back off. For instance, at the point when you're tempted to accept the offer, hesitate, look the interviewer in the eye, and directly ask, "Is that the best you can do?" Keep looking her in the eye and say nothing until she responds. It takes some guts, but it can work wonders. Whatever she says, respond by saying, "I'm excited about the position, but I'd like to go home and think about everything we discussed. Would it be okay if I get back to you tomorrow morning?" This gives her a chance to trade a slight increase in her salary offer for your immediate acceptance.

Leasing versus Buying an Automobile **44**

I'm still waiting for someone to give me one good reason for a Die Broker to take out a car loan to buy a car rather than lease it.

I love the fact that you can walk into a dealer's lot, put down a deposit of around $300, fill out a simple credit application, and drive away in a brand-new car. You get to drive around in that car for three years, each month paying about half of what you would have had you taken out a loan and bought the car. Since most manufacturers' warranties last for three years, you can be pretty certain not to have any repair expenses other than routine maintenance. When the three years run out you simply exchange the car for a new one, this time putting even less money down because your initial deposit just gets rolled over into the new lease. To sum up: By leasing you're spending less each month and you're getting a better car. The only drawback that I can see is that you'll be making a monthly car payment for as long as you need a car.

If you took out a loan to buy the same car, your monthly payments would be about twice as large, slashing your stream of income. You would probably have to put more money down, since few lenders offer 100 percent financing, reducing your savings.

Granted, at the end of the loan term you'd own the car and wouldn't need to make further payments. However, you'd own an asset that has probably depreciated dramatically rather than maintained or increased in value. And, while your loan payments might end, they'll be twice what lease payments would be on the same vehicle. That means you'll end up saving money only if you keep the car for more than six years. Keep most of today's cars for six years and you'll be facing some major repair bills.

There are only two times when I can see buying a car rather than leasing it. If you need a second car for minimal local use—the classic "junker" to get you to and from the suburban train station—save up some money and pay cash for it. If you've got so much money that you can lay out the cash to buy an extraordinarily durable vehicle that maintains its value, go right ahead. In other words, if you can buy what you need with cash—whether it's a brand-new Mercedes or a used Yugo—without feeling any pain, do it. If you can't, lease.

Life Insurance   45

In Woody Allen's film *Take the Money and Run* the harshest punishment for convicts in a southern chain gang is to be locked into a small wooden hut . . . with a life insurance salesman. If you've ever had an insurance agent put down roots in your kitchen, you'd probably agree. Not only do they couple the hard-sell sleaze of used-car dealers with the guilt-inducing guile of funeral directors, but they're also as hard to get rid of as athlete's foot.

The bad news is, even though you're planning to Die Broke, you still need life insurance. The good news is that for you it's actually a very simple purchase—so simple you won't need to deal with an agent or broker.

Life Insurance Is Just Insurance
That means it's not an investment or a forced savings plan. Insurance companies have great track records as insurers but lousy track records as investors. They're the last people I'd have invest my clients' money. The only advisers who encourage insurance as an investment are those who make money selling it. That also means the only kind of life insurance you should concern yourself with is term. Forget all the propaganda and marketing you've heard about whole, universal, and variable life insurance. It's all nonsense, especially that line about term being "temporary" and whole life being "permanent."

You actually don't need permanent life insurance. As soon as you have sufficient savings of your own, you can drop the insurance.

(The only time whole life insurance makes sense for you personally is when you're over seventy and therefore can no longer get affordable term coverage but want insurance to pay for your funeral and any debts left after you die.[20] Since this is actually "funeral insurance," not life insurance, a discussion of it is included in chapter 33 on funerals.)

You're Insuring Income, Not Life

You need life insurance for one simple reason: to protect your survivors from a premature, permanent loss of your income. (Disability insurance protects *you* from a *temporary* loss and is discussed separately.) If there's no one who depends on your income, there's no need for you to have life insurance. The emotional, psychological, and spiritual pain that comes with the loss of a loved one is beyond measure. And anything that cannot be measured in dollars and cents should not be insured.

Everyone wants to take care of loved ones. No one wants their survivors to worry about a thing. It's natural to want them to be able to continue living as they did when you were alive. But even though it's a natural sentiment, it's still a mistake.

You cannot look at insurance emotionally. If your goal is to "take care of your family forever," you'll never have enough insurance. You'll be falling back into the old rules: sacrificing the present for the future and attempting to make your financial life immortal.

You cannot be replaced. No matter how much money is paid to your survivors upon your death, it won't compensate for your loss. That's why you have to put ideas of financial immortality out of your mind. Not speaking with insurance agents and brokers will help in this regard, since they're trained to make you feel that money can, in some measure, replace you. Focus on the financial impact of your loss, not the emotional impact: How will the loss of you or your spouse effect the family's income?

You need to define income broadly. A stay-at-home spouse who cooks, cleans, and cares for children may not have an actual income,

---

[20]Okay, I take that back. I can think of one other scenario when it might make sense: If you're over seventy, have a young family that depends on your income, and don't have enough savings to take care of them on your own.

but his or her unpaid work frees up a share of the income of the spouse who works outside the home. That means the life of a stay-at-home spouse who does such housework should be insured. On the other hand, unless your child brings home an income that contributes to the maintenance of the rest of the family, his or her life should not be insured.

They Need Enough to Get By . . . for a Little While

So how much insurance do you need? I'd start with enough to replace the income that would be lost, for as long as it takes the survivors to adjust their lifestyles to the permanent loss of the income.

Let's face it, they may never adjust emotionally or psychologically to the loss. They can, however, adjust financially fairly quickly. If they need to cut their spending to pay for housecleaning and child care, they'll do it. If they need to sell the home because they can't cover the mortgage and maintenance with just one income, they'll do it. If they need to go back into the job market rather than stay home with the kids, they'll do it. I generally tell my clients to start their estimates with enough coverage to replace the insured's income (or equivalent contribution) for three years. In my experience I've found that's enough time for a family to mourn, face their financial circumstances, and adjust their lives.

Remember: Trying to provide so much insurance protection that the survivors don't have to *ever* change their lives is absurd. Their lives *are* changed—there's no getting around that, regardless of how much money is dumped in their laps after the funeral. Besides, making adjustments is part of the healing process.

Changing their lives to fit their new economic circumstances can help them see that change is both possible and necessary to recover from grief. The life they led prior to your death is over. It's time to turn the page and start a new life.

Adjust Coverage to Fit Your Circumstances

That being said, don't think that the three-year figure is a hard-and-fast number. It's just a starting point, one you need to adjust to your own unique circumstances.

If your spouse is un- or underemployed, but younger than age forty-five, odds are he or she will be able to reenter the job market and will eventually remarry. But if he or she is older, it will be much tougher to get a job, and a second marriage isn't likely. If the latter is the case, additional coverage might be justified.

Similarly, if you have an outstanding debt other than your mortgage, you should certainly make sure it's covered by your death benefit. Let's say you borrowed $20,000 from your brother for help in launching a business. Since you're a Die Broker, there will be nothing in your estate to cover the debt. Rather than passing the burden on to your survivors, cover it with insurance.[21]

What About a Child's College Education?

I don't think your life insurance should automatically cover the cost of your child's college education. If your child is already in college, and you're paying the bills, simply replacing your income for three years should provide enough to continue paying the bills, especially since with your income gone they'll qualify for more financial aid. If your child is in middle school or high school, three years' worth of income will offer them more than enough time to adjust their sights and make necessary financial arrangements (see chapter 8). And if your child is still young, it's way too early to predict where, or even if, he or she will want to go to college. It's foolish to spend on life insurance to pay for your daughter's Harvard education when she may want to become an actress instead. Use the money you save to send her to Paris.

What About the Mortgage?

People reflexively want to pay off their mortgages. However, that's not always the best thing to do—it depends on the survivors' income and their relationship to the home.

If the house was *never* intended to serve as a "family home" forever, I'd suggest *not* providing any added benefit for the mortgage. I'd advise the survivors to use their three-year cushion to either increase their income sufficiently to continue paying the mortgage or, if that's

---

[21]However, do not, under any circumstances, take out life insurance sold by either your credit card company or your mortgage lender. Not only is it more expensive than regular life insurance, but it limits the flexibility of the beneficiaries. If your spouse doesn't want to pay off the mortgage, he or she is out of luck. If you feel the need to cover this or another debt, simply make sure there's enough in your regular life insurance to pay off the loan(s).

not possible or desirable, sell the home, pay off the mortgage, and buy a new dwelling that *is* affordable and that they *do* intend to live in for the rest of their lives.

If the house in question *is* the one that was always intended to serve as a "family home" for the rest of the person's life, then I think it's important to do everything possible so the survivor can stay there if he or she wishes. But rather than trying to cover the entire mortgage through insurance, I'd suggest providing enough to pay the mortgage down to a level that's manageable.

Let's say you've followed my advice and bought your second home first. You and your spouse intend to spend the rest of your lives in this home. Your family's total income is $150,000, $100,000 of which comes from you. My suggestion would be to provide enough additional life insurance so your spouse could pay off two-thirds of the outstanding mortgage. In effect, that would bring the mortgage down to a level comparable to the survivor's income.

What About Double Indemnity?

Great movie. Dumb idea. How you die should have no impact on your death benefit.

What About Second-to-Die Insurance?

If its primary purpose is to pay the tax on a estate, second-to-die life insurance makes no sense for a Die Broker. After all, you're not going to leave an estate. However, if you're worried about a child who may not have the capability to support him or herself even as an adult, second-to-die insurance is probably a good idea (see chapter 64).

A Narrow but Important Choice

Throwing out all forms of whole life insurance simplifies your choices dramatically, but you've still got one shopping decision to make. There are two types of term coverage: annually renewable term and level-premium term (also called reentry term).

The premiums on an annually renewable-term policy start low but increase a little bit every year (or every three or five years). However, the insurer can't cancel your coverage or increase your fee due to a decline in your health. In fact, once you pass the first medical exam you never have to take another. You can generally keep renewing the policy every year up until around age seventy. Of course, if you've saved and invested, your need for life insurance coverage should be well past by then.

The premiums on level-premium term policies start out a bit higher than those on annually renewable-term policies, but they stay the same for ten or more years. Over the length of a level-term policy you'll generally pay less than you would for a similar annually renewable term policy. However, when the period of coverage runs out, you must take a medical exam if you want continued coverage. While you won't be denied coverage (since you'll have bought a policy that's guaranteed renewable), your premiums could jump dramatically.

Which type of term coverage should you opt for? If you've already got a savings and investment plan in place and you're confident you'll be able to build up your net worth enough to be a self-insurer in, say, twenty years, opt for level term. If you don't yet have a savings and investment plan in place and you're not as confident about your investment acumen, get an annually renewable term policy.

Let Your Fingers Do the Walking

Once you've decided how much you need and what kind of term policy you want, the shopping is fairly simple. Term insurance is like a commodity. A certain amount of coverage costs just about the same wherever you look. The differences between premiums come from the fees, administrative costs, and different profit margins of individual insurers.

Forget about going to a broker or an agent—you don't need them for this purchase and they'll just try to talk you into whole life coverage. Instead, turn to the telephone and the Internet. Call and/or log on to one of these free quote services:

- InstantQuote (http://www.instantquote.com)
- MasterQuote (800-337-5433)
- Quicken InsureMarket (http://www.insuremarket.com)
- QuickQuote (http://quickquote.com)
- Quotesmith (http://www.quotesmith.com)
- SelectQuote (800-343-1985)
- TermQuote (800-444-8376)

You'll be asked or prompted to enter relevant information (age; smoker or nonsmoker; amount, length, and type of coverage; occupation; etc.) and then provided with a series of quotes. Some services provide just the lowest five premiums, others provide more than 150 options. You'll then be asked to fill out an application over the telephone or on-line. Don't.

Each of these services is actually an insurance brokerage. While they work on greater economies of scale than the guy with the storefront next to your local Department of Motor Vehicles, they still only offer quotes from the insurers they represent. That's why you should get quotes from at least three of them in order to get a true sampling of all that's available.

If you're particularly industrious and extremely healthy, consider calling these companies for individual quotes as well. All are direct insurers:

- Ameritas (800-552-3553)
- Charles Schwab/Great-West Life (800-542-5433)
- USAA (800-531-8000)
- Zurich Direct (http://www.zurichdirect.com)

These insurers will also prompt you to fill out an application. Don't. You first need to check the health of all your potential insurers.

Make a list of the three to five lowest bidders overall. Then let your fingers do the walking.

A. M. Best is the rating service that rates more insurers than any of the other firms, so I'd start with them. Write down the list of insurers you're thinking of buying a policy from and call (908) 439-2200. You'll receive a Best ID number for each of the insurers you're interested in. Then call Best's automated ranking line at (900) 420-0400. You'll be prompted to enter the ID numbers to receive the latest Best rating of the insurers. It will cost you $2.50 per minute to use this automated service.

I wouldn't stop there, however. Every rating firm has its own criteria. Play it safe and make sure more than one of the rating services gives your insurer high marks. The second call I'd place would be to Weiss Research at (800) 289-9222. For a fee of $15 it will provide you with an oral report on a company. Obviously, ask for reports only on insurers that you've already learned Best rates highly.

Now you'll have a list of insurers rated highly by two services. As a final check, call the three other firms that rate insurers: Moody's at (212) 553-0377; Standard & Poor's at (212) 208-1527; and Duff &

Phelps at (312) 368-3157. They all provide one free quote over the telephone. Ask each for a rating of one of the insurers you've found were highly rated by both Best and Weiss. That will give you three independent judgments on three of your candidates.

If you've more than three candidates, or aren't satisfied with just three judgments, check all the candidates by using Standard & Poor's ratings on the Insurance News Network Website at http://www.insure.com. If you don't have Internet access, you can find books listing Moody's and Standard & Poor's ratings in the reference section of a good library.

Now, simply select the cheapest coverage from the healthiest insurer. From beginning to end the whole process will take half the time and be far less annoying than if you'd met with a broker or agent.

Living Trusts

46

Nearly every day in Florida and Arizona there's a seminar on living trusts being held at some retirement community's clubhouse. They usually begin with a charming lawyer standing up and telling the audience a series of horror stories about probate. The lawyer then segues into a presentation about how a living trust can keep an estate from going through probate. He might even imply that a living trust offers tax savings—even though it doesn't. The conclusion is a sales pitch about how living trusts can be set up easily and affordably. The seniors applaud appreciatively and then make appointments with the attorney.

I think the whole process is a farce. Probate isn't the nightmare it's made out to be (see chapter 57), and even if it was, a living trust wouldn't eliminate the need for your will to go through it. While they do have one very specific advantage, more than anything else living trusts are ways for lawyers to make more money.

What Is a Living Trust?

I think the well-respected personal finance author Jane Bryant Quinn put it best when she wrote that a living trust is like a "mirror maze in a fun house, where you see yourself in every glass." When you set up a living trust, you take whatever assets you'd like to transfer and hand them over to the trust. You no longer own them, the trust does. They are controlled by the person named trustee. The fun starts when you realize that you can name yourself trustee. (In some states you can even name yourself beneficiary as well, but that's another issue entirely.) Basically, the trust is a legal obfuscation.

Property placed in a living trust passes directly to a named beneficiary (or beneficiaries) when you die. The transfer doesn't need to be approved by a probate court, as it would have had it been accomplished in a will. But there's a catch.

Trusts May Not Keep Your Estate from Having to Go Through Probate

Only that property formally placed in the trust bypasses probate. Anything you buy subsequent to the formation of the trust that you fail to then actually transfer to the trust must go through probate. Few people, once having set up the trust, realize that they must continue to sign newly acquired assets over to it in order to keep them from going through probate.

Let's say you set up a living trust at age sixty-five. Two years later you buy a new car. A year after that you leave your job, sell your home in the Northeast, move south, start a consulting business, and buy a condominium apartment with some of the proceeds from the sale of your home. You deposit the rest into certificates of deposit until you see what your expenses will be and can figure out how much of an annuity to buy. You're walking back to your new car from the bank when a ninety-eight-year-old woman who can't see over the dashboard of her white Lincoln Town Car runs you over. Your dying thought is that at least your heirs won't have to go through probate. Wrong. You didn't transfer ownership of the car you bought to the trust. The new apartment was owned by you, not the trust, as was your new business, as were those certificates of deposit. All of those assets must be transferred by will and, therefore, must go through probate.[22]

The One Real Use for Living Trusts

In my eyes the one legitimate use for living trusts is privacy. Probate is a public process. People will be able to see exactly what

---

[22]There is a way around this: You need to have a "pour-over" will drafted. That guarantees that any assets or property you own that you forgot to transfer are added to the trust after you die.

assets you owned, what they are worth, and who they were transferred to, if they are passed by will and go through probate. For most people that's not a big deal. But if the deceased is famous, or infamous, it's likely the media will be there at the court to report on the whole process. If you think your financial life might be fodder for the media and you want to keep asset transfers private, your best bet is to set up a living trust.

Naturally "Avoiding" Probate

More and more assets are naturally bypassing probate these days. That's because wills are concerned solely with property that's owned individually or commonly *and* that does not have a named beneficiary. Jointly owned property—such as a checking account with two names—and property with a named beneficiary—like your pension savings—passes without regard to a will. Personal property, assuming no one files a complaint, also passes, not by will, but by private agreement among the family (see chapters 30, 57, and 72).

For Die Brokers over a certain age, there probably won't be any other assets to worry about. Most other investment funds will have been annuitized so they'll no longer be in the estate. And real estate will be subject to a reverse mortgage so it will be used to pay off the loan rather than pass to the estate. In all likelihood, the assets of Die Brokers will pass almost entirely outside of their will, so probate won't even be a minor concern.

Living Wills   47

Whenever a patient is determined to have only a short time to live, either due to advanced illness or a terminal injury, a health care provider is obligated to ask whether he wants to continue treatment. If the patient is conscious and mentally competent, he can answer for himself. If the patient isn't capable of answering, decisions can become very complicated and difficult.

Some doctors immediately turn to spouses and family members, following a statutory hierarchy—typically spouse, parent, child, sibling, etc., but generally not including an unmarried "significant other." Other doctors, for whatever reason, refuse to accept family judgments and insist the court appoint a guardian to make decisions.

Making Decisions When You Can't

Living wills are designed to avoid all these problems. They are formal documents that express an individual's wishes and beliefs about the extent of medical care to be used in the case of terminal injury or illness. They are supposed to answer your doctor's obligatory questions when you no longer can, freeing she, your family, or a court-appointed guardian from the responsibility of making decisions for you.

Laws differ from state to state about exactly how binding these documents are and how they should be phrased. (An attorney in your state will know the preferred form. It should take her about an hour to draft both a living will and its complementary durable power of attorney for health care.) However, when push comes to shove, just about any form is acceptable as "clear and convincing evidence" of a patient's wishes, as long as it has the right number and type of witnesses and clearly expresses those wishes.

Eliminating Potential Gaps and Loopholes

Living wills should be witnessed by two impartial adults. Impartial means they can't stand to inherit your estate, be in charge of your medical care, be legally responsible for paying your health care bills, or work for your health care provider. Once again, the easiest way to deal with this issue is to sign the document at your attorney's office so she and one of her associates can serve as witnesses.

As for expressing wishes clearly, a good attorney will have the right boilerplate language available. However, most such language provides for the continued provision of nourishment and fluids. (Almost all states require "comfort care," such as the wetting of a patient's mouth, always be provided.) It is usually very difficult for loved ones to make the decision to withhold nourishment and fluids, even if they know no suffering will be involved and it will speed the end. That's why it's important your living will specifically address the issues of nourishment and fluids. Many states actually require that language okaying the withholding of nourishment and fluids be in a separate section with an additional signature and two different witnesses.

Another important area that should be addressed by your living will is the difference between refusing to start treatment and stopping treatment that's already under way. Legally, there's actually no difference between the two acts, but many health care providers don't know that. They're often afraid that withdrawing treatment exposes them to legal liability. By making sure your living will expressly authorizes the withdrawal of treatment as well as the nonprovision of treatment, you avoid another potential problem for your survivors.

Finally, Die Brokers may need to make an additional, even more uncomfortable consideration.

The Die Broker's Special Dilemma

The survivors of someone who has pursued the traditional financial path actually *benefit* financially from pulling the plug. That's because there's often a sizable life insurance policy and/or a large estate that could be drained by prolonged, expensive end-of-life care. I'm not suggesting that ever enters into their decision making, or that it should—I'm just pointing out that their financial and emotional needs may be best served by the same decision.

The survivors of Die Brokers, on the other hand, may be *hurt* financially by pulling the plug. That's because there's apt to be disability insurance, an annuity, and perhaps a reverse mortgage that all pay out a certain amount of money . . . while the person is *living*. In this case, financial and emotional needs are not served by the same decision. Once again, I'm not suggesting that will or even should enter into *their* own feelings. However, *you* may want to address this dilemma in your living will.

Neither Permanent nor All-Encompassing

Living wills are easily changed or revoked. In fact, some states require them to be updated or at least reaffirmed periodically—usually every five or seven years. Rather than tearing up an old living will, it's better to cross out the contents, write that you're revoking the document and replacing it with a new one, and sign your name. That way it will be clear to everyone that the old living will was actually revoked and no longer accurately expresses your wishes.

Finally, it's important to recognize that a living will isn't sufficient to address all the potential problems your survivors may face if you're not capable of making your own decisions.

Living wills come into force only when a patient is deemed to be terminal—they have nothing to do with patients whose lives are just intolerable. Living wills deal only with life-support issues—they don't impact decisions like whether or not an operation should be performed on someone who's unconscious or incompetent. Finally, living wills cannot necessarily force a doctor to do or not do anything—they simply state your wishes. If they have a conscientious objection to carrying out your wishes, they are supposed to transfer you to another doctor, but if they're real zealots, they may resist and put up a legal battle. You'll eventually win, or die before a decision is reached . . . but only after your family has been put through hell. In order to solve or mitigate these problems you need a second legal document: a durable power of attorney for health care (see chapter 28).

Long-Term Care Insurance **48**

I really want to be able to tell you to take out long-term care insurance as soon as possible . . . but I can't.

In a better world it would fit Die Brokers like a glove. But the industry is a snake pit of lying salesmen, onerous provisions obscured by arcane language, fly-by-night insurers looking to make a quick buck, and horror stories that are all too common. There's little federal or state regulation or control over the business, and what few rules are in place are hardly ever enforced.[23] It really is a disgrace.

There is a tremendous need for long-term care insurance—not just for Die Brokers but for everyone. Neither Medicare nor Medigap policies cover extended stays in nursing homes or long-term custodial care in the home. Both must be paid for out of personal savings. About 43 percent of Americans who turn sixty-five will eventually spend some time in a nursing home. Twenty-five percent of those who do will stay in the home for at least a year, running up a bill of between $30,000 and $50,000.

[23]As this book was being written, Congress passed, and the president signed, The Health Insurance Portability and Accountability Act. Among its other provisions this bill has elements that try to make the coordination of benefits between long-term care policies and Medicare easier and try to clarify the tax treatment of long-term care insurance premiums and expenses. As part of this latter effort it says that only premiums on long-term care policies that are guaranteed renewable and that offer nonforfeiture options to guarantee benefits if the insurer goes out of the business will be deductible. This is only a first baby step down the road of regulating these policies and doesn't change my mind about them one bit.

That means at an age when their income is likely to be very low, some folks will be paying about twice the cost of a year at Harvard to have someone help them take a bath and change their bedpan. After saving for their entire lives they could end up going broke in a year and finding themselves on government assistance. Those who have the time and savvy to plan in advance are forced to deceive the government and artificially impoverish themselves, in effect taking money away from the truly deserving poor (see chapters 7 and 49). These folks are certainly dying broke, they're just not getting to enjoy their lives in the process.

This is just the kind of scenario at which insurance should theoretically excel: protecting against a rare but potentially disastrous circumstance. And make no mistake about it, the insurers are aware of the market. In fact, it's the hottest product in the insurance business. In 1987, the first year the Health Insurance Association of America kept records on the product, about 100,000 policies were sold. The next year the number jumped to 1.1 million. In 1989 1.5 million were being sold. And by 1990 it was 1.6 million. In 1987 only 75 companies sold long-term care insurance. By 1990 the number had climbed to 130. The shame is that most of the products being sold are inadequate, and those policies that actually do what they advertise are so expensive that only the wealthiest of people can afford them.

What Do They Really Cover?

There are three different types of policies that fall under the general title long-term care insurance: the first covers stays in nursing homes; the second covers health care in the home; the third covers both. However, it's essential you're clear on exactly what's meant by terms like "nursing home" and "home health care."

When they first came out, many of these policies defined "nursing home" narrowly as a skilled nursing facility that provides twenty-four-hour medical care by licensed personnel. Few people stay in such facilities for very long. Long stays—the ones that you need coverage for—are more apt to be in intermediate and custodial care facilities. Thankfully, most (but not all) policies today don't distinguish between the three levels of care.

However, you still need to be careful about what the policies categorize as eligible facilities. Some say they'll pay for custodial care, but only if it's provided in a skilled or intermediate care facility, ruling out most "adult homes" that are specifically designed to provide custodial care. Other policies say facilities must be over a certain size or have a certain type of medical staff available constantly.

Home health care is even more problematic. What most people need is someone to come in and make them a meal, clean up, run errands, and help them wash and dress. Unfortunately, that's not what insurance companies consider home health care. Some pay only for skilled care provided by registered or practical nurses or occupational or physical therapists. Others pay for licensed home health aides who will help with bathing, dressing, and moving from one place to another, but not with homemaking services. Only a few companies will pay for such services, and they generally have very strict limits on how much they'll pay. The best policies will also pay for these services in adult day care centers.

Not Everyone Can Get Coverage

Some long-term care insurance companies are very picky about who they'll cover, turning down about half of those who apply. If you've had a stroke, diabetes, asthma, high blood pressure, eye problems, cancer, or hip replacement surgery, you may be turned down, forced to wait for coverage, and/or charged a higher premium. Still, it's better to deal with a company that's selective than one that accepts everyone.

That's because many of the companies that will sign up everyone use an insidious practice called "postclaims underwriting." Once a claim is filed, the company checks the accuracy of the application and the candidate's medical history. If the claim is filed within two years of when the application was accepted, and the company discovers something that would have led it to reject the application, it can deny benefits and/or cancel the policy. If there are fraudulent statements on the application, claims can be denied no matter how long it has been since it was first filed. Unfortunately, this isn't just an admonition against lying. There have quite a few instances in which agents, eager to collect their commission, make honest mistakes or fill out the application "creatively," either with the client's tacit cooperation or on their own volition.

Qualifying for Benefits Is Difficult

Being able to buy a policy that pays for the right kind of care is one thing. Actually qualifying for benefits is often something else entirely.

The best policies say that you qualify for benefits if your doctor says you need the care. Most policies, however, say that in order to qualify for benefits, care must be medically necessary due to sickness or injury. Some add that you must first spend a certain number of days in a hospital. Obviously, not everyone who enters a home, particularly those who need only custodial care, are doing so because of a specific sickness or injury, or after a hospital stay. Even if you were entering the home because of a particular problem, the insurer, not your doctor, would be the one who decided if care was "medically necessary." And remember, it's in the insurer's interest to define medical necessity very narrowly.

Other policies say you're eligible for benefits if you can't safely perform a number of "activities of daily living," such as eating, remembering to take your medication, using the toilet and maintaining continence, bathing and dressing, or walking or moving from one place to another—say, from a bed to a chair. While this should be more realistic than the sickness/injury qualification, it depends on how the insurer defines "safely" and "activities of daily living" and how many deficiencies are required to qualify for benefits. And once again it's the insurer, not a third party, who makes those judgments.

Many early policies explicitly refused to cover Alzheimer's disease. Gratefully that's now illegal—however, some insurers still try to get around paying benefits to Alzheimer's sufferers. If the insurer uses the activities-of-daily-living standard and won't pay benefits to those whose only problem is memory loss, someone who has Alzheimer's but is otherwise physically fit can be refused coverage.

How Much Will That Benefit Really Help?

No long-term care insurer says it will pay your nursing home or home health care bills for you. What it says is it will provide you with a monetary benefit for every day you need those services. For nursing home care, benefits range from around $40 to over $200 a day. For home health care the benefits could be daily ($50 to $150), hourly ($5 to $20), or up to a lifetime maximum ($30,000 to $60,000). Policies that cover both nursing home and home care often simply pay half the nursing home benefit for in-home care. These benefits can last either for as short a period as one year or for your entire lifetime. Benefits can also start immediately or after a waiting period of from twenty to a hundred days, during which time you're paying the bills. As you might imagine, the larger the benefit, the longer it lasts, and the sooner it starts, the higher the premium.

The major problem with this system is that you're selecting a benefit today that you may not be receiving for another twenty or thirty years. Let's say today's average nursing home stay costs $100 a day. You're sixty-five and you buy a policy that pays exactly that as its daily benefit. If you're unlucky enough to need to use the policy right away, you'll be fine. But what if you're in good health and don't need to claim a benefit until you're eighty-five? Well, if you assume a moderate inflation rate of 5 percent a year, that nursing home is going to cost you about $265 a day in two decades. After paying the premium for twenty years, you're not even going to have half your bill covered. The scenario is worse for someone who buys the policy when he's fifty-five. If he doesn't file a claim until he's eighty-five, and we assume the same 5 percent rate of inflation, he'll be facing daily bills of more than $432 with only a $100 benefit.

The solution is pretty obvious: take out an inflation protection rider, just like the one you've probably got on your disability and homeowner policies. Unfortunately, the inflation protection offered on long-term care insurance policies is generally both inadequate and expensive.

Some insurers deal with inflation risk through "premium inflation notes." These give policyholders the periodic opportunity to buy added coverage at the new rate for their age without having to prove their continued insurability. Of course, the price for this added coverage can be quite high. In addition, some policies stop offering future opportunities to those who pass one of these periodic offers.

Other insurers simply sell a rider that increases the benefit by a percentage each year. Not all such riders compound the increases, however. Using that same $100 benefit from our earlier example, you can see the difference: A 5 percent yearly increase that's compounded would result in a benefit of $265 in twenty years; if it's not compounded, it results in a benefit of only $200.

To make matters worse, some insurers offer inflation protection for only a limited number of years—from ten to twenty years—or up until you're a certain age—usually eighty or eighty-five. Buy one of these policies when you're young, say fifty, and your benefit will be frozen at what's likely to be a less than sufficient level.

The charges for inflation protection either are factored into a level premium—adding between 25 and 40 percent to the bill—or become simply a reflection of the added benefit—you pay 5 percent more for a 5 percent increase in benefit. These added fees come on top of already high costs.

What's the Bill?

There are so many possible variations to these policies that talking about average costs has limited value. Still, in order for you to get some idea of the numbers, you can figure that a combined nursing home/home health care policy, paying about $100 a day for nursing home care and $50 a day for home care, for four years, after a thirty-day waiting period, with inflation protection, would cost a fifty-five-year-old from $625 to $700 a year, a sixty-five-year-old from $1,250 to $1,400 a year, and a seventy-five-year-old from $2,500 to $2,800 a year. Of course, if you increase the size and length of benefits and/or decrease the waiting period, the premiums will go up.

While these policies are guaranteed renewable, their premiums aren't etched in stone. Most of the policies have "level premiums," which means rates don't go up based on a policyholder's increasing age. However, rates can and do go up if the insurer has to pay out more claims than it projected. With companies currently cutting rates in order to capture market share, odds are they'll climb once claims start rolling in. In other words, today's bargain may be tomorrow's dog.

What About a Group Policy?

The increasing popularity of long-term care insurance has led some employers—generally large corporations—to offer it as an employee benefit. Usually employees are offered one set plan and must pay the entire premium themselves.

There are some advantages to these group policies. First, they're usually a bit cheaper than individual policies. Second, every employee who applies is often accepted, regardless of medical history (spouses and parents are carefully screened, however). And third, you can usually buy group policies at a younger age than individual policies.

Unfortunately, there are disadvantages too. Group policies rarely have inflation protection. Worse yet, they're not always portable. If you can't take a policy with you, paying the same rate when you switch jobs (and as we know, you *will* be switching jobs), you'll have thrown those premium dollars away.

Group policies make sense in one scenario: someone who wants coverage who wouldn't be able to buy it on his own and can take the policy with him when he leaves.

So What's a Die Broker to Do?

Now you know why I called long-term care insurance a nightmare. Of course, you didn't buy this book just to hear how bad things are, you want some answers and advice. Okay, here's my best advice.

If you're under sixty-five years old, forget about long-term care insurance for the time being. This market is growing so rapidly and is so filled with poor products and outright rip-offs that even the most laissez-faire Republicans will eventually agree it needs federal regulation and standardization similar to what was done to clean up Medigap. Buying when you're young will save you money. However, you're gambling that the policy you buy now will still look good five years from now. My advice is to wait and count on things getting better. If they don't, you'll have to spend a little more; if they do, you'll own coverage in which you can have added confidence.

If you're sixty-five years old or older, buy the best policy you can afford from a healthy insurer. (See chapters 11 and 45 to learn how to check insurers' health.) Become as much of a self-insurer as possible by opting for the longest waiting period. Insist on inflation protection that uses compounding. Get as high a benefit as you can, but for only a year. Most people don't require care for longer than that, and a year will give the family enough time to make any needed financial or lifestyle changes (see chapters 8 and 45). If you're single, your spouse is in ill health, and/or you live far from other family, get combined nursing home/home health care coverage. If you're married and your spouse is in good health and/or you have close family nearby, consider getting just home health care coverage.

Regardless of your age, resolve to adopt the Die Broke program and start converting your assets to income and start spending it as soon as you reach sixty.

Medicaid   49

Medicaid is a joint federal and state program established in 1965 (at the same time as Medicare) designed to take care of the medical needs of the indigent. Sounds straightforward, right? Well, it has become anything but. It's a political, economic, and ethical morass that shows no sign of clearing up anytime soon. Luckily for you, as a Die Broker you may be able to sidestep this swamp. (Your parents, on the other hand, *will* need to deal with this issue. You can help them out by going back and rereading chapter 7.)

As you've figured out by now, one of the secrets to not going broke *before* you die is to establish and maintain an adequate safety net of insurance coverage: health, disability, and Medigap. With those in place you and your family should have fewer worries about your ever becoming poor enough (naturally or artificially) to qualify for Medicaid.

Obtain and keep up good comprehensive and major medical health insurance coverage (see chapter 35) until you qualify for Medicare (see chapter 50) at age sixty-five, and then supplement your protection with Medigap (see chapter 51) coverage. That will ensure you'll be able to pay any doctor and hospital bills.

Take out disability coverage (see chapter 25) to ensure you'll have an income to pay your other premiums even if you're unable to work. If the long-term care insurance industry (see chapter 48) has cleaned up its act by the time you're sixty-five, consider taking out a policy that will cover nursing home and/or at-home care.

Finally, resolve to Die Broke (see chapter 5) rather than build up an estate. That way you'll already have made use of or given away your assets—you'll have neither the need nor the urge to artificially impoverish yourself.

As you know from reading chapter 7, I have some real ethical difficulties with the whole issue of Medicaid planning. I can accept it as a necessary evil for those who, like your parents, have no other choice. But I have a great deal of trouble with promoting it for people who have time to make other arrangements. By taking advantage of legislative loopholes and savvy financial planning, middle- and even upper-income people can qualify for an underfunded program designed to help the truly poor; in effect, those who "have" can take funds away from those who don't. What's even more disturbing to me is that some of these same "haves" spend their younger years bemoaning federal and state spending on entitlements.

Medicare   **50**

First the good news. You don't have to retire to qualify for Medicare; the day you turn sixty-five, whether you're working or not, you can get health insurance from Uncle Sam. Now the bad news: Uncle Sam's not the best insurer around. Medicare is another one of those federal programs that is simultaneously a success and a fiasco.

Created in 1965 (along with Medicaid—see chapter 49), Medicare was supposed to make sure elderly Americans wouldn't have to worry about paying for medical care by providing them with guaranteed health insurance. It *has* done a great job of making sure the elderly can afford care for "acute illnesses": serious yet finite conditions like heat attacks, strokes, and broken hips. However, it doesn't do such a good job at helping people afford preventative or custodial care. Instead of Medicare being comprehensive health insurance coverage, it has evolved into decent coverage for hospital stays, surgery, and postoperative care that needs to be supplemented with other major medical and long-term care plans.

Medicare has also been an utter flop at controlling health care costs. Senior citizens' average out-of-pocket spending on medical expenses has doubled (after accounting for inflation) since Medicare was enacted, from about $1,600 in 1961 to about $3,305 in 1991. And on top of that they need to spend at least another $1,000 annually, on average, for their own supplemental insurance policies to cover the gaps in Medicare coverage.

Mind Your As and Bs

Medicare is actually a two-part package: Medicare Part A and Medicare Part B.

Medicare Part A provides, with some limitations,[24] coverage for hospitalization and surgery, stays in skilled nursing facilities, some home and hospice health care, and blood transfusions. To qualify you must be eligible to collect Social Security or be the dependent of someone qualified to collect Social Security. (Others, such as noncitizens and government workers who don't participate in Social Security, can obtain Medicare for an annual premium.) Medicare is funded by 1.45 percent tax on salaries, with no cap on contributions. Since, as a Die Broker, you'll still be working while you're collecting benefits, you'll actually be paying 1.45 percent of your salary for your Medicare.

And that won't be all you're paying. If you want major medical–style coverage you'll need to apply and pay for Medicare Part B. That covers—again with limitations, conditions, copayments, and deductibles—medical expenses, lab services, some home health care, outpatient hospital treatment, and blood transfusions. The premium for this coverage currently amounts to about $50 a month, or $600 a year. (It increases each year at the same rate as the Social Security cost-of-living adjustment, and jumps 10 percent every year you're eligible and not working that you don't apply.) If you were retired and collecting Social Security and opted for Medicare Part B, the premium would be deducted from your Social Security check. However, since you're a Die Broker, you'll have to pay this yourself.

Getting the Boss to Foot the Bill

That doesn't mean it has to come out of your paycheck, though. Federal law requires all employers who offer health insurance to their employees to also offer it to over-sixty-five employees and their

---

[24]As you might have guessed, the limitiations and exclusions for Medicare coverage are just as, if not more, confusing than those you've come to expect from your current private health insurance. Listing them here would take up lots of space and time. Besides, between the time this was written and the time you read it the rules may change. Instead, I'd suggest you make a few telephone calls and do some side reading. First, call the Social Security Administration at (800) 772-1213 for the location of your local SSA office. They'll have some info that can help. Second, contact the American Association of Retired Persons (AARP) at (800) 424-3410 and ask for their relevant brochures and booklets. Third, head over to your local bookstore or library and look for books on the topic. The best that I've run across are *Medicare Made Easy* by Charles B. Inlander and Charles K. MacKay (Addison-Wesley, 1989) and Consumer Reports' *Medicare/Medigap: The Essential Guide for Older Americans and Their Families* (Consumer Reports Books, 1990).

spouses. That means you could just keep your employer's plan and not take out Medicare Part B until you're no longer covered at work. As long as you've been covered at work, you won't have to pay the annual 10 percent premium increases when you do apply. You could also keep your employer's plan, pay for Medicare Part B coverage on your own, and use it as secondary insurance. However, what's more than likely to happen is that your employer will ask you to switch to Medicare Part B and offer to pick up the cost of the premium—it will probably cost less than keeping you on his or her group policy.

Apply on Time

Everyone has his or her own seven-month window, centered on the month you turn sixty-five, to apply for Medicaid. You can apply as early as three months before your sixty-fifth birthday. If you do, your coverage will begin the day of your birthday. If you wait until the month you turn sixty-five, coverage will begin the first of the next month. If you procrastinate and wait until after you turn sixty-five, there's a two-month wait for coverage to kick in. And if you really drag your feet and fail to apply within three months after your birthday, you'll have to wait until the general enrollment period—January 1 through March 31—to apply and your coverage won't start until July.

Retiree Health Benefits and Medicare

Even though you're not retiring in the traditional sense, there's nothing that says you can't collect retiree pension benefits from a longtime employer while working for someone else who may or may not provide health insurance. If you're covered by a retiree health plan, you can still collect Medicare when you turn sixty-five. In this case, the retiree plan becomes secondary insurance or Medigap coverage.

Filling the Gaps

Medigap is supplemental private insurance that covers many of the costs Medicare Parts A and B won't. While private, it is strictly regulated by both the federal government and the individual states. That makes it so complex it merits a separate chapter (see chapter 51).

Taking out your own long-term care insurance (see chapter 48) is another way to cover the gap between what Medicare covers and what you'll actually need. However, the industry is as perilous as Medigap used to be, so for the moment I'm hesitant about encouraging you to buy a policy unless you're already over sixty-five.

Putting Together a Package of Plans

After reading this chapter it should be obvious why health care is one of the great conundrums of American life. Right now there's no simple solution to the problem of post-sixty-five health care coverage: Everyone has to fashion his or her own individual crazy quilt of different insurance policies into the best protection he or she can afford. Still, I think I can safely suggest a general plan for Die Brokers who turn sixty-five.

Assuming you've followed the advice in other chapters, you'll have good health and disability coverage already in place. Apply for Medicare Part A three months before your sixty-fifth birthday—you have been paying for it all your life and will continue to pay for it as long as you collect a salary, so you might as well get something for your money.

Next, go to your employer and discuss the situation. Remember, he or she cannot refuse you continued coverage if it's offered to everyone else.[25] Still, you don't want that to be a potential roadblock to your continued employment. It's possible you can work out a deal in which your employer picks up the cost of Medicare Part B and maybe even a Medigap policy rather than keeping you on the company's group policy.

If you're paying for your own health insurance, either because you're not covered through an employer or you're self-employed, simply shift your coverage and premium dollars to Medicare Part B. Then (after reading chapters 51 and 48) analyze what you need in a Medigap pol-

---

[25]Surprise, surprise—the law is a quite complex. It says employers must provide "equal" benefits to employees regardless of age. Clearly it costs more to provide some benefits (including health insurance) to older workers than younger workers. While an employer cannot force older employees to contribute more, he or she can give them smaller benefits. However, if participation in the company plan is voluntary, older employees can be charged more as long as the increase represents the actual premium. If the employer pays the whole premium for employee coverage he or she must do so for older workers as well, even though it will raise costs. If the employees pay the entire premium themselves, older employees will have to pay more for the same coverage. If the employer and employees split the cost of the premium, the employer must pay the same percentage of every employee's premium, regardless of their age.

icy and perhaps a long-term care policy to cover the inevitable gaps in coverage.

This time I'll give you the bad news first: Odds are you'll need at least some form of Medigap policy. The good news is the total cost for Medicare Part B and your Medigap policy will be quite a bit less than you were paying for coverage before you turned sixty-five.

Medigap Insurance 51

The third and least well known of the old-age health insurance programs, Medigap is actually a type of private supplemental coverage.
Its purpose, as the name implies, is to cover the gaps in Medicare coverage. It's important, particularly for Die Brokers, because unless covered, those gaps can turn into huge black holes sucking away all your
disposable dollars.

Even though Medigap coverage is private, it's highly regulated by
both federal and state governments. That's because prior to regulation
the business was home to more than its share of con men and rip-off
artists, eager to scare the elderly and take their money. (They've now
moved into the long-term care insurance business.)

Because it's so tightly controlled and administered, and still quite
affordable, Medigap offers Die Brokers their best first chance to cover
the holes in Medicare coverage. Long-term care insurance (see chapter
48), still largely unregulated and very expensive, should be used only
by the handful of people sixty-five or over who can afford to gamble
with the premiums.

Buy It ASAP

There's no question you need Medigap coverage. Health care costs
have risen so high that even if you're just responsible for the
deductible and coinsurance you'll be facing big bills. If your surgeon

or doctor charges more than Medicare deems "reasonable and customary," or you need a procedure Medicare's bean counters don't think is necessary, your out-of-pocket costs for health care could bankrupt you.

There's also no debate about when you should buy it. If you apply within six months of first being covered by Medicare Part B, insurers *must* sell you the policy you want, even if you're a high risk or have a preexisting condition. They can, however, refuse to cover you for that preexisting condition for the first six months of the policy. After that six-month window, insurers can refuse to sell you some or all their Medigap policies and can charge much higher rates on the policies they *will* sell you.

All Medigap plans must be guaranteed renewable—that means once issued, they can't be canceled as long as you pay the premiums.

So much for the easy decisions. Now you've got to select what category of Medigap policy you want.

Ten Potential Choices

The federal government has authorized ten different standardized Medigap insurance plans, labeled A through J. Each individual state, however, has the right to decide which and how many of the ten plans are offered for sale to its residents. That means a resident of, say, New York may be able to choose from all ten, while a resident of Wyoming may have only five choices.

The basic coverage, Plan A, is offered in every state and must be offered by every company that sells Medigap insurance. It covers:

- All the coinsurance payments you'd be responsible for if you were hospitalized for over sixty days
- All the coinsurance you'd have to pay for nonhospital care (Medicare Part B)
- The first three pints of blood you'd need, whether in or out of the hospital
  The ultimate coverage, Plan J covers:
- All the coinsurance payments you'd be responsible for if you were hospitalized for over sixty days
- Your deductibles for all hospitalization expenses
- All the coinsurance and deductibles you'd have to pay for nonhospital care (Medicare Part B)
- The first three pints of blood you need

- Your coinsurance charges for days 21 through 100 in a skilled nursing facility
- 100 percent of any doctor's fees above the approved amounts
- Foreign emergency medical care
- At-home recovery costs
- Prescription drugs
- Preventative medical care

The other eight plans offer various coverages in between these two extremes. Choosing from among them can be quite confusing. Thankfully, every insurer selling Medigap policies must provide you with a comparison chart showing exactly what each plan does and doesn't cover, as well as the charges for each. (See the chart on page 249.)

You can also call your local Social Security office and have them send you their free brochure *Guide to Health Insurance for People with Medicare*. Just remember to follow that up with a call to your own state's Department of Aging, since each state has its own package of plans.

You should also write or call the United Seniors Health Cooperative (1331 H Street, NW, Suite 500, Washington, DC 20005; (202) 393-6222) and ask for their free analyses of Medigap policies.

Choosing a Plan

The secret to choosing which plan is right for you is examining your particular needs, circumstances, and personal budget. For instance, while it might sound nice to get coverage for any doctor's fees above the allowed limits, it's now moot: Such excess charges are now illegal. Similarly, coverage for prescription drugs makes sense only if you're spending a lot of money on drugs each year; the coverage is quite expensive and still requires a 50 percent copayment. That means you could end up spending more for this coverage than you could ever get back.

Comparison-Shop

After you have selected one or two plans that seem right, your next step is to comparison-shop. This part is actually quite easy. The government requires that every Plan A policy, for instance, not only offer the same exact coverage but also look the same and use identical wordings and definitions. The only variations are the premium and alacrity with which the insurer responds to claims.

Get three quotes for each type of plan you're considering: one from a large group, like the American Association of Retired Persons (601 E Street NW, Suite 500, Washington, DC 20049; (800) 424-3410 or (202) 434-2277) or your union or trade association; a second from your state's not-for-profit health insurer, like Blue Cross/Blue Shield; and a third through your local independent insurance broker (see chapter 41).

Next, speak to your employer. Many employee health plans can be turned into Medigap plans once you qualify for Medicare (see chapter 50). In other cases, employers will ask you to find your own policy but will pay the premium.

As a general rule, group policies, such as those offered by AARP, are cheaper than individual plans. Just make sure the initial price quote isn't a lowball that will jump dramatically in two or three years. While all Medigap plans are guaranteed renewable, there are no restrictions on how much or how often premiums can be increased.

After you've got your price quotes, investigate the reputation of the insurers for settling claims. Check with your state's office of insurance to see if it compiles any relevant statistics, reports, or studies. Then contact local and national senior citizen advocacy groups to see if they've any information you could use. Finally, take a trip to the library or out on the Internet to find *Consumer Reports'* most recent story rating health insurance companies.

Consider Alternatives

You definitely need some kind of policy to fill the gaps in your Medicare coverage, but that doesn't mean it has to be a Medigap policy. Consider these three alternatives that may be available in your state:

• There's a trial program called **Medicare Select** available in fifteen states. It provides a Medigap type of coverage for considerably less than traditional Medigap policies, by requiring you to use specified hospitals and doctors, just like an HMO. It has all the benefits *and* all the disadvantages of traditional HMOs (see chapter 35).

• Speaking of HMOs, some sell streamlined **Medigap-style HMO plans** to nonmembers.

• There are also a handful of states that offer their own **state Medigap insurance** plans.

Part of a Package

The final thing to consider when shopping to solve the Medigap puzzle is long-term care insurance (see chapter 48). No Medigap plan covers long-term stays in a nursing home or an assisted living home, or long-term home health care or assistance. The only way to get such coverage is to buy it separately.

MEDIGAP INSURANCE PLANS

Plan Benefits*	A	B	C	D	E	F	G	H	I	J
Hospital coinsurance days 61–90	✓	✓	✓	✓	✓	✓	✓	✓	✓	✓
Lifetime reserve coinsurance days 91–50	✓	✓	✓	✓	✓	✓	✓	✓	✓	✓
365 hospital days—100%	✓	✓	✓	✓	✓	✓	✓	✓	✓	✓
Medicare Pts A & B blood	✓	✓	✓	✓	✓	✓	✓	✓	✓	✓
Medicare Pt B coinsurance	✓	✓	✓	✓	✓	✓	✓	✓	✓	✓
SNF coinsurance days 21–100			✓	✓	✓	✓	✓	✓	✓	✓
Medicare Pt A deductibles		✓	✓	✓	✓	✓	✓	✓	✓	✓
Medicare Pt B deductibles		✓				✓				✓
% Medicare Pt B excess charges						100	80		100	100
Emergency foreign care			✓	✓	✓	✓	✓	✓	✓	✓
At-home recovery				✓			✓			✓
Prescription drugs								✓	✓	✓
Preventative care					✓					✓

*Just remember, most of these benefits have ceilings above which the insurer will not pay.

There's a problem with this approach, however. Long-term care insurance is very expensive and very risky. You need to sit down and figure out if long-term care insurance makes sense for you today. (I think it does only if you're currently sixty-five or older.) If it does, then you need to compare your potential Medigap and long-term care policies so you're not paying for duplicate coverage.

If it doesn't make sense for you, all you can do is make sure your Medicare and Medigap policies work together as a package, covering as many health crises as you practically can.

Money Market Accounts **52**

Money market accounts are the Die Broker's equivalent of the piggy bank. Since they're as secure as a savings or checking account but offer greater interest and are more flexible than a certificate of deposit, they're the perfect place to temporarily park your savings until you're ready to invest them in something more productive.

The only real disadvantages of money market accounts are: they often let you write only a limited number of checks per month (usually three) for no less than a minimum amount (usually $250 or $500); and they usually require a minimum balance of between $1,000 and $2,500. But for Die Brokers those really aren't problems. It's doubtful you'll ever write more than three checks a month on the account or write checks for small amounts, since you'll be using those checks only to make investments. The minimum balance (along with your emergency certificates of deposit) can simply be viewed as the cash portion of your investment portfolio.

I recommend opening your money market account at the same bank or credit union where you have your checking account (see chapter 21) and your set of emergency fund certificates of deposits (see chapter 18). That way it will be easy to move funds between them if you must.

Mortgage Loans

53

While Die Brokers should abandon serial house ownership (see chapter 39) they should adopt serial mortgage financing.

Back when it made economic sense to buy a house, own it for a short time, and then sell to buy another, it also made sense to take out an adjustable-rate mortgage (ARM). The advantage of an ARM was that the interest rate was generally locked in for a short period of time at a lower rate than a comparable fixed mortgage. The idea was that you could take advantage of that low rate, and then, just when it started to climb, you'd be ready to sell the property. If you were going to stay in the house for only a few years, it didn't matter what the interest rate would do over the long term.

Today, Die Brokers are looking for a home rather than a house, a place where they can stay for the rest of their lives. That means long-term concerns now come first. As a result, I'm encouraging my Die Broker clients to take out fixed-rate mortgages. While they may be a bit more expensive initially than an equivalent ARM, at least you know they will never climb. And with your income apt to be erratic in the twenty-first century (if it isn't already), that's important. If interest rates eventually drop two points or so below the fixed rate, you can always refinance.

Similarly, the standard advice used to be to take out a thirty-year mortgage, since that would lower your monthly payment. Since you were going to be selling the house soon anyway, it didn't matter that it would take longer to build up equity. Today, Die Brokers should seriously consider a fifteen-year mortgage instead. While the monthly payments *are* slightly higher, your equity builds more than twice as fast. That will let you take out a home equity loan for renovation work that much sooner.

We used to think we'd own three or four homes in our lives: a starter house, a second house, maybe a trophy house, and then a retirement home. Now we know the best approach is to buy just one, but maybe to take out three or four mortgages on it: an initial fixed-rate mortgage, a refinanced fixed-rate mortgage, maybe a home equity loan (see chapter 36), and then finally a reverse mortgage (see chapter 62).

Mutual Funds

54

I'm convinced that when historians look back on the latter part of the twentieth century, they'll universally say that the single most important development in personal finance was the emergence of the mutual fund.

The magic is quite simple: By bringing together a large number of small investors, mutual funds are able to compile a big enough pot of cash to assemble a more diversified portfolio than any one small investor could amass on his or her own. In effect, the small investor is leveraging his or her money to get a far greater or safer yield than would otherwise be possible. I can't come up with a single investment that's not made safer by investing through a mutual fund. That's why one of the fixed laws of the Die Broke program is:

Invest only through mutual funds.

Avoid the temptation to ever become a stock picker. Even if you think you've stumbled across a sure thing—the next Microsoft, for instance—don't bite. At least don't take such a discrete bite. If you must play a hunch, do so through a sector fund that includes your sure thing. Granted, if it is the next Microsoft, you won't make as much money. But if it's not, you won't have lost your shirt. And as a Die Broker you're counting on turning that shirt into an income to support yourself when your salary drops. When a Die Broker takes a long shot, he's not betting his children's future, he's betting his own.

That being said, not every mutual fund is a winner. And thanks to their incredible popularity there are now more than five thousand of them. There are businesses, publications, newsletters, and on-line services whose sole purpose is to measure and chart the performance of all these funds. It has become as difficult, if not more so, to pick mutual funds than it was to pick individual stocks. That's why my suggestion is to cancel your subscriptions to all those tracking services and instead rely on the wisdom, knowledge, and expertise of your financial planner.

Pensions

55

Just because the IRS calls something a retirement pension or account doesn't mean it has to be used for exactly that purpose.

Even though, as a Die Broker, you don't believe in retirement, you should still be taking full advantage of every retirement pension device you can. If your employer offers a 401(k), fund it to the max. If you're self-employed, put as much money in your SEP or Keogh as you possibly can. Why? Because whatever money you put in these accounts is tax deferred. That can dramatically increase the effective yield on whatever investments are made through these pensions. The more of your savings you can put in tax-deferred pensions, the faster your net worth will grow.

Of course, those taxes will have to be paid at some time, since the IRS will eventually force you to start withdrawing money from these pensions—generally six months after your seventieth birthday.

Rather than looking at these instruments as pensions, Die Brokers should look at them as their own wonderful version of tax-deferred annuities. In effect, they're investments funded with pretax dollars that grow tax deferred, which will then turn into streams of unearned income just at the time when your earned income will be dropping. They, along with your remaining earned income, the payments from the immediate annuities you buy with your other savings, and the payments on your reverse mortgage, will make up the total stream of income you'll be living off of for the last two decades of your life.

Pre- and Postnuptial Agreements **56**

I think prenuptial agreements have gotten a bad rap. Whenever they're mentioned, the image that comes to mind is of a rich old man forcing his poor young wife to sign away her rights to half his money should they divorce. They seem to memorialize the lesser financial status of women. But that need not be the case. In fact, prenuptial agreements, properly understood and placed in the right context, may actually be more valuable and applicable to women than men.

A nuptial, or marital, agreement is simply a legal document defining the ownership of assets within a marriage and outlining what effect the dissolution of the marriage would have on the ownership of those assets. A prenuptial agreement is one signed prior to the marriage, while a postnuptial agreement is one signed after the marriage takes place. Most often, these agreements are used to ensure that assets owned by one spouse prior to the marriage remain entirely the property of that spouse and his or her estate. There are three times when I believe such agreements aren't just acceptable but essential.

The Most Common, and Most Important, Prenuptial: Second Marriages

While the agreements involving rich men and their trophy wives get all the ink, most prenuptial agreements are prudent documents signed by older couples of similar economic status who are remarrying. Generally one or both parties have children from a prior marriage, and the couple doesn't intend to have any children together. Both spouses are usually coming to the relationship with already established financial lives—probably including real estate and investment portfolios. Each individual wants to make sure that the assets acquired prior to the marriage—often through the efforts of a deceased spouse—remain in the original family. Should they divorce—more common in second marriages than first—they want to leave the union with at least as much as they brought to it. Should they die unexpectedly, without having used up all their assets, they want them to go to their own children rather than to their new spouse and subsequently to his or her children.

Most of these agreements divide the assets of the couple into three categories: those brought to the marriage by the wife, those brought to the marriage by the husband, and those acquired during the marriage. The most common arrangement is for the assets brought to the marriage to remain the property of the individual spouse, reverting to that spouse in case of divorce or passing on to that spouse's children should he or she die. The assets acquired during the marriage are generally to be split by the parties should they divorce or to pass to the surviving spouse when one dies, and then, if need be, to all the children from both prior marriages.

In my mind, these agreements are absolutely essential for all men and women entering second marriages.

Another Valid Prenuptial Scenario: Female Financial Independence

With women marrying for the first time later in life than in previous generations, more of them are bringing their own assets to the relationship. The thirty-year-old women about to get married for the first time may already own an apartment or home. She could have an investment portfolio on her own, through her retirement plan at work, or both. Having worked hard to establish financial independence, she should not give it up just because of a marriage, especially since, if she intends to have a child, she may have to leave the job market for a time. These premarriage assets can be a financial security blanket, providing the kind of financial independence that women all too often lose in marriage. If she retains those assets independently (perhaps selling her apartment and investing the proceeds in her portfolio), she will never find herself stuck in an unhappy marriage because she's financially dependent on her husband.

While you might think that what was good for the goose would be good for the gander, I don't believe so. Most studies show that women end up in worse financial shape after a divorce, while men, after a couple of shaky years, actually end up in a better financial position than when they were married. That's due to income inequality between the sexes, women taking time off to have children, and the propensity of judges to limit support awards to working women. Whatever the cause, it's a situation that can't be ignored. So if it's just a matter of bringing sizable personal assets into a first marriage, I think a prenuptial is justified if it's for the woman's protection. Of course, like most rules, there's an exception.

A Third Valid Use: Protecting the Family Business

Anyone who owns a share of a family business should have a prenuptial agreement, not for his or her own protection, but for the protection of the other owners of the business. If you get married without signing a prenuptial, and you divorce, your spouse could be entitled to one-half of your share of the business. If the business was a source of income for you during the marriage, it will continue to help the divorced spouse, if deemed necessary by a court, when that income flows as alimony. Of course, the agreement can be written (as can all prenuptials) to allow for a change in terms should the marriage produce a child or end due to your death. In those cases it would probably be proper for the child or widow to retain an ownership interest.

Probate

57

It's remarkable how a system designed to ensure justice can become the embodiment of injustice. That's exactly what has happened to probate.

Probate is the legal process by which a court makes sure that a will is valid and that property is passed to the right person(s). It was supposed to defend the deceased and the rightful recipients of bequests. Unfortunately, it occasionally became a quagmire. Estates were sometimes tied up for years by lawyers who were making huge hourly fees by either challenging or defending the provisions of a will. Judges, with other cases they thought were more pressing on their dockets, let cases run on interminably. Meanwhile, assets sometimes lost value through neglect or inattentive management, while people who might be in desperate need of a bequest waited and waited. As the number of horrible anecdotes increased, probate became the legal equivalent of root canal—something horrible to be avoided at all costs.

In response, a new industry sprang up to help people avoid probate. Many of the same lawyers who were making money on probate saw the way the wind was blowing and started peddling living trusts (see chapter 46) designed to avoid probate. In effect, they were swapping one profitable line for another. Those who were now making money on helping people avoid probate spread the horror stories, real or apocryphal, fanning the flames.

But back at the probate ranch other individuals were reforming the system. Today, despite what I'm sure you've heard, probate is not a nightmare.

Most states have simplified the process, streamlining probate for wills that are passing estates to spouses, that aren't being contested, and/or that are of smaller sizes. Personal property transfers—"Who gets Grandma's candlesticks?"—are usually handled by private agreement among family members rather than through probate. Jointly owned property—such as bank accounts with two names or homes with two names on the title—are available instantly.[26] Property that has a named beneficiary—like an IRA or a life insurance policy—is also transferred immediately.

Court clerks have been trained to help guide family members through the paperwork so they can handle the process themselves. Of course, an attorney can be used—generally the one who helped draft the will—and in most straightforward cases will be able to do the job speedily and for a very reasonable fee.

If the will is a simple one—assets passing to a surviving spouse—there aren't a lot of heirs to notify, you're not in a big city, and no one is contesting it, the court could take up the issue and validate the will within two weeks of it being filed. Some elements of more complex wills—such as the sale of real estate or valuable personal property—could stretch the process out longer, but generally the other more direct transfers will be made right away. By and large the average estate is fully settled and distributed within six months.

Simply put, probate isn't the nightmare it's made out to be. If you have a comprehensive will drawn up by an experienced attorney, and if you take the simple precaution of talking to your family and having a joint owner or a beneficiary named for most of your property, it will be a breeze for your survivors. There's absolutely no reason to go to great or costly lengths to avoid probate.

---

[26]When both spouse's names are on a checking account, for instance, the surviving spouse will be able to continue writing checks to pay for living expenses with no discernible interruption.

Real Estate Investment Trusts   **58**

Unless I'm misreading the signs, real estate investment trusts (REITs) are going to be the next trendy investment. And while they're not for everyone, they may be right for some Die Brokers.

A REIT is like a mutual fund, except the pool of money from different individuals is invested in real estate. By law, 95 percent of a REIT's annual earnings must be distributed to the investors. That's what has made them hot—the top-yielding REITs are outperforming the stock market—and what may make them a savvy buy for an older Die Broker looking to generate an income from his or her accumulated savings.

Theoretically, REITs do for real estate investing what mutual funds did to stock investing: By forming a pool and putting money in a number of properties, they make it more accessible and safer for the small investor. REITs are traded like stocks or closed-end mutual funds, so their price depends on supply and demand as well as their income production. However, since they're less heavily traded than stocks or closed-end mutual funds, they're not as easy to sell.

Three Types of REITs to Look At, and One to Buy

Equity REITs invest in income-producing properties like apartment and office buildings, hotels, shopping centers, and commercial real estate. There are REITs that buy just one type of property, or that stick to investing in just one region, while there are others that take a more balanced approach, buying different types of properties all over the country. A REIT can be a passive investor—simply financing a developer—or it can be an active investor, buying, developing, and managing its own projects. The performance of equity REITs is tied to the overall stock market in the short term but to the real estate market in the long term.

Mortgage REITs invest in construction loans and mortgages primarily, while receiving some ownership income from their investments. Hybrid REITs, as you might guess, combine both approaches.

Over their brief history, equity REITs have offered the steadiest growth and the best dividends, and the funds that specialize and take an active role have done the best of all. If you're going to invest in real estate, they're the avenue I recommend you follow.

Watch Your Step

But you've got to be careful on this path. This is a relatively new type of investment, and there are still some land mines yet to be avoided.

First, make sure you steer clear of any REITs that have a finite life and promise to dissolve in a set number of years, distributing huge profits to shareholders. These are just the latest variation of the notorious real estate limited partnerships (RELPs) that brought grief to so many famous investors in the 1980s. They charge very high fees and, when they dissolve, may not be able to sell their holdings for anything near what they're projecting.

Second, watch out for start-up REITs, particularly initial public offerings. Sure, you can get in on the ground floor, but there's no track record on which you can make a sound investment judgment. Basically you're handing your money over blindly. Personally, I think that's an awfully big mistake.

Third, beware of any REIT that's tied closely to one particular sponsor or developer. It could simply be a backhanded way for a developer to come up with money cheaply or to bail himself out of an illiquid portfolio.[27] REITs should be independently managed and operated

---

[27]While this book was being written there was a scandal of one such real estate developer, based not far from where I live, who used an REIT to turn his entire estate into cash.

by individuals whose primarily interest is in how the REIT performs.

Work with your financial planner if you're considering a REIT investment. Find out exactly what the REIT buys, how its stock has performed, and what kinds of dividends it has paid out. Make sure the REIT is paying its dividends with operating capital rather than with funds it held in reserve or raised by selling off property. If a REIT isn't making enough to meet its obligations from its operations, it's headed for big trouble. Similarly, check the REIT's annual reports and financial disclosure statements for signs of any possible conflict of interest. If you or your planner detect even a whiff of inside dealing, stay away.

As long as you're aware that real estate isn't the boom market it once was and you don't expect it to make you rich overnight, investing in an established large, actively traded REIT can be an excellent way for a Die Broker to generate a good income from some of his or her accumulated savings.

Renter's Insurance   **59**

Those who rent homes or apartments or who own cooperative units are definitely not adequately protected by their landlord's or association's insurance. If a fire destroys the cabinets you added to the kitchen or burns up your stereo equipment, you're not covered. If a visitor trips over your rug and breaks his ankle, you're not covered. The landlord's or association's policy protects only what was already there when you moved in: the structure and the original permanent fixtures. It doesn't protect your personal property or additions or renovations you've made, nor does it provide you with any personal liability coverage. For that kind of very necessary protection you need to take out your own coverage.

You've got a couple of options to investigate. The standard renter's or coop owner's policy is called HO-4. It covers seventeen or eighteen different risks to your personal property up to the amount you choose, which should be its replacement value. (Renter's policies are so inexpensive that I don't think it makes any sense to insure for less than what it would cost to replace your possessions.) This basic coverage is fine for those who haven't made major permanent additions to their apartment.

A step-up is a policy called HO-6. This adds coverage of damage to additions and renovations you've made to the apartment to the standard personal property coverage. Anyone who has, for instance, redone an apartment's kitchen or bathroom should opt for this coverage. Be aware that there's usually a limitation on this added coverage of up to 10 percent of the face value of the policy. If you've made renovations worth more than that amount, buy additional coverage.

Finally, check into your liability protection. Both HO-4 and HO-6 policies usually provide a small degree of liability coverage, perhaps $100,000. For a small added charge you can often buy another $200,000 or $400,000 of liability protection.

Consider buying your renter's and auto protection from the same insurer. That usually results in a discounted premium, and often gives you the opportunity to buy inexpensive umbrella liability insurance (see chapter 71) that boosts both your coverages dramatically. (For other tips on saving money see chapter 38.)

Résumés

The biggest résumé mistake is not realizing who a résumé should be written to help. A Die Broker's résumé shouldn't be written to help himself; it should be written to help his prospective employer. Let me explain.

Résumés are negative screening devices. Potential employers scan through résumés quickly looking for anything to disqualify the candidate. They begin by looking for lack of experience and expertise to weed out those who are clearly unqualified. But there are also some subjective analyses. Some eliminate candidates from schools or companies they don't like. The guy who was rejected by Harvard might have an irrational automatic bias against those who were accepted. Others discard résumés of candidates who have worked for one company for too long or who have jumped from one company to another too often. Their goal is to trim the number of candidates to a pile they can easily manage.

You should write a résumé that, first, minimizes potential negatives and then maximizes positive achievements. That's the best way to get through the screening process and be invited for an interview. After all, that's the most you can ask of your résumé: to get you an interview. It's how you perform at the interview that will determine whether you actually get the job.

Most potentially negative factors come from your career chronology, so I think it's best to stress your personal attributes and achievements instead. Those attributes and achievements should all focus on the one thing companies care about: making more money, whether by increasing revenues, decreasing costs, or saving time.

Your résumé should list your achievements *and* translate them into bottom-line improvements, either in dollars and cents, percentages, or lengths of time. If you don't have exact numbers, estimate—just don't go crazy. All realistic figures will be accepted as true.

If you're looking for a job in another industry, phrase your achievements using the new industry's jargon. That immediately demonstrates your skills and experiences are transferable to the new industry.

Cover Your Gaps

Even though your résumé stresses bottom-line achievements, you'll still need to write up a career chronology. Every employer will want to know where you've worked and for how long. Just make sure you put your chronology after your list of achievements, so the person reading your résumé will have to go through all those impressive positives before coming up against potential negatives. There are also ways to mitigate those negatives by formatting your career chronology in the right way.

If you have an unusually long series of short stays, make sure you include salary figures and job descriptions that illustrate each move was made for good reasons.

If you've been with one company for a long time, show internal progression by treating each promotion, change in responsibility, or salary increase as a separate entry.

If you have any time gaps, eliminate them by showing how the time was used productively—to write a book or go back to school, for example.

Show How Interesting You Are

Most people include a list of their interests as a way to fill up the last bit of white space on a page. That's a waste. Instead, use them to answer some questions you can't be asked, make some subtle points you couldn't otherwise, and take some shots at making a personal connection. For example, by noting that you run marathons you demonstrate you're a nonsmoker who's in good health—two things an interviewer wants to know but can't ask. By noting you're interested in chess you imply you're a problem solver. And by noting you're interested in something very specific—say, the works of Patrick O'Brien—you could make a connection with another enthusiast.

Retirement Communities 61

As much as I personally dislike retirement communities, I can see that they make sense for some people . . . but not you. The better ones do offer a safe, comfortable environment, with facilities and activities geared to those who have chosen to pursue the traditional retirement path. However, for Die Brokers, intent on not retiring, they can be deadening. Not only aren't they home to people of diverse ages, but they tend to naturally divide along ethnic, religious, racial, and sometimes even geographic lines. They're almost like tribal burial grounds, where people return to their own to die/retire after having been out among the diverse world. I don't think they're conducive to remaining an active player in the world.

Besides, they have their own odd economic profile. When a community is being built, prices are set by the developer. Units in the first few phases are priced lower as a sales inducement and because the development isn't complete. The closer to completion the development gets, the higher the prices get. The last few units open will be the most expensive. Once there are no more open units, prices are set by the resale market. For about five years, this will be healthy, as people who wanted to get into the community earlier but couldn't buy their way into a still-new community. However, after five years, prices stagnate. Other new communities being built will attract the next batch of retirees. Those who bought into a community will now remain in place and all age together. As they get older, the value of their units will drop. No new retirees will want to move into a community where the people are older than they are. The only reason they'll do so is that it's cheaper. The older the residents get, the harder units will be to sell and the further prices will drop.

Units in retirement communities are one of the few real estate investments that are almost guaranteed to decrease in value as time goes on. The only reason to buy one is if you really want to downsize your living quarters and you think that at some point you'll need the care services that the community provides.

For a Die Broker it makes more sense to buy one home you'll be happy living in for your entire life, in a community you'll be happy living in for your entire life (see chapter 39).

Reverse Mortgages **62**

Reverse mortgages are traditionally viewed as the chemotherapy of the personal finance world: emergency maneuvers with potentially dire side effects, to be used only when there's no other choice. But for Die Brokers they're a panacea: a marvelous financial tonic with no downside that can truly boost quality of life.

Because up until now they've been talked about only in frightened whispers, there are a lot of misconceptions about reverse mortgages. Let me try to clear them up.

In a conventional mortgage, an individual borrows a large sum of money to buy a home and pays it back, with interest, at regular intervals over as many as thirty years. The lender retains a security interest in the home, in proportion to the outstanding balance of the loan. When the mortgage is paid off completely, the borrower has full title to the home.

In a reverse mortgage, an individual borrows against the value of a home they own. The lender pays money out in a set monthly amount, in a lump sum, or in the form of a line of credit. The loan term can be as long as the borrower lives, as long as the borrower lives in the house, or a predetermined period. The borrower retains full ownership of the home. When the loan comes due, it must be paid off by the borrower or his estate. The total due cannot be more than the value of the home.

(An important caveat: At the time this book was written you could not yet take out a reverse mortgage on a vacation home, secondary residence, cooperative, mobile home, manufactured house not attached to a permanent foundation, rental properties of more than four units, or a home on leased land. As more private lenders enter this market, I believe these exceptions will gradually disappear.)

VIEWING REVERSE MORTGAGES IN CONTEXT

Reverse mortgages sound pretty straightforward. But it's only when you look at them in context that the incredible advantages they offer Die Brokers come into sharp focus.

Let's say you're a Die Broker who's about to turn seventy. Following the program, you continued on the job until you were sixty-seven and then left to start your own home-based consulting practice. Also following the program, twenty years ago you and your spouse bought a home that you were comfortable staying in the rest of your lives. In order to compensate for your shrinking income, at sixty-seven you decided to take a portion of your investment portfolio and turn it into a lifelong income by purchasing an annuity. After three years on your own you've decided to stop growing the business and to just maintain your current client roster and cut your hours. You know that will mean another drop in your income. How can you and your spouse compensate for it? By taking out a reverse mortgage.

Since both you and your spouse are seventy, and your home is valued at $200,000, you take out a mortgage that pays you $550 a month for as long as one of you lives there. Since this money is a loan, not income, it's tax-free, making it effectively worth even more. In addition, since it's not income, it doesn't affect your Social Security or Medicare benefits, nor will it ever be counted against your Medicaid eligibility, as long as you spend it. When the last one of you leaves the house (in a pine box according to plan), the loan will come due. Your kids will sell the house (it wasn't *their* dream home, and you never intended to leave an estate anyway) to pay the loan. According to the terms of the loan, if it sells for more than the amount you owed, the bank gets to keep the profit; if it sells for less, the bank takes the loss—they can't go after your kids for the difference.

It's a no-lose situation: You turned a major asset into a lifelong, tax-free stream of income, while getting to retain use of that asset for as long as you lived, without leaving any potential financial burden on your children. Where's the downside? There is none for a Die Broker.

Payouts Can Fit Your Needs

Reverse mortgages can be paid out in four different ways, depending on your needs. Seniors looking to consolidate high-interest debt or to make a specific home renovation can opt for a lump-sum payout. Those who want flexibility can choose a credit line payout, usually taking the form of a checkbook. Die Brokers will probably do best selecting the monthly payment option, though some may want to investigate combination advances that couple an initial lump sum with a monthly payment.

Loan Terms Can Fit Your Needs

Similarly, the term of a reverse mortgage can be selected based on your individual needs. Term loans are for a fixed period of time—say, ten years. Usually, these are selected only by extremely old borrowers— say, in their nineties. Lifetime loans are a fairly recent innovation. They guarantee a monthly payment regardless of where you live. However, in order to accomplish that they combine an annuity purchase with the mortgage, which may make part of the monthly payment taxable. Die Brokers should generally opt for tenure loans, which pay out as long as one of the borrowers remains in the home. This is a particularly good choice if you've followed my advice on real estate and have purchased a home you'd be happy living in for the rest of your life.

By the way, interest rates on reverse mortgages are usually higher than those on conventional mortgages and, tied to a public index, are adjustable either monthly or annually, generally with built-in limits on how high they can rise or how low they can fall.

Potential Pitfalls

While I don't think they're anything to lose sleep over, there are some potential pitfalls you need to be aware of.

First, the amount you receive will be determined by the value of your home, your age and life expectancy, and the lender's underwriting and interest policies. Just as no lender will give a regular mortgage for 100 percent of the value of a home, no lender will give a reverse mortgage for 100 percent of its value. Since lenders are gambling on market values and your age, most will play it safe and lend only from 50 to 75 percent of its value. The older you are, the more they'll lend, since odds are you won't live long enough to collect more in payments than the home is worth.

Second, the fees and costs on reverse mortgages can be higher than for regular mortgages. That's why I suggest rolling these fees into the loan itself so they're settled when the loan comes due—though not every reverse mortgage lender will let you do that.

Third, not every reverse mortgage is federally insured. As a Die Broker likely to take your money in monthly payments, you may see that as a concern. But you can either simply opt for a federally insured lender (the FHA) or spend the time to investigate the financial health of the private lender. That shouldn't be tough for you since you'll have already investigated your insurers and the company issuing your annuity.

And fourth, if the surviving spouse is permanently forced into a nursing home, the loan will have to be repaid. However, in most cases that will happen only if it becomes medically impossible for the person to *ever* return home. Short-term convalescent stays in a nursing home—the kind you're most likely to experience—won't affect the loan. And since the monthly payments won't effect eligibility, they can serve as an excellent financial adjunct to Medicare and Medicaid home health care benefits.

Built-in Safeguard

What has made reverse mortgages a very safe product to buy is that the driving forces behind the industry have been the AARP and the federal government, not the financial services industry. That has resulted in one very important safeguard being built into the products right from the start: All reverse mortgages must be nonrecourse loans. That means the lenders can look only to the value of the home for repayment and cannot turn to any other assets or income from any other source. If you end up borrowing more than your home can be sold for, the lender has to eat the loss.

The flip side of that is that some of the private lenders want to take all or a share of any profit that results from the sale of your home. I don't have a problem with that, as long as they pay for it somehow, either in increased monthly payments or payments that extend to your lifetime, not just your tenure in the home. After all, as a Die Broker you're not concerned with conserving money for the next generation. You should be happy to trade potential future profits for increased cash in your hand.

Potential Lenders

While reverse mortgages haven't yet become a mass market financial product, a surprising number of national, state, and local lenders are out there. Here are the two major national lenders:

- The **Federal Housing Administration** (FHA) offers federally insured lump-sum, credit line, tenure, and combination reverse mortgages to homeowners sixty-two and older through a variety of local lenders. For a list of FHA lenders in your area call your local FHA or Department of Housing and Urban Development office.

- The **Federal National Mortgage Association** (Fannie Mae), the quasi-governmental agency that buys up mortgages, packages them, and then resells them on Wall Street, is now the largest player in the reverse mortgage market. You can get a list of local Fannie Mae reverse mortgage lenders by calling (800) 732-6643. Here are some of the major regional lenders:

- Transamerica Corporation, one of America's largest financial services companies (more than $35 billion in assets), has moved into the reverse mortgage market in a big way through its **Transamerica HomeFirst** subsidiary. While it offers lump-sum, credit line, tenure, and combination reverse mortgages to homeowners over sixty-five, it has made waves by being the first to also offer lifetime loans. Not all its products are available in every state. For information on its offerings call (800) 538-5569.

- Household Bank (more than $32 billion in assets) is another private company that has become a major player in the reverse mortgage market. Its **Household Senior Services** subsidiary offers lump-sum, monthly payment, and credit line products in thirteen states. For information call (800) 414-3837.

- The **Individual Reverse Mortgage Account** is a Mount Laurel, New Jersey–based reverse mortgage lender that offers products in eight states. For information call (800) 233-4762.

- **Home Income Security Plan** of Louisville, Kentucky, lends in at least seven states. For information call (800) 942-6550.
- San Francisco's **Providential Home Income Plan** offers reverse mortgage products in at least five states. For information call (800) 441-4428.

For More Information

- A state-by-state list of lenders, a guidebook titled *Home-Made Money: Consumer's Guide to Home Equity Conversion*, and a periodic bulletin on reverse mortgages titled *Reverse Angle* are all available by writing: AARP Home Equity Information Center, Consumer Affairs Section, 601 E Street N.W., Washington, DC 20049.
- An excellent book on reverse mortgages, *Your New Retirement Nest Egg: A Consumer Guide to the New Reverse Mortgages* by Ken Scholen, is available for $24.95 from the National Center for Home Equity Conversion, 7373 147th Street W., Apple Valley, MN 55124, (612) 953-4474.
- A report titled *How Senior Citizens (and Their Adult Children) Should Shop for a Reverse Mortgage* by Robert J. Buss is available for $4 from Tribune Media Services, 435 N. Michigan Avenue, Chicago, IL 60611.

Savings Accounts 63

Savings accounts are just about useless, not only for Die Brokers but for everyone. Checking accounts earn just as much interest and offer far greater utility. Money market funds earn more interest and are just as flexible. And certificates of deposit earn more interest and are just as secure.

The only use I can see for a savings account is as a tool to teach your children about banking, saving, and interest (see chapter 8)—but only if you can talk your local bank into letting your child set up an account with no minimum balance. Credit unions and local savings banks will usually agree to that as long as the child is under eighteen and is the one who actually controls the account.

Second-to-Die Insurance   64

One of the most popular new life insurance products around is second-to-die life insurance. It's just what its name implies: a policy that covers two individuals' lives and that pays a benefit only after both have died.

Second-to-die is so popular because it's being promoted as an estate-planning device. A couple takes out a second-to-die policy in the amount of the estate taxes their children would have to pay. (Inheriting spouses aren't liable for estate taxes.) Not only is the policy pretty cheap, since two people have to die for it to pay off, but it will allow the heirs to pocket the whole value of the estate. As a Die Broker you don't have to worry about estate taxes, since you won't be leaving an estate. However, that doesn't mean second-to-die policies are worthless.

If you have a child or dependent who you don't believe will ever be able to fully take care of him or herself financially, a second-to-die policy might make sense. As long as even one parent is alive there will presumably be someone to help provide for the child. Then when both potential sources of support are gone, the child can turn to the insurance benefit for support. The advantage of second-to-die in these circumstances is that it covers your specific need in the most cost-effective manner.

Don't rely on an insurance broker to determine how much money a special-needs child might need. Instead, talk to someone like a social worker who is familiar with your child's particular case and who knows the kind and type of government and community care that might be available.

Social Security

65

Social Security will never be the lifesaver for baby boomers that it was for their grandparents or parents. The numbers just don't add up.

As I explained in chapter 4, when you collect Social Security you're not getting back your own money; your funds are coming from the subsequent generation. That means that baby boomers, a very large generation likely to live a very long time, will be relying on Gen Xers, a very small generation, to pay their Social Security. Due to increased benefits, the burden of Social Security is difficult today, with a small generation (your parents) receiving benefits from a very large generation (you and your fellow boomers). When it's *your* turn to collect, the burden on your younger siblings and children will be unmanageable. Some things will have to change.

However, I don't think Social Security will ever become a means-tested program. That would destroy the political consensus supporting the program. If Social Security payments go only to those below a certain economic level, the program will become as unpopular as every other welfare system. That means you can rest assured that you'll get something. But I don't think you can count on getting as much as your folks. I think you can assume that changes will be made in three areas: cost-of-living increases will probably be reduced; further incentives and penalties will likely be created to encourage late claims and discourage early claims; and benefits will probably be taxed much more often and heavily than they are today.[28] Having said all that, let me answer the most common questions my clients ask me about Social Security, based on today's regulations.

What Will My Benefit Be?

The Social Security Administration (SSA) uses a very complex formula to figure out what your full retirement benefit (they call it your primary insurance amount, or PIA) will be. I'm oversimplifying, but in a nutshell, it adjusts your annual incomes for inflation, selects your thirty-five highest-earning years, averages them, turns that annual average into a monthly average, then gives you a weighted percentage of that number. The weighting is regressive, so the less money you made, the higher percentage of it you'll actually get back. Rather than go into any more detail and get you totally confused, I suggest you call the SSA at (800) 937-2000, or visit their nearest office, and ask for Form SSA-7004. Fill it out, return it to the SSA, and six weeks later you'll receive an estimate of what your full benefit would be. Of course, the younger you are the less accurate this will be.

If you're just interested in ballpark figures I can tell you that if you're forty-five and have averaged about $40,000 a year in income, you'll probably receive around $1,200 a month. For every $10,000 less in average income, subtract $200 a month; for every $10,000 more, up to $60,000, add $200.

Of course, under current rules, that benefit, like all Social Security benefits, will be adjusted upward for inflation every year.

When Can I Start Collecting It?

In 1983, as a first step to deal with America's changing demographics, the SSA instituted changes affecting when individuals can collect *full* Social Security benefits, based on what year they were born.

If you were born before 1938, you can still collect full benefits when you turn sixty-five. But if you were born between 1938 and 1942, you have to wait an added two months for every year past 1937. For instance, if you were born in 1938 you can't collect full benefits until two months after you turn sixty-five; if you were born in 1940

---

[28]Right now, if a Social Security recipient's income reaches a certain level, he owes income taxes on 50 percent of his benefit. If his income reaches a second, higher level, he owes taxes on 85 percent of his benefit. I think it's a good bet that in the future those levels will drop and those percentages will rise.

you can't collect full benefits until six months after your sixty-fifth birthday; and if you were born in 1942 you have to wait until ten months after you turn sixty-five to collect your full benefits.

If you were born between 1943 and 1954, you can collect full benefits on your sixty-sixth birthday. But if you were born between 1955 and 1959, you too will have to wait an added two months for every year past 1954. For example, someone born in 1955 can't collect full benefits until two months after their sixty-sixth birthday; someone born in 1957 has to wait six months after they turn sixty-six; and someone born in 1959 has to wait until ten months after they've blown out sixty-six candles.

Anyone born in 1960 or later must now wait until they are sixty-seven to collect their full benefit.

Do I Get More by Delaying My Claim?

Social Security has always given bonuses to those who delay claiming their full benefits. That's because the system is designed to pay you the same total lifetime amount regardless of when you begin to collect. So the earlier you collect, the lower your benefit, and the later you collect, the higher your benefit. (The first amount you collect remains your base benefit for life, though it will be adjusted for inflation.) If you were born before 1938, you get an added 3 to 4 percent a year for each year you wait to claim your full benefit. If you were born in 1938, you get an added 6.5 percent per year. Those born in 1939 and 1940 get a 7 percent bonus for each year they wait, while those born in 1941 and 1942 get a 7.5 percent annual bonus. If you were born in 1943 or later, you'll get an 8 percent bonus for each year you wait. (In addition, all the cost-of-living adjustments for the years you haven't collected are figured in and compounded as well, increasing the benefit even more.) Whatever year you were born, all bonuses now stop accruing at age seventy.

Can I Collect Partial Payments Earlier?

Anyone, regardless of when they were born, can start collecting Social Security at age sixty-two, as long as they are retired.[29] However, you can't collect a full benefit. How much would you get? Once again,

---

[29]The Social Security Administration right now has a very flexible and subjective view of what retirement means for someone who is self-employed. If you work fewer than fifteen hours a week you're definitely retired. If you work more than forty-five hours a week you're definitely not (obviously).

thanks to the new regulations enacted in 1983, that depends on your birthday. If you were born before 1938, you'd receive 80 percent. The percentage then drops a bit for every year after 1937 that you were born, until you reach the years from 1943 to 1954, where it's set at 75 percent. Then the percentage starts dropping again, a little bit each year from 1955 to 1959. It levels off finally at 70 percent for those born in 1960 and after.

Can I Work and Still Collect Social Security?

Right now, if you're between the ages of sixty-two and sixty-four and collecting Social Security, you can bring home up to $8,040 in earned income (salary) without it affecting your payment. For every $2 you earn over that amount, your Social Security will be reduced by $1. Let's say you're sixty-three, are collecting Social Security, and earn $10,000 from a home-based consulting business. That's $1,960 above the maximum ($10,000 − $8,040 = $1,960). As a result, your Social Security payments will be reduced by $980 ($1,960 ÷ 2 = $980).

Under current rules, if you're between the ages of sixty-five and sixty-nine and collecting Social Security, you can bring home up to $11,160 in earned income without it affecting your payment. For every $3 over that, your benefit will be reduced by $1. So if you were still earning $10,000, your benefit wouldn't be affected. However, if you were bringing home $15,000, you'd be $3,840 over the limit ($15,000 − $11,160 = $3,840). That would mean your benefit would be reduced by $1,280 ($3,840 ÷ 3 = $1,280).

Once you turn seventy, you can earn as much as you'd like and still receive your full benefit.

By the way, it's a mistake to not report your earned-income status to the SSA. They'll learn about it from the IRS and will then ask you to pay back any overpayments, along with a hefty penalty far outweighing any interest you could have earned on the money.

How Do Spousal Benefits Work?

If both you and your spouse qualify independently for Social Security, you can each collect your own individual benefits. Your

But if you work hours somewhere in between fifteen and forty-five, the SSA says your work status depends on what you do and how long you're doing it. In order to get an idea of how your situation might be treated, contact the nearest SSA office and schedule an appointment.

spouse alternatively could receive up to 50 percent of your benefit. He or she can select whichever method will pay more money. However, he or she can't collect a share of your benefit until you actually start collecting. So let's say you and your spouse both independently qualify for Social Security. You continue to work, but your spouse doesn't. She can claim her individual benefit. Once you decided to collect, she can then choose to continue receiving her benefit or to receive 50 percent of yours, whichever is higher.

Your ex-spouses can also claim benefits of up to 50 percent, as long as they were married to you for at least ten years, they haven't remarried, and they aren't eligible for an equal or larger benefit based on their own or another ex-spouse's earnings.

There's no limit to the number of spouses and ex-spouses who can claim benefits based on your account, and those claims have no effect on the payments you'll receive. Theoretically, Social Security could be pay you a full benefit, 50 percent of your benefit to your current spouse, and 50 percent of your benefit to however many ex-spouses you have, as long as they qualify.

What's the Die Broke Social Security Strategy?

First, keep your fingers crossed that there won't be a radical change in the system, keeping you from at least getting back what you've paid in over your working life.

Second, you can make certain assumptions. The system will always reward recipients for collecting later and punish them for earning substantial outside income; however, at a certain age it will stop issuing rewards and exacting punishments. That means there will always be a magic point at which your benefits max out *and* you can earn as much outside income as you'd like. Right now, that magic point is age seventy. (That's convenient, since it's also the age when you should also be annuitizing most of your assets.) That may change, however, in order to compensate for the system's altered demographics.

And third, whatever happens, Die Brokers should do all they can to delay claiming their Social Security until they reach that magic age. By waiting until then you guarantee you'll receive your largest possible benefit and yet incur no penalty for earning as much outside income as you can.

Stockbrokers 66

Let me ask you a question. Would you go to a Chevy salesman for unbiased advice on what sports utility vehicle to buy? Of course not. You know he's going to tell you to buy a Blazer. Then why would you go to a stockbroker for investment advice? He's going to tell you to buy stocks or stock-based mutual funds, because that's what he sells.

Granted, as a Die Broker, you will in fact have more of your money in equities, and for a longer time, than most people. But that doesn't mean you need a stockbroker to help you select those equities. A good fee-only certified financial planner (see chapter 31) can be just as skilled in analyzing stocks and mutual funds as a stockbroker. She has no bias either toward or away from stocks, has no "morning line,"[30] and will also have expertise on other nonequity topics—such as annuities, charitable remainder trusts, and reverse mortgages—that you'll be needing as you shift your portfolio from a growth to an income orientation.

If you need yet another reason to steer clear of stockbrokers, how about this: They make money both when you buy and when you sell stocks. In other words, they make their money even when they give you bad advice.

[30]Every day stockbrokers receive their brokerage firm's "morning line," which suggests what type of investments they might suggest to individual clients that might also help the firm's institutional clients.

Stocks   **67**

I think it's safe to assume you didn't turn to a book called *Die Broke* to get your first schooling in the worlds of personal finance and investing. That's why I'm not going to take up your time with rudimentary explanations and definitions. You probably already know that stocks have, over the past seventy years, outperformed every other investment around. And, if you read chapter 9 on the Die Broke program, chapter 12 on asset allocation, and chapter 54 on mutual funds, you also know I'm a big proponent of putting the bulk of your savings in equity-based mutual funds and keeping them there for the long haul. So why do I have a chapter on stocks?

It's because I want to offer a word of warning, an observation that, I believe, has been lost in all the enthusiasm surrounding the stock market. Yes, "stocks have historically outperformed all other investments," but the often overlooked and misunderstood word in that now hackneyed phrase is "historically."

When you look at the performance of all investments over the nearly seventy years since the Great Depression, stocks do indeed win out. However, that doesn't mean stocks have always been the peak performers in smaller periods of time. There have indeed been decades when stocks did not do as well as other investments. Stocks haven't grown at a steady rate—their climb has been erratic, marked by dramatic declines as well as increases. And since you're not starting your investment life at an early enough age to assume you'll have your own seventy-year period to work with (we are all living longer, but not *that* much longer), you can't automatically assume stocks will *always* be the peak performers during the remainder of your investment life.

I wouldn't be at all surprised if in the near future we live through a decade or so when bonds actually outperform stocks. If you don't pay attention to these types of short-term economic trends and simply blindly rely on the historical record, you could seriously jeopardize your chances of living rich before you Die Broke.

Yes, by all means invest the bulk of your savings in equities and keep them there as long as you can. But don't think that your initial investment decisions are etched in stone. Keep abreast of what's going on economically. You don't need to obsessively chart your portfolio daily and react to every little blip in the market, but you do need to regularly reexamine your portfolio and your plan annually. You can't read this book, set a course, put your financial life on autopilot, and assume everything will work out the way you want. You've got to remain fully in charge and in touch with your financial life if you plan to live rich and Die Broke.

Summer, Weekend, and Vacation Homes   68

Buying a summer, weekend, or vacation home can make a great deal of sense for a Die Broker who (a) has the money, and (b) who currently owns a house he can't see himself and his family living in for the rest of their lives.

Rather than bailing out of your current home completely, you can keep it and buy a summer, weekend, or vacation home you can eventually turn into your long-term full-time home. This approach has worked very well with clients of mine who own apartments in New York City.

One way to employ this kind of tactic is to look in communities that aren't made up solely of part-time residences. For you to ever move in full-time you'll need year-round services and facilities. For instance, many of my New York clients who have done this have purchased older homes in the small exurban towns and villages beyond commuting distance to Manhattan, rather than buying in the traditional shoreline vacation communities.

Another good tip is to look for a property below what you can theoretically afford—because it's either smaller, in worse shape, or with fewer features. That will make it easier to carry on your current budget. The property could then be upgraded to the level you'd like either when your income increases or when you can use the proceeds from the sale of your current full-time home.

You could make this kind of purchase more affordable by using the home as a replacement for vacations. Of course, for that to work it has to be more than just a rationalization—you have to really stop spending on vacations and divert the funds to the house.

My weekend home has done more for my quality of life than any other purchase I've ever made. And since it has become a wonderful gathering place for all my children and grandchildren, it has also become the greatest gift I have ever made to my family.

You know how all those other books about personal finance and investing tell you that there's no such thing as a risk-free investment? Well, they're wrong.

U.S. Treasury bonds are backed by "the full faith and credit" of the U.S. government. They aren't rated since they're considered to be safer than the top AAA rating. While we can all gripe and moan about how inept and corrupt politicians are, when push comes to shove, there's nothing more economically certain on this earth than the financial solidity of the United States of America.

I've been surprised in recent years to find that most of my clients seem to know more about stocks, bonds, and mutual funds than they do about U.S. Treasury bonds. I suppose that's because they're staid and mundane investments, associated with dowager aunts and other risk-adverse old folk. So, while I assumed you had a knowledge of those other investment instruments, I don't feel comfortable doing the same in this chapter. Just think of the following as a brief civics lesson.

Different Names for Different Maturities

Treasury bills, commonly called T-bills by the cognoscenti, are very short term U.S. government bonds with maturities of thirteen, twenty-six, or fifty-two weeks, that are sold weekly or monthly at a discount, with a minimum face value of $10,000. You don't receive interest payments when you buy a Treasury bill. Instead, you buy it for less than its face value, but then receive the full face value at maturity. The exact amount of this discount is determined by an auction that takes place on the day the bond is sold, with large institutional investors doing the bidding. The income you make when a Treasury bill matures is exempt from state and local taxes.

Treasury notes are short- to medium-term U.S. government bonds with maturities of from two to five years. The smallest denomination for two- and three-year notes is $5,000; for four- and five-year notes the minimum value is $1,000. Treasury notes pay interest semiannually. That interest income is exempt from state and local taxes.

Treasury bonds are medium- to long-term U.S. government bonds with maturities of from either five to ten years, or ten to forty years, sold in minimum denominations of $1,000. They pay out their state and local tax-exempt interest income semiannually.

All of these U.S. government securities can be purchased directly from a Federal Reserve bank on the day they are issued, either by mail or in person.[31] They can also be purchased from banks and brokers, but that entails an added fee. If you intend to hold a U.S. Treasury bond until it matures, it makes sense to buy it directly. If you intend to sell it in the secondary market prior to maturity, it's better to buy it through a broker, since you'll need his services to sell it.

What Are They Good For? Late-in-Life Laddering

For the average Die Broker, U.S. Treasury securities don't really have much use. While they're as secure as Fort Knox, they don't provide the kinds of returns most people need from such a sizable investment. If all you were looking for is a way to bring some balance to your equity-heavy portfolio, a bond-based mutual fund would probably be a better bet.

But for a well-off Die Broker, individual U.S. Treasury securities can be used as yet another technique to generate unearned income later in life when earned income has dropped. Funds that aren't put into annuities in your mid-sixties can instead be invested in a series of

---

[31]For information on finding the nearest Federal Reserve bank, the dates of auctions, and how to buy through the mail, call the Bureau of the Public Debt at (202) 287-4113.

Treasury securities with staggered maturities so as not to lock yourself into a potentially poor interest rate. For instance, rather than buying one large seven-year bond, you could buy ten smaller bonds with maturities from one to ten years. That gives you an opportunity to take some advantage of interest-rate movement each year while also protecting you from adverse shifts in interest rates. Depending on your age and wishes, as each bond comes due it can be used to buy another annuity, used for living expenses, made part of a gift or charitable contribution, or even rolled over into another bond.

Trip Insurance 70

I've always had a morbid fascination with those vending machines at airports that sell flight insurance. Has anyone ever collected on one of those policies? Somehow I doubt that an insurer who uses vending machines spends a great deal of time and effort contacting beneficiaries to let them know they're entitled to another $100,000. So what do you do if you buy one? Do you use the Airfone to call your spouse and say the bad news is your flight's about to crash, but the good news is you bought a $500,000 policy at the airport?

The whole concept of insurance that pays off if you die in a certain manner is crazy. To begin with, every life is priceless. Life insurance should be focused on the financial needs of the survivors, not the circumstances of death (see chapter 45). Your family's financial needs are no different if you die from a heart attack at your desk or in a plane crash in the Rockies.

However, despite the absurdity of it, I do end up with travel insurance when I drive. That's because I belong to the American Automobile Association. It includes a small auto accident life insurance policy in with my annual membership. I didn't join the AAA because of the life insurance—I really love their triptiks and tour books as well as the emergency road service. Still, I've let my family know that if anything happens to me on the road, they're entitled to an added benefit—as should you if you're similarly covered.

Umbrella Liability Insurance   71

I used to think umbrella liability insurance made sense only for the wealthy. That was until I heard about the $5 million cup of coffee. You remember the story: A woman had bought some piping-hot coffee from McDonald's and was driving to work with the paper cup pinned between her thighs. She hit a bump, scalded herself, and convinced a jury that McDonald's owed her $5 million in compensation. In a place and time where that can happen, everyone with more than two nickels to rub together needs to think about umbrella liability coverage.

Auto and homeowners' insurance policies generally provide from $100,000 to $300,000 worth of protection from lawsuits. If you're sued and the legal fees and damages total more than the ceiling on your coverage, you need to tap into your assets. If you don't have sufficient assets to pay the fees and judgment, your salary can be garnisheed.

Most Die Brokers, even though they aren't preoccupied with building up their net worths, will likely have more than $300,000 in assets. Perhaps more important, they will certainly *appear* to have far more than that because they're more likely than most people to spend their money. And that's what really counts in this instance: appearances. Personal injury attorneys generally decide how much they should seek in damages by examining the lifestyle of the defendant, not the injuries of their client. If you and your spouse live in a nice area, hold down mid- to upper-management positions, and drive one or two late-model cars, you could easily be hit with a $1 million lawsuit.

You could protect yourself from such suits related to auto and home accidents by upping the liability coverage on both those policies. However, buying a separate umbrella liability policy will not only be cheaper, it will provide you with more protection.

Umbrella policies cover you not only from home and auto-related suits but from accidents involving watercraft, aircraft, nonowned motor vehicles, and at rental properties, as well as personal injury suits claiming libel, slander, wrongful eviction, and defamation of character. (Typically, suits from business activities, intentional acts, and sexual harassment claims are excluded.) And these policies not only pay any damages but all your legal fees as well, whether you win or lose the case. That's pretty impressive.

What's even more impressive is that you can get $1 million of this kind of coverage for as little as $150 a year. Rates vary by region, by how many cars and homes you own, and by the age and records of the drivers in the family. (Most claims under umbrella policies are triggered by automobile accidents.) The standard $1 million in added coverage is enough for most people, but you can buy even greater protection at decreasing rates. For instance, the person who pays $150 annually for a $1 million policy would pay about $225 for a $2 million policy and around $260 for $3 million in coverage.

For most people, the most affordable umbrella liability coverage will come from the same insurer that covers their autos and home. The insurer will usually insist you purchase up to a specified amount of liability coverage under those two policies—say, $300,000 each—and will then sell you $1 million in additional protection at a very affordable rate. Not only will you get the best deal by ganging up your coverage in this way, but it will also facilitate the payment of claims.

Remarkably, two out of every three Americans die without a will, or intestate. As a result they give up control over not just how their remaining assets are divided but also over who controls them. Even more disturbing is that by dying intestate a parent hands control of a minor child's fate to the state. That's why I think dying without a will is the ultimate abdication of personal control and responsibility.

If you die without a will, the court will appoint an administrator to dispose of your assets, since you haven't named an executor. The first thing the administrator will do is make sure the administration fees are paid. Then he'll turn to the state's formulas as to how to divide up your estate. That could mean your spouse will have to split the estate with your grown children, your parents, or your siblings, regardless of her financial need; your long-term companion could get nothing; your business might have to be sold instantly rather than given to a spouse or child; your stepchildren or grandchildren might get nothing; or, if you have no family, the state rather than your lifelong friend could get all your assets. If you die without having named a guardian for your minor children, the court will appoint one, almost automatically opting for a family member—either a parent or sibling.

Everyone Needs a Will Early On

While it's your intent as a Die Broker to leave no estate, you don't know when you're going to die. If you don't live long enough to turn your assets into income, but you do live long enough to accumulate assets, you'll actually end up with quite an estate, regardless of your aversion to the concept. If you have a will, you can make sure that at least the spirit, if not the letter, of your Die Broke philosophy is carried out. For instance, the money can be given entirely to your spouse, who agrees with your Die Broke philosophy and who will then spend it and give it away much as you would have wished. Or an executor who supported your philosophy could be named to follow in your footsteps.

The time to have your first will drafted is when you begin to accumulate assets or have a child, whichever comes first. Don't make the common mistake of not drafting wills because you're part of a married couple. While it's unlikely, you could both die simultaneously, leaving the state to take care of your children and assets.

You can minimize the property that will have to be transferred through your will by making sure most of your assets are either jointly owned or have a named beneficiary. Still, there's apt to be some assets you'll own individually, even if they're primarily personal property. Besides, there are still the guardianship issues to be concerned with.

Don't Do It Yourself

Don't try to save money by using a do-it-yourself will kit. Such computer programs and preprinted forms reflect traditional financial views, not those of a Die Broker.[32] In addition, your life, your attitude, and your assets are all unique and deserve to be treated as such. Finally, a do-it-yourself will is much more likely to be thrown out by the courts as invalid. The risks outweigh any possible savings, since a competent attorney can draw up a simple will in less than an hour, if you come to her office with a clear idea of how you want your assets distributed. An experienced attorney can walk you through the entire process, ensuring that the will is written so explicitly that your estate gets divided up exactly the way you intended.

Die Brokers Need to Include Letters of Instruction

One added element that I'd suggest be added to every Die Broker's will is a letter of instruction. This is an inventory of all your personal

---

[32]By the way, handwritten statements and video- or audiotaped messages are generally *not* accepted as valid wills.

possessions, spelling out exactly who should get what when you die. Most wills give the executor control over the exact disposition of personal property—I've found that's an awful responsibility. More often than not family disputes arise, not over the stock portfolio but over the parent's collection of teaspoons. That's because personal property carries the most sentimental value. In fighting for these objects, family members are really battling for their fair share of the deceased's love. This is only exacerbated at the death of a Die Broker. The *only* tangible things a Die Broker's hoping to leave behind are personal possessions—that's going to give them inordinate value to heirs. Your final gift to your heirs should be to spare them from any possible fight over your bones.

Index

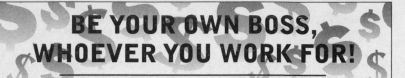